Greenhill
Books

THE KNIGHTS OF ISLAM

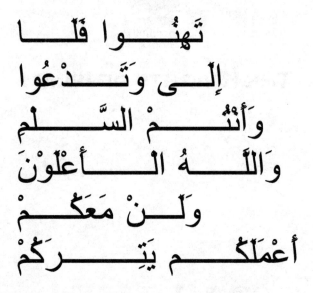

فَلَا تَهِنُوا وَتَدْعُوا إِلَى
السَّلْمِ وَأَنْتُمُ الْأَعْلَوْنَ وَاللَّهُ
مَعَكُمْ وَلَنْ يَتِرَكُمْ أَعْمَالَكُمْ

Therefore, you shall not waver and surrender in pursuit of peace,
for you are guaranteed victory, and GOD is with you. He will
never waste your efforts.

Koran 47.35

THE KNIGHTS
OF ISLAM

THE WARS OF THE MAMLUKS

JAMES WATERSON

Greenhill Books, London
MBI Publishing, St Paul

FOR M&M&37

Greenhill
Books

The Knights of Islam: The Wars of the Mamluks

First published in 2007 by Greenhill Books, Lionel Leventhal Limited,
Park House, 1 Russell Gardens, London NW11 9NN
www.greenhillbooks.com
and
MBI Publishing Co., Galtier Plaza, Suite 200, 380 Jackson Street, St Paul,
MN 55101-3885, USA

British Library Cataloguing-in Publication Data
Waterson, James
The knights of Islam : the wars of the Mamluks
1. Mamelukes 2. Military art and science – Egypt – History
– Medieval, 500–1500 3. Islamic Empire – History, Military
4. Islamic Empire – History – 1258–1517
I. Title
962'.02

ISBN-13: 978-1-85367-734-2

Library of Congress Cataloging-in Publication Data available

For more information on our books, please visit
www.greenhillbooks.com, email sales@greenhillbooks.com
or telephone us within the UK on 020 8458 6314.
You can also write to us at the above London address.

Edited and typeset by JCS Publishing Services, www.jcs-publishing.co.uk
Maps drawn by Red Lion Prints

Printed and bound in Great Britain by Creative Print and Design (Wales),
Ebbw Vale

CONTENTS

Maps and Illustrations

The chapter end illustrations are Mamluk blazons showing rank and office.

Maps

Illustrations

Acknowledgements

I T IS THE NORM to give thanks to all who have suffered during the writing of a book but here the list is comprised of only one, my dear wife Michele. The list of those to whom I feel indebted also includes Michele for her translations of French, Italian and Chinese for me. I would also like to thank Peter Furtado of *History Today* magazine and my editor Kate Baker. Many thanks also to Bean Edge and Jimmy Reilly for their superb images and illustrations.

FOREWORD

THE EVENTS AND PEOPLE covered by this book are relatively unknown to Western readers. This is a shame, because they are hugely significant. One reason they are under-reported, at least in books for general readers, is that the story is one of great complexity. Once upon a time, the world of Islam in the Middle East had a certain grand simplicity, but by the thirteenth century this had long been destroyed by schisms and rivalries. From the late eleventh century, Christian Europe had intruded; in a 200-year adventure that now seems like a malign expression of religious fanaticism, Crusaders of many nationalities established four states along the eastern Mediterranean coast. And then, in the mid-thirteenth century, came the Mongols into the Middle East springing from the heart of Central Asia. It was in this stew of nationalities and religions that the Mamluks – former slave soldiers who rose to rule Egypt – aspired to restore Islam through a two-front *jihad*. In just over thirty years, they stopped the Mongols dead in their tracks and drove the Crusaders back to Europe.

If the Mamluk dynasty had not arisen, the Middle Eastern world might well have evolved in a very different way. In the mid-thirteenth century, the Mongol Empire still retained a sort of unity, linked by the vision and genius of its founder Genghis Khan, whose destiny (so his heirs claimed) was to rule the whole world, which to them meant Eurasia and Japan. Since his death in 1227, they had shown that this was indeed a possibility, with their assaults westward across southern Russia into Eastern Europe (1241–2) and the seizure of most the world of Islam (1255–60) they reached the shores of the Mediterranean, where they made contact with the Crusader states. Some Crusaders were ready to welcome the Mongols, because they appeared to be implacable enemies of Islam and some capitulated, as did many of the Muslim princes, and so Syria fell. In the summer of 1260, Mongol armies were on their way south, intending to take Egypt. Success there would have given them an astonishing boost: the control of an Islamic empire with two capitals, Baghdad and Cairo, access to the Mediterranean, ports, naval expertise, armies expert in siege warfare – and then what? Byzantium? Europe? What would Eurasian history have been like, with Qubilai Khan, the master of Xanadu, ruling from the Pacific to the Atlantic?

Luckily, we never knew, because the Mamluks stopped them, in one of history's most significant battles at Ayn Jalut, or Goliath's Spring, near Nablus, sixty kilometres north of Jerusalem, where the Jezreel Valley runs up against the Gilboa Hills. It was high summer. The Mongols' horses were short of water and fodder, and their manpower was reduced as over half of their army had returned to Persia when news came of the death of the Mongol Great Khan, Mongke. Even then, against most armies of the day, the Mongols would still have had the strength to win. But not against the Mamluks, whose rigorous training and astonishing commitment to the military arts made them more than equal to the Mongols. The Mongols were superb mounted archers but so were the Mamluks and they were also trained to fight with lances and swords to a level far exceeding anything Mongols could match. At Ayn Jalut, the Mongols died almost to a man, a catastrophe that turned the Mamluk–Mongol struggle for supremacy into a cold war stalemate punctuated by some of the bloodiest battles of the medieval period until the end of the Mongols' Persian regime in 1335.

The Mamluks were also experts in siege warfare, able to deploy catapults of a size and in numbers unthinkable in previous times in the Middle East. Under their greatest Sultan, Baybars, the Mamluks took on the Crusader castles that had defied even the *jihad* of Saladin. Having brought both Egypt and Syria under his rule, Baybars dealt so many hammer blows to the Crusaders that, by the time of his death in 1277, they were already obviously doomed and the last Crusader city fell to the Mamluks in 1291.

Baybars himself emerges as one of the most gifted military leaders of the Middle Ages, as ruthless and as brilliant in military and political terms as Genghis Khan himself. He fought wars on several fronts, against Mongol Persia, Armenia, the Crusader states and in Nubia. He was also a wily diplomat, reaching out to Byzantium, the Golden Horde (those other Mongols who ruled southern Russia), Sicily and Spain. He built canals, improved harbours and took a leaf out of the Mongols' book by setting up pony-express and carrier-pigeon services that could carry messages across his kingdom in three days. He also had the brilliant idea of installing his own Caliph in Cairo to legitimise his dynasty, re-establishing Islam's religious leadership after its destruction by the Mongols when they seized Baghdad in 1258. He was without doubt a truly complete military man and was expert in the martial pursuits of hunting, polo and jousting.

Behind the Mamluk Sultans lay an army committed to the rule of Islam – committed, in short, to the ideal of *jihad* that runs through Islamic militancy in its most extreme and individualistic form to the present day. This book describes social and political realities that can be traced back to Baybars and to the high point of Mamluk power in the second half of the thirteenth century.

Thereafter, for another two centuries, the Mamluk Empire struggled to maintain itself as it entered upon a long decline. Conservatism and corruption of the old martial ways were major causes of this slow collapse, but in the end, however, despite heroism and unlikely victories against enemies that far outnumbered its own small forces, it succumbed under the dual assault of economic competition with the new European colonisation of the Indian Ocean and of the rising power of the Ottoman Empire. Even after being subsumed into the Ottoman Empire at the beginning of the sixteenth century the Mamluks remained the archetypes of the kind of chivalry and military honour to which Ottoman princes aspired.

This, in brief, is the epic sweep of James Waterson's book, with its astonishing array of themes and characters.

John Man

Key Events Timeline

632   Death of the Prophet Muhammad.

651   Arab conquest of the Middle East and Persia virtually complete.

716   North Africa and Spain under Arab control.

732   Arab advances into Europe halted after battle of Poitiers. Islamic Empire continues expansion into the Turkish lands east of the Oxus River, Mamluks – slave soldiers – begin to be imported into Islam from Transoxania and from the Caucasus.

750   The Abbasid revolution in Persia, civil war within Islam. Turkish Mamluks prove themselves superior to Arab levies.

833   The caliph al-Mutasim builds the first army of Mamluks in Iraq and begins a fledgling Mamluk military aristocracy.

1055   The Saljuq, a Turkish tribe, come from the East and take control of the Islamic Empire of Persia, Turks become the dominant military power in Islam.

1071   The Battle of Manzikert, the Byzantine field army is destroyed by a Saljuq force of Mamluks and Turcoman levies.

1099   The First Crusade, launched in response to Byzantium's calls for aid following Manzikert takes Jerusalem. Turcoman troopers make the only effective Muslim resistance to the Crusade's progress. Their phenomenal archery assaults annihilate the People's Crusade, nearly destroy the main Crusader army at Dorylaeum and wipe out the Crusader armies of 1100 and 1101.

1187   Saladin destroys the Crusader field army at Hattin and retakes Jerusalem. The Mamluk core of his army sustains the Muslim response to the Third Crusade.

1244 The Battle of La Forbie. The Sultan of Egypt's Mamluk army defeats a combined Crusader and Syrian Muslim army.

1249–50 King Louis IX of France crusades in Egypt. His army is defeated by the Mamluk Bahriyya regiment of Cairo who then mutiny against their Sultan and seize power, the Bahri Mamluk Sultanate is born.

1258 The Mongols invade the Middle East, sacking Baghdad and killing the Caliph.

1259 The Mongol conquest of Syria begins; the Mamluks are called on to surrender by the Mongol Ilkhan Hulegu.

1260–4 Mongol civil war between Ariq Boke and Quibilai for the Great Khanate distracts Hulegu from Syria.

1260 The Mamluk Sultan Kutuz defeats the Mongols at Ayn Jalut and the Mongols evacuate Syria. Kutuz is murdered by the emir Baybars who usurps the throne.

1261 The Mongols are defeated again in Syria at Homs, Baybars takes up *jihad* against the Crusaders, makes the Royal Mamluk regiment the core of his new model army and lays the foundations of the Mamluk military state.

1262–5 Crusader castles and cities begin to fall under Baybars's assaults; Caesarea, Haifa and Nazareth are taken. A cold war of espionage, raiding and dirty tricks begins between the Mongols and Mamluks.

1263 Baybars secures an alliance with the Mongol Golden Horde of Russia against the Ilkhan Hulegu. A long border war between the two Mongol khanates begins.

1266 Sis, the capital of Armenia, the ally of both the Crusaders and of the Mongols, is sacked by the Mamluk emir Kalavun in a devastating campaign.

1268 Jaffa and Antioch fall to Baybars's siege engines.

1270 King Louis's final Crusade to Tunis fails.

1271 Crak de Chevaliers falls to Baybars. Prince Edward of England crusades in Syria and attempts joint operations with the Mongols. His plans fail and he is nearly killed by one of Baybars's assassins.

1272 Baybars brings Nubia under Mamluk control. He and Kalavun defeat the Mongols at al-Bira in the Jazira.

1274 Armenia's capital is sacked once again by the Mamluks.

1277 Baybars campaigns in Anatolia and destroys a Mongol army at Abulustayn. Baybars dies in Damascus and is succeeded by his son Baraka.

1277–9 Mongol emissaries are sent to the European courts in numerous attempts to secure an alliance against the Mamluks.

1279 Baraka is deposed by a military clique. Kalavun is elected as the new Sultan.

1281 The Second Battle of Homs. The Mamluks narrowly defeat a vast Mongol army. Thousands of Mongols are slaughtered during their retreat.

1282–94 Huge internal difficulties in the Mongol Ilkhanate with civil wars, continued conflict with the Mongol Chagatay Horde to the east and total mismanagement and destruction of the Persian economy.

1289 Tripoli is the last of many Crusader cities and castles to fall to Kalavun in his continuation of Baybars's *jihad*.

1290–1 Kalavun dies. His son al-Ashraf succeeds him and finally extinguishes the Latin Kingdom of Outremer by destroying Acre.

1293 Al-Ashraf launches a disastrous campaign against Shiites, Druze and Christians in Lebanon's mountains and is later killed by a group of Mamluk emirs. A series of puppet Sultans, the sons of Kalavun, are put up by Mamluk juntas.

1295 The gifted Mongol Ilkhan Ghazan reforms the Ilkhanate and its army.

1299 Ghazan invades Syria and routs the Mamluks at Wadi al-Khazindar but fails to destroy their field army. Mamluk resistance from castles and citadels, particularly at Damascus causes the Mongols to evacuate the country by 1300.

1300 Ghazan invades Syria again but turns back in the face of impassable floods and bitter cold.

1303 Ghazan's final attempt on Syria meets with total defeat of his army by the Mamluks at Marj al-Suffar. He dies soon after. The new Circassian Mamluks fight particularly bravely at the battle.

1310–41   The long reign of the Mamluk Sultan al-Nasir and the final collapse of the Ilkhanate. Corruption becomes rife in the Mamluk Sultanate.

1347   The Black Death comes to the Middle East.

1341–89   Al-Nasir's sons and grandsons are used as puppets by a series of military juntas.

1346   The House of Osman, a small Anatolian warrior confederation, is employed in the Byzantine civil wars. It soon begins its own conquest of the Balkans to form the Ottoman state.

1365   The Crusade of Peter of Cyprus sacks Alexandria, Mamluk naval weakness is exposed.

1389–1402   The Ottoman Sultan Bayezid destroys the Balkan Crusade at Nicopolis, encircles Byzantium, expands into Anatolia and threatens the Mamluk Sultanate.

1400–2   Tamerlane, in his mission to recreate the empire of Genghis Khan, invades the Middle East. He defeats the Mamluks bloodily at Aleppo. He sacks Aleppo and Damascus and then defeats Bayezid at the Battle of Ankara. He dies on his way to invade China in 1405.

1402–22   Almost continuous revolts in Mamluk Syria and political chaos in the Mamluk Sultanate as Circassian Mamluks and Bahri Mamluks wrestle for power. The Ottomans regain their power in Europe and in Anatolia as Tamerlane's empire disintegrates.

1422–38   Reign of Sultan Barsbay, a Circassian Mamluk. He raids Cyprus many times, builds an effective navy and pacifies Syria. The Mamluk Sultanate is briefly renascent.

1453–81   Mehmed II, the Ottoman Sultan, conquers Constantinople, subdues Anatolia and conquers the Black Sea area whilst the effects of plague and corruption send the Mamluk military state into a renewed decline.

1468–96   The reign of Kayitbay. After initial disasters against the Turcoman warlord Shah Suwar he eventually defeats him, crushes Bedouin revolts in Egypt and Syria and repeatedly defeats the Ottomans in the war of 1485–91. Despite Kayitbay's brilliant reign, the Sultanate is both economically and politically nearly exhausted.

1497   The Portuguese round Cape Horn and enter the Indian Ocean.

1501–16   The reign of al-Ghawri following political chaos in Egypt. He attempts reform of the army by expanding its use of firearms and his ship-borne riflemen defeat the Portuguese in a naval war around the Red Sea between 1505–16.

1504–14   The rise of the Safavid dynasty in Iraq and Persia. The Safavids raid Mamluk lands and threaten Ottoman possessions in Anatolia. The Ottoman Sultan Selim the Grim defeats them at the Battle of Chaldiran and moves against them again in 1516.

1516   Al-Ghawri, fearing Selim's increasing power, forms a mutual defence pact with the Safavids and brings his field army into Syria. Selim's vast Ottoman army is nearly defeated by the 944 men of the Royal Mamluk regiment but al-Ghawri dies on the battlefield, the Mamluks of Aleppo desert under their emir Khair Bey and the Mamluk army is subsequently slaughtered by the Ottoman field artillery.

1517   Selim moves onto the conquest of Egypt encouraged by Khair Bey. He defeats and captures the last Mamluk Sultan, Tumanbay, among the Pyramids and executes him, hanging him amid the lamentations of Cairo's populace from the city's main gate.

1518–1797   Mamluks are employed by the Ottomans on campaigns and as a local defence force in Egypt. As the Ottoman Empire declines, Mamluk emirs accrue power again and become almost independent of Istanbul's control.

1798   Napoleon campaigns in the Middle East and defeats the Egyptian army in a matter of hours. When he leaves Egypt he takes a Mamluk bodyguard and Mamluk regiment with him.

1805   The new Ottoman viceroy Muhammad Ali takes up office in Cairo.

1811   Muhammad Ali massacres Mamluk leaders in the Cairo citadel, a few Mamluks flee to Sudan and survive there until 1820 when they are finally exterminated by Ottoman troops.

THE SULTANS AND KHANS

BAHRI MAMLUK SULTANS

Shajar al-Durr (Sultana)	1250	al-Nasir Muhammad	
al-Mu'izz Aybeg	1250–7	(3rd reign)	1310–41
al-Mansur 'Ali	1257–9	al-Mansur Abu Bakr	1341
al-Muzaffar Kutuz	1259–60	al-Ashraf Kuchuk	1341–2
al-Zahir Baybars	1260–77	al-Nasir Ahmad	1342
al-Sa'id Baraka Khan	1277–9	al-Salih Isma'il	1342–5
al-Adil Salamish	1279	al-Kamil Sha'ban	1345–6
al-Mansur Kalavun	1279–90	al-Muzaffar Hajji	1346–7
al-Ashraf Khalil	1290–3	al-Nasir Hasan	
al-Nasir Muhammad		(1st reign)	1347–51
(1st reign)	1293–4	al-Salih Salih	1351–4
al-Adil Kitbogha	1294–6	al-Nasir Hasan	
al-Mansur Lachin	1296–8	(2nd reign)	1354–61
al-Nasir Muhammad		al-Mansur Muhammad	1361–63
(2nd reign)	1298–1308	al-Ashraf Sha'ban	1363–77
al-Muzaffar Baybars	1308–10	al-Mansur 'Ali	1377–81
		al-Salih Hajji (1st reign)	1381–2

CIRCASSIAN MAMLUK SULTANS

al-Zahir Barkuk		al-Musta'in	
(1st reign)	1382–9	(Caliph and Sultan)	1412
al-Salih Hajji		al-Mu'ayyad Shaykh	1412–21
(2nd reign)	1389–90	al-Muzaffar Ahmad	1421
al-Zahir Barkuk		al-Zahir Tatar	1421
(2nd reign)	1390–9	al-Salih Muhammed	1421–2
al-Nasir Faraj		al-Ashraf Barsbay	1422–38
(1st reign)	1399–1405	al-'Aziz Yusuf	1438
al-Mansur 'Abd al-'Aziz	1405	al-Zahir Chakmak	1438–53
al-Nasir Faraj		al-Mansur 'Uthman	1453
(2nd reign)	1405–12	al-Ashraf Inal	1453–61

al-Mu'ayyad Ahmad	1461	al-Zahir Kansawh	1498–1500
al Zahir Khushqadam	1461–7	al-Ashraf Janpulat	1500–1
al-Zahir Yalbay	1467	al-'Adil Tumanbay	1501
al-Zahir Temurboga	1467–8	al-Ashraf Kansawh	
al-Ashraf Kayitbay	1468–96	al-Ghawri	1501–16
al-Nasir Muhammad	1496–98	al-Ashraf Tumanbay	1516–17

OTTOMAN SULTANS TO 1520

Osman	1300–24	Murad I (abdicated)	1421–7
Orhan	1324–62	Mehmed II (abdicated)	1437–8
Murad I	1362–89	Murad II (reascended)	1438–51
Bayezid I	1389–1402	Mehmed II	
Civil War		(reascended)	1451–81
(Suleyman–Mehmed		Bayezid II	1481–1512
–Musa)	1402–13	Selim I	1512–20
Mehmed I	1413–21		

THE GREAT KHANS

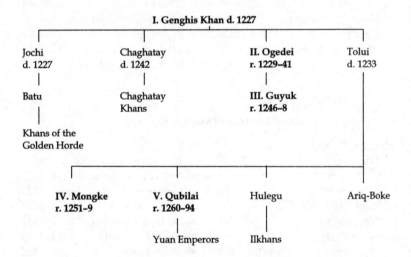

KHANS OF THE GOLDEN HORDE TO 1359

Batu	d. 1255	Tole Buqa	r. 1287–90
Sartaq	r. 1256–7	Toqta	r. 1291–1312
Ulaghchi	r. 1257	Ozbeg	r. 1313–41
Berke	r. 1257–67	Tinibeg	r. 1341–2
Mongke Temur	r. 1267–80	Janibeg	r. 1342–57
Tode Mongke	r. 1280–7	Berdibeg	r. 1357–9

THE ILKHANS OF PERSIA

Hulegu	d. 1265	Baidu	r. 1295
Abagha	r. 1265–82	Ghazan	r. 1295–1304
Teguder Ahmad	r. 1282–4	Oljeitu	r. 1304–16
Arghun	r. 1284–91	Abu Said	r. 1316–35
Geikhatu	r. 1291–5		

A Note on Transliteration, Titles and Dates

There are many, many ways of rendering Turkish, Arabic and Mongolian into English. I have generally opted for the most commonly used forms of names rather than the more accurate and scholarly forms simply because the vast swathe of names that the reader encounters whilst reading any history of the medieval Middle East means that any familiar faces are welcome. Therefore, for example, I have Saladin rather than Salah al-Din and Genghis Khan and not Chingiz Khan.

This also applies to the transliteration of many of the Mamluk names encountered in the text. This has thrown up anomalies in that I have used a mix of transliteration methods but the reason for this is that I want readers to be able to find the names of these characters in both the secondary sources I have consulted and in the translations of primary documents that are available and these were originally translated under different systems of transliteration. My transliteration of individual characters' names and titles is however, needless to say, consistent throughout.

Of course the events of the medieval Middle East were commonly recorded by contemporary writers in the Arabic calendar, based on a lunar cycle and dated from the *hijra*, the prophet's flight from Mecca to Medina. I have used the Christian calendar as the text is for a Western audience and I want readers to be able to parallel the events described with what was happening in Europe at the same time.

MAPS

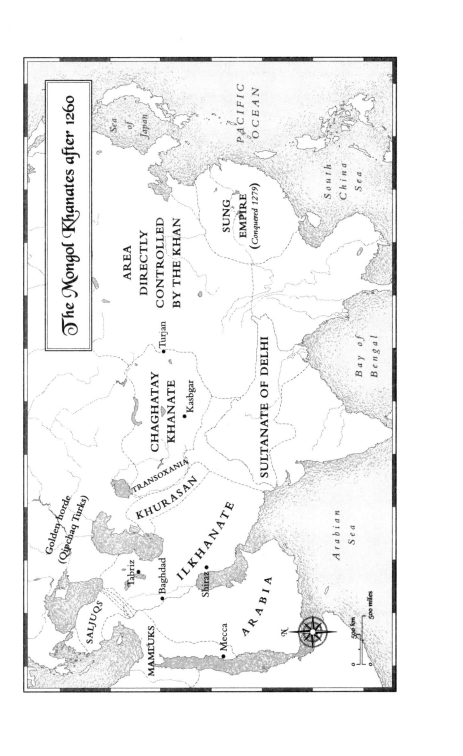

The Mongol Khanates after 1260

Sea of Japan

PACIFIC OCEAN

South China Sea

AREA DIRECTLY CONTROLLED BY THE KHAN

SUNG EMPIRE
(Conquered 1279)

Bay of Bengal

• Turfan

CHAGHATAY KHANATE

• Kasbgar

SULTANATE OF DELHI

TRANSOXANIA

KHURASAN

Golden horde (Qipchaq Turks)

ILKHANATE

• Tabriz
• Baghdad
• Shiraz

Arabian Sea

SALJUQS

ARABIA

MAMLUKS

• Mecca

N

0   500 km
0   500 miles

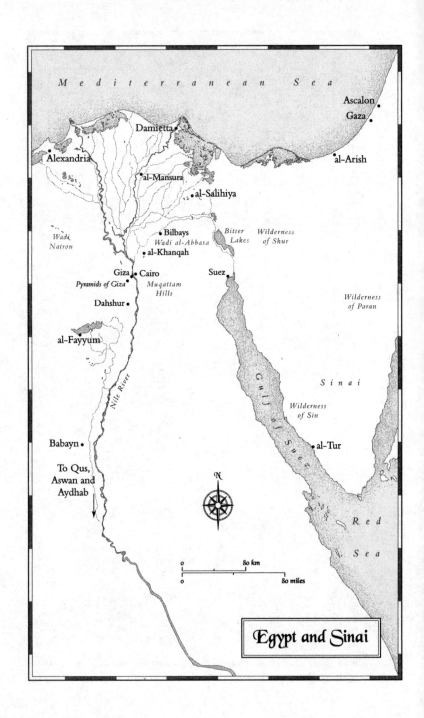

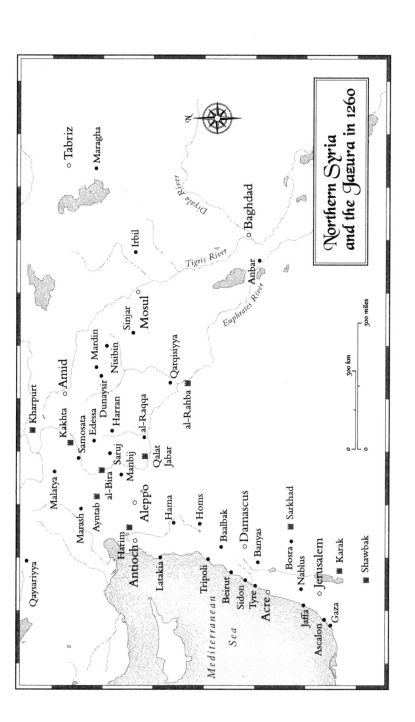

Northern Syria and the Jazira in 1260

Qaysariyya

Tabriz
Maragha

Kharpurt

Malatya
Marash
Ayntab
Kakhta
Samosata
Amid
Mardin
Dunaysir
Nisibin
Sinjar
Irbil
Mosul
Anbar
Baghdad

Harim
Antioch
Aleppo
al-Bira
Saruj
Manbij
Edessa
Harran
al-Raqqa
Qalat Jabar
Qarqisiyya
al-Rahba

Latakia
Hama
Homs
Baalbak
Damascus
Banyas
Bosra
Sarkhad

Tripoli
Beirut
Sidon
Tyre
Acre
Nablus
Jerusalem
Karak
Shawbak

Jaffa
Ascalon
Gaza

Mediterranean Sea

Diyala River
Tigris River
Euphrates River

300 km
300 miles

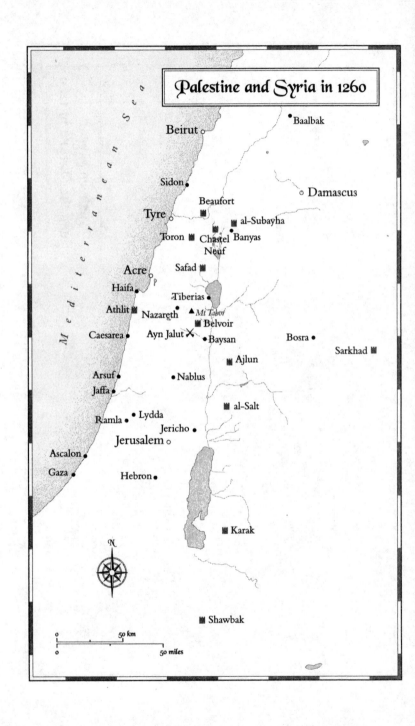

Palestine and Syria in 1260

The Middle East after Tamerlane, 1405

0 — 400 km
0 — 400 miles

N

GOLDEN
HORDE
KHANATE

EMPIRE
OF
TAMERLANE
(TIMURIDS)

GRAND DUCHY
OF
LITHUANIA

P. OF
MOLDAVIA

P. OF
WALLACHIA

GENOESE
TRADERS

CIRCASSIANS

Black Sea

Caspian Sea

K. OF
GEORGIA

TREBIZOND

Constantinople

OTTOMAN EMPIRE

BEYLIK OF
KARAMAN

WHITE
SHEEP TURK
CONFEDERATION

BLACK SHEEP TURK
CONFEDERATION

Knights of
St John
(Rhodes)

KINGDOM
OF CYPRUS

Mediterranean
Sea

Persian Gulf

MAMLUK
SULTANATE
OF EGYPT
AND SYRIA

MAMLUK
PROTECTORATE OF
ARABIA

Red Sea

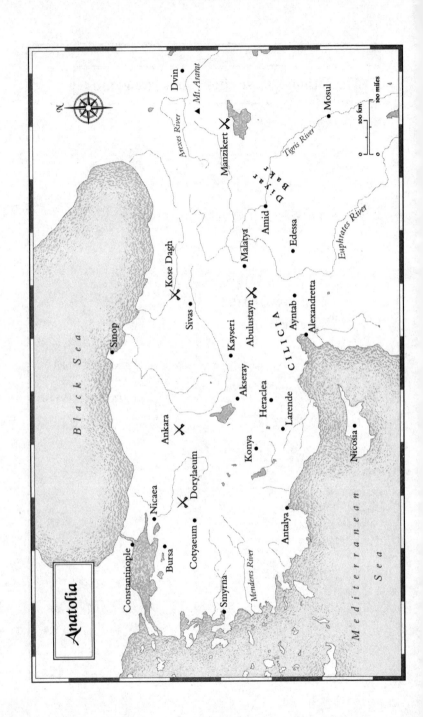

1

STRANGERS FROM A STRANGE LAND

THE MAMLUK ENIGMA

> They became to Islam a source of reinforcement and an enormous army, and to the Caliphs a protection and a shelter and invulnerable armour, they were as the mail worn under a cloak . . .
>
> *Amr' ibn Bahr of Basra, known as al-Jahiz 'the goggle eyed',*
> *d. 869*

THE MAMLUKS AND THE Mamluk Sultanate are a study in contradictions. They were slave soldiers from the barbarian steppes beyond the lands of Islamic civilisation who became lords in the Empire of the Arabs and saved Islam's holy places from the Mongol rage. They were born pagans and yet formed the machine of *jihad* that ultimately destroyed the Crusader kingdom of Outremer and re-established Islam's hold over the Levant. They were, at one distinct point in history, the greatest body of fighting men in the world; the quintessence of the mounted fighter reaching near-perfection in his skill with the bow, lance and sword. These often unlettered automatons who were just as often almost strangers to the Arabic tongue developed a martial code and sophisticated military society that at its apogee had parallels with both Western chivalry and Japanese *bushido* in its complex ideas of the meaning of warrior life, its scientific approach to war and its passion for the soldier's way of life.

Yet the Mamluks have disappeared from history's view in a way that has not been allowed to happen to the Knights of the West and the Samurai. The reasons for this are complex but are chiefly related to Arab nationalism in the late nineteenth and twentieth centuries, a nationalism that required the obscuring of the historical achievements of other racial groups in the central lands of Islam, the conquests in Europe and the longevity of the Ottoman Sultanate that has tended to shade from Western eyes the accomplishments of earlier Islamic dynasties and to the gun – a great leveller of men that eventually took away all the advantages of those whose way of life was entirely devoted to martial training with traditional weapons.

The Mamluks' disappearing act is, however, strange given that the Battle of Manzikert in 1071 – in which the Byzantine army was decimated and the Greek Emperor Romanus Diogenes captured – was a victory achieved by Alp Arslan's Mamluk regiments for his uncle the Sultan of the Sunni Muslim world. This debacle led to the pleas of Byzantium to the West for succour, resulting in the First Crusade's eventual capture of Jerusalem. Saladin's recapture of the city following the pivotal Battle of Hattin in 1187 and his long campaign against Richard the Lionheart and the Third Crusade were both built on an army that had Mamluks at its core. In 1250 the Mamluk regiments of Egypt defeated one of the largest Crusader armies ever to enter the fray and then bloodily seized power from their masters, the descendants of Saladin.

In 1260 their new state claimed an immense victory, the defeat of the Mongols at Ayn Jalut in Syria. Mongol forces who had bludgeoned their way down through China, the world's most developed state, had dismembered the eastern Islamic Empire, placed Russia under a yoke and annihilated the cream of eastern European chivalry at the battles of Liegnitz and Sajo in 1241 were finally halted by men who were decidedly similar to themselves. The state subsequently created by the Mamluks in Egypt and Syria had a longevity greater than that of either the Mongol Yuan Dynasty in China or of the Latin Crusader kingdom. It waged long and complex wars against the Mongols, Crusaders and Ottomans that required the total involvement of the state and its economy as well as exceptional diplomacy and governance.

The above events have shaped the history of the world and the world we live in today. All will be returned to in the course of this story, but the point here is that the Mamluks, their Sultanate and their deeds should not be hidden in the darkness of history. They have left us enough evidence of the splendours of their time. The *Furusiyya*, the military manuals of the Mamluk Sultanate are Islam's equivalent of the Chinese classic, *Sunzi Binfa*, (*The Art of War*), and their armourers, architects and craftsmen have produced some of the world's most perfect works of art and architecture.

But then there is the question of slavery and of slaves who were soldiers. The idea of slavery is repugnant to modern eyes and this is, undoubtedly, another reason why the martial code of the Mamluks is not shown the same reverence as are the Western chivalric codes and the Samurai way. To understand the Mamluk Sultanate, then, it is vital to understand the concept of the slave soldier in early Islam, the society that bought boys to make them into warriors and the lands that bore this soldier stock.

The expansion of the Arab Empire in the years following the Prophet Muhammad's death in 632 had been phenomenal. Certainly the long war between Sassanian Persia and the Byzantines (603–28) that had totally exhausted both of the main powers in the region had been of assistance and by 651 Egypt, Syria, Iraq, Iran and much of North Africa had all come under Arab control either by conquest or by treaty. By 716 they had conquered Spain with armies of newly converted Berbers and their progress up into France was only halted by the heroism of Charles Martel at the week-long battle of Poitiers in 732. In the East they crossed the Oxus River and penetrated into what is today Pakistan. The greatest resistance to the progress of their forces in Asia was in Transoxania as they pushed up from Khurusan and to the east of the Caspian Sea. Here they were encroaching on Turkish homelands and here they found their first slave soldiers to supplement the limited manpower available from the Arabian Peninsula.

It was perhaps too much of a good thing. All this success left the Arab leaders with something of a dilemma: the division of the spoils. The problem was threefold, firstly the Arab clans argued over who was entitled to the largest share of the tax yield on non-Muslims in the newly conquered lands – those with long loyal service or those who had been most successful in terms of territorial gain, whether they were latecomers to the faith or not. Then there was the problem of conversion, which radically changed the character of the Arab Empire as non-Arabs took up Islam en masse. There was no active move to convert non-believers as every Muslim was, in theory, entitled to a salary drawn from the *jizya*, the tax levied on non-Muslims. Mass conversion both emptied the pot and of course made the pot smaller. Finally there was a problem with the Arab armies themselves – they simply weren't Arab anymore. Persian commanders and Berber chiefs had brought with them groups of their men wholesale into the Islamic army as they defected from the Byzantine and Sassanian armies. Furthermore, as the Arabs of the original conquests were now garrisoned far away from their original homelands tribal loyalties disintegrated as they formed new attachments to their garrison towns and the armies' allegiances were as likely to be to a local governor or general as to the Caliph in Damascus.

The tensions within the empire came to a head in 750 with the Abbasid Revolution. The revolution started in Persia and it is possible to see it as a Persian revolt against the Arab Umayyad Caliphate in Syria, but there was more to it than that. The Abbasids were also Arabs but they tempted non-Arabs to join them with a vague message promising a more just and equitable society. Khurasan was the starting point for the revolution. The Khurusani army was used to fighting with the Turks and were the best troops in Islam; they won a series of victories over the Umayyad armies and the Abbasids came to power but were unable, essentially, to salve the disaffection within the Islamic Empire for the idea of an 'Arab Kingdom'. Conversion continued to fuel economic, racial and religious discontent throughout Islam. The early Abbasid Caliphate spent its time suppressing peasant revolts and attempting to stop breakaways by powerful and distant governors. Their Caliphate was unrecognised in Spain and a rival Umayyad Caliphate there endured until the Christian Reconquista of the eleventh century. In 788 the Idrisid Kingdom broke away in North Africa and Syria slipped into civil war among petty princes. Then there were revolts in both Transoxania and Khurasan; it is particularly notable that both these insurrections were instigated by imams, an indication of the abundance at that time, as in our own, of self legitimising militant Islamic leadership amongst the grass roots. The Tulunid Dynasty of Egypt sprang from an all too powerful local governor who had been a slave soldier and was at least quasi-independent of the Abbasids from 868, and eastern Iran was lost in 867 to the Saffarid Dynasty.

The Abbasid Caliphate was therefore becoming more and more of an irrelevance outside Iraq. Islam, the force that had united Arabia and made possible the empire, was now making it ungovernable; it was no longer a tool of power to be wielded only by the Caliphs and they had to cast about to find new bricks to support their house. They needed to re-establish the authority of the Caliphate and to find new resources of power, however repressive, to do their bidding in the suppression of rebellion in the revenue-bearing lands. This was a tacit acknowledgement that the Arab Empire as a working system was finished and a military dictatorship was the inevitable outcome of this crisis. The Abbasids did control Iraq but even there they were hostages to the powers that had delivered them the Caliphate. The Khurusani Arab troops who had become Persianised from long-term garrisoning in Khurasan were settled in Baghdad as a powerful Caliphal guard but their loyalty was dubious. They were liable to support any candidate for the Caliphate who was willing to bring advantages to their new homeland of Khurasan and the ambitions of the powerful families there. The Caliph al-Mamun (r. 813–33) had to pay off the Khurasanis after a civil war with his brother by making Khurasan practically independent in 821. This praetorian dilemma led the Caliphs then to look beyond the lands of Islam for their new army, an army of soldiers who were personally dependent on their master, who were beyond the reach of the harmful ideology of Islam as preached by the intelligentsia, free of ties to kin and to homelands and whose entire *raison d'être* was service to their lord and prepossession with the skills of the warrior. The solution was to be an army of slaves. As discussed above, slave soldiers already had a history of employment in the young Islamic Empire, but it is at this point that the Arabic word for slave, *mamluk*, starts being used by the chroniclers of the time to describe these men along with the Arabic word for boy, *ghulam*, an obvious indication of the youth of these Mamluks when they first entered service. The chroniclers' application of specific words to the phenomenon of the slave soldier in the early ninth century is strong evidence that the use of Mamluks accelerated greatly in this period and that systematic harvesting of Turkish boys from the steppes of Central Asia and southern Russia had now begun on a huge scale. The Islamic geographer and scholar Yaqut (d. 1229) tells a distinctly uncharming story of life in these steppe lands.

> If a man begets a son, he would bring him up and provide for him and take care of him until he reaches puberty. Then he would hand him a bow and arrows and drive him from the family home crying. 'Go fend for yourself!' Henceforward he would treat him both as a stranger and a foreigner. There are also among these people those who will sell their sons and daughters. *

There are always harsh customs in hard lands. It is difficult for modern readers to fully understand the reasons for such actions but the fact that the sale of children has occurred in so many places across the world at so many different times requires at least a brief investigation into the practice. Generally, agrarian societies have tended to sell girls rather than boys, perhaps because crop farming is labour intensive, especially in the absence of plough animals, but the Turks of Central Asia did not undertake settled farming; the steppe is a treeless plain where sedentary agriculture is impossible. The Turks survived as nomadic herders of sheep and they supplemented the family's diet to a great extent with hunting. Survival was marginal

---

* D. Ayalon, 'The Mamluk Novice: On his Youthfulness and on his Original Religion', *Revue des Etudes Islamiques*, vol 54, 1986.

during hard winters and the ground would not support large densities of inhabitants. Surplus children were an encumbrance to the survival of the family unit and the boys might become a possible challenge to the authority of the *paterfamilias*. Indeed, one way of reading Yaqut's passage is that if you are prepared to kick your adolescent son out of your home and never acknowledge his existence thereafter, you may as well receive some profit from his departure and from your investment in his young life.

In common with other nomadic peoples the Turks engaged with the sedentary peoples to their south in order to trade animal products – wool and meat – in exchange for finished items. Perhaps children too were brought to trading posts for inspection and sale and perhaps they were sold at puberty because at this point their parents may have found the cruel but necessary arithmetic of calculating how many of their offspring would survive childhood easier to undertake. Certainly the chronicler al-Istakhri (d. 951) assures us that trading of slaves was a common practice within steppe communities. It is notable, however, that Yaqut only says there are *some* who were willing to sell their children. Kidnapping of children and raids on families by slaving gangs must also have occurred to satisfy the needs, which were great and increasing, of the Islamic states for Mamluk novices.

Yaqut's short exposé of the customs of the steppe peoples must also mean that there were a number of unattached pubescent boys roaming around the steppe. It is possible that such individuals might be tempted to gather at known points for entry into the slave-dealing system. This idea still applies *mutatis mutandis* to the recruitment of Ghurkhas into the British Army, where young would be recruits muster for examination and the successful leave their homeland for a military life. We might be tempted to call these young Turks volunteers, but if the other life options are uniformly bleak, calling this choice voluntary might be a little strong.

Boys just approaching puberty were ideal in every way for both the slave traders and their clients in the Islamic lands. The logistics of moving child slaves are much less complex than that of moving adults; security, both in terms of possible revolt and of escape are much less of a concern. Furthermore, the relationship between the slave trader and his child slaves was close, with the slave trader acting as a surrogate parent during the journey and in the slave markets. Sometimes the slave traders offered a kind of after-sales service: they would continue to care for the Mamluk novice after he was purchased, during his military apprenticeship and right up to manumission and the boy's full entry into the service of a lord.

From the buyer's point of view these boys were young enough to allow for moulding to their lord's needs whilst, as Yaqut's passage indicates, they had already taken up the bow and would certainly, given the nature of steppe life, have had at least rudimentary if not advanced skills in horsemanship. The Mamluk's personal dependence on his lord, which classically lasted until the death of one of the parties, was a direct result of the social displacement that the boys underwent at a young age and the need to form new ties in an alien environment. The level of personal attachment was then like that of a court favourite but with an essential difference. The Mamluk, because of his entire dependence on his lord, would undertake menial tasks that no favoured or intimate associate would agree to perform. Al-Tabari (d. 923) records the Caliph al-Mahdi as saying that he might raise a Mamluk during an audience and have him sit at his side so close that their knees would rub and then at the end of the audience he would order the same man to groom his horse and the Mamluk would go, without taking offence, to the Caliph's horse. The Caliph complained that if he asked any nobleman to do the same he would receive only complaints and refusals.

The paganism of the Turkish people of Central Asia in the medieval age was also convenient. Islam has a *sharia* interdict on the enslavement of Muslims, but this did not apply to unbelievers. It was acceptable to enslave Jews and Christians but not entirely desirable; the Christians and Jews were 'People of the Book', so whilst they were inferior to Muslims in that they had not received the full revelation of the Koran they had some shared heritage with the Muslims. This is not to suggest that enslavement of Christians did not occur in the period before the establishment of the Ottoman Empire – it did, but compared to the trade in pagans it was very limited and occurred generally in the western lands of Islam where capture of Christians was more common and there were no other sources available. Certainly in later years more Christians were taken as the process of Islamisation had begun to occur in the traditional harvesting grounds of Central Asia. Even then, Christian Slavs – *Saqaliba* – were more likely to be castrated and used as eunuchs than as Mamluks in the eastern Islamic world. The Ottomans certainly harvested Christian boys in the Balkans for the Janissary Corps and enslaved Muslims, but more of that later.

The Mamluk revolution really began with Caliph al-Mutasim (r. 833–42) and his desire to produce a Mamluk military aristocracy. He wanted his Mamluks to be much more than just front-line troopers, he planned for them to be totally immersed in military culture and capable of being promoted to the highest positions in the state. He personally supervised the training and the apprenticeship that they passed through to gain entrance to the military caste. He had been a witness to the civil war between his older brothers al-Mamun and al-Amin who had been Caliphs before him. The lesson of this confrontation for al-Mutasim seems to have been twofold: first, that al-Amin had lost the war and his life because he had relied on Arab forces that were markedly inferior to the Turkish levies of al-Mamun and secondly, that it was the fact that a good proportion of al-Mamun's troopers were Mamluks that made all the difference. A tale that circulated after the war may also have influenced al-Mutasim in his course of action. The story was that Al-Amin's governor of al-Ahwaz was losing a battle and his command was about to be overrun; he told his Mamluk bodyguard to flee and to leave him to fight alone but his men replied:

> By Allah! If we do so we would cause you great injustice. You have taken us from slavery and elevated us from a humble position and raised us from poverty to riches. And after all that, how can we abandon you and leave you in such a state? No, instead we shall advance in front of you and die under your

steed. May Allah curse this world and life altogether after your death.*

They then dismounted and hamstrung their horses. They died, to a man, fighting around their master.

During the early years of al-Mamun's Caliphate al-Mutasim started buying Turkish boys in Baghdad's slave markets and he even arranged direct purchases from Turkistan. His private Mamluk army only numbered three thousand men by the end of his brother's reign but it was, for its size, one of the most formidable forces within Islam at this time due to its troops' discipline and high level of training and the Caliph often relied on al-Mutasim and his Mamluks for the suppression of revolts. By 828 al-Mutasim was governing Syria and Egypt as the Abbasids re-established a degree of control over the Islamic lands and he used his Mamluks to pacify these unruly provinces. On his accession to the Caliphate al-Mutasim cut all the Arabs from the salary roll of the state, and by so doing he ensured that the standing army would no longer be drawn from the tribes of the Arabs. He redirected the funds to his new model army, an army made up of slave soldiers from the fringes of the empire and strongly Turkish in origin but without any true home except that given to them by the Caliph.

The home he gave them was founded in 836 and can still be traced out in the desert beside the river Tigris about eighty miles north of Baghdad. The site of the city of Samarra is over thirty miles long. It required its own canal system to meet its need for water and was chiefly composed of huge walled compounds with endless successions of living quarters, courtyards, racing tracks and game enclosures, halls, harems and a grid-like web of boulevards and side streets to link each zone. The city was designed to be self-sufficient and to seclude the ruler from the ruled and, just as importantly, to shield his Mamluk military elite from possible sources of sedition that might tempt them to break their loyalty to the Caliph. Such was the extent of this

---

* Cf. D. Ayalon, 'The Military Reforms of Caliph Al-Mutasim, Their Background and Consequences', in D. Ayalon, *Islam and the Abode of War*, London: Variorum Reprints, 1994.

separation that those on the outside, totally ignorant of the activities of the sequestered few inside, used imagination to replace hard fact and these daydreams gave to the world the tales of the Thousand and One Nights. Even within Samarra the Mamluks were housed in self-contained quarters that were separated from the civilian sections of the city.

Within these barrack ghettoes, al-Yaqubi tells us, Mamluk marriages took place to slave girls specially imported by the Caliph, as marriage to local civilians was forbidden. Mosques were also built for the Mamluks' exclusive use; even prayer was not an activity to be shared with the general community. Religious teaching and the process of conversion to Islam was deliberately perfunctory. It was desirable that Mamluks maintained an innocence of doctrine; obedience to Allah, keeping to the *sharia* and undivided loyalty to the Caliph was more than enough. No complex theological arguments that might confuse the clear thinking of these automatons were introduced.

We are unable to assay just how impressive al-Mutasim's new model army could have been. The fissures that had begun to erupt in the Islamic Empire in 750 were, by the ninth century, well advanced and the Caliph himself did not live long enough to guide his project fully. As the Islamic Empire splintered politically the Abbasid Caliphate found itself further and further away from the frontier zones of Transoxania and Afghanistan. The Samanid and Saffarid Emirates dominated the eastern Islamic lands in the ninth century and the Mamluks employed by these states on the Transoxanian border proved themselves able warriors.

During this period of fighting against forces that were racially akin to themselves but distinctly from outside the *Dar al-Islam*, the 'Abode of Islam', the Mamluks were exposed to the influence of *ghazi* fighters for the faith who volunteered to do battle with the infidels in the *Dar al-Harb*, the 'Abode of War' beyond the Islamic lands. These men propagated *jihad* through their actions and preaching and, whilst Mamluks never evolved into *ghazi* fighters per se, *jihad* entered into the Mamluk lore along with faithfulness to the lord who manumitted them, loyalty to the corps, a reverence for weapons and warfare and an innate understanding that the man of arms and the martial way of life was totally superior to the civilian and civilian ways. This lore would find its full expression under the Mamluk Sultanate of Egypt and Syria between 1260 and 1517 but its origin was in the ninth century, far away from the Levant. Some idea of how essential war – of any variety – was to the Mamluk self-view and *amour propre* can be garnered from this short passage from an archery manual of the Mamluk Sultanate, 'As man is built of four foundations: namely bone, flesh, blood and arteries, so is the compound bow in as much as wood to bone, horn to flesh, sinews to arteries and glue to blood'.

And as to how they were viewed by the Arabs, Al-Jahiz relates a tale of how, whilst waiting for the Caliph in blazing midday heat in full battle array, Arab troopers of the army dismounted and flopped down beside the road whereas, despite the Caliph's delayed arrival, his Mamluks remained mounted and in good order. Al-Jahiz was amazed by the stamina of the Turks but also, at the end of the passage he asks, 'whatever happened to us?'*

---

* Ayalon, 'The Military Reforms of Caliph al-Mutasim'.

2

Under Siege

Steppe People and Crusaders

But why did they not dare? Why did so many people and so many kingdoms fear to attack our little kingdom and our humble people? Why did they not gather from Egypt, from Persia, from Mesopotamia, and from Syria at least a hundred times a hundred thousand fighters to advance courageously against us, their enemies?

From the Historia Hierosolymitana of Fulcher of Chartres. c.1115

A T THE BEGINNING OF the tenth century the Khitans,* a Turco-Mongolian people from north of the Great Wall of China, swiftly subjugated a large area of what is today Mongolia and of Northern China. The Khitans were strong enough and China was weak enough at this point for the Khitans to take a dynastic name, the Liao, and rule as emperors in Northern China from 907 to 1125. When the Liao started to place garrisons in the Central Asian steppe in an attempt to control and tax its peoples the Turks knew it was time to leave and they headed west. The steppe peoples were on the march.

The most important clan from this movement were the Saljuqs, they entered the Islamic lands early in the eleventh century and became Sunni Muslims but continued raiding westwards across the Islamic lands and completely defeated the Ghaznavids, another Turkish dynasty that had been founded

---

* The Khitans were misnamed the *Khitai* by Westerners. From this comes Cathay, which later came to mean China generally.

by the Mamluk Sebuktigin and had carved out an empire in Persia, Afghanistan and the Punjab in a battle in which the Saljuqs deployed an army almost entirely made up of horse archers – unheard of in previous times. The Saljuq leaders were able to convince the Abbasid Caliph that, as Sunnis they were preferable to the Shiite Buyids who had been in effective control of Persia until their arrival and certainly much preferable to the Fatimids, a Shiite dynasty that had grown up in North Africa, conquered Egypt and Syria in the late tenth century and looked set for further moves against the Sunni world.

The Abbasid Caliphs acted as ciphers to the Saljuqs, who were now the real power in the Sunni world, taking the title of Sultan and who were the forerunners of the Mamluk Sultanate of Egypt in many ways. They showed the total superiority of mounted warriors and of cavalry warfare over armies that deployed infantry as their main force and used cavalry as an auxiliary arm. They also maintained the Mamluk system to ensure that they had a core army of trusted troops. The extended Mamluk bodyguard or *askari* of a Saljuq lord were the only truly trusted troops in the empire. The Turcomen – the tribal Turks who had never become involved with government and over whom even the Saljuq Empire's most senior leaders had only a tenuous hold – could only be relied on for short campaigns that offered booty.

The Saljuqs also extensively developed the Islamic *iqta* system. An *iqta* was similar to a fief for a Western knight in that it provided the *askari* trooper's salary. However, in many ways the *iqta* was more complex in that it could be a 'share' of an industry such as the spice trade or a tract of agricultural land. The owner did not need to be resident on the land from which the *iqta* was drawn as the government managed it for him. Furthermore the *iqta*, in theory, was not hereditary as a fief was. The distribution of *iqta* by the Sultan was, though, like the Western fief in that it was a way of maintaining the loyalty both of the Sultan's personal bodyguard and of his emirs. Both of these uses for the *iqta* would apply later in the Mamluk Sultanate, paying salaries and buying loyalty.

The Saljuq Sultans, as the new champions of the Sunnis, began to push to the west to meet the Fatimid threat. By doing so they almost inadvertently clashed with the forces of the Byzantines. The Greek Emperor Romanus Diogenes had been spoiling for a showdown with the Saljuqs. He had brought his army into Anatolia in 1071 and he rushed into battle without really thinking about what he was doing. The armies met in a valley near Manzikert on 19 August or perhaps to Byzantine eyes they didn't meet – as the Greeks advanced the Turks just fell away, certainly there were Turkish archers riding up and down the flanks, showering the Byzantines with arrows and then fleeing but there was no force to engage with. The Byzantines kept coming on up the valley but still there was no real contact. Towards the end of this day of futile pursuit the Emperor decided that he could not move any further from his camp and the army turned back to retrace its steps. At that moment, when the Byzantine army was stretched out along the valley, in the process of changing their grouping for the return journey and whilst the van had become separated from their rearguard, the Saljuqs attacked. The mounted and heavily armoured Mamluk archers of the *askari* poured into the Byzantine column and broke it up and lightly armed Turcoman auxiliaries rode down the Byzantines' flanks adding their arrows to the onslaught. Many of the Greeks' mercenaries fled the field immediately, as did the Byzantine nobles who were the Emperor's rearguard. The incredible impact and fury of the Turkish assault is testified to by the recollections of Michael Attaleiates, who fought with Romanus Diogenes on that day. 'It was like an earthquake: the shouting, the sweat, the swift rushes of fear and not least the hordes of Turks riding all around us . . .' The Emperor managed to mount some resistance to the onslaught, his army was much larger than the Saljuq force, and at one point it looked as if the Turks would have to break off the attack. It was the discipline of the Mamluk *askari* that ensured victory; they refused to give up the field and by doing so drew the Turcoman auxiliaries back to the fight. The Byzantines were crushed and Romanus was taken prisoner. The important mission of returning the captured

Emperor to Byzantium in order to raise his own ransom was undertaken by a bodyguard of one hundred Mamluks.

Looking back from nearly a thousand years later, the Turkish tactic seems very simple and it seems incredible that Romanus fell into the trap but the feigned retreat was a complex exercise, requiring that the enemy be engaged to a degree sufficient to tempt him on. It must also be noted that medieval armies were difficult to command and control in the field. This meant two things: the more Romanus' army was kept on the move the worse the communication inside the army became, and in order to deliver a swift, killing stroke the troops of the Saljuqs needed to be well drilled and practised in manoeuvres in which they moved and acted as one body. The Mamluk *askari* were at the core of such discipline, but skills acquired in the grand hunts of the Turkic peoples also applied here and it is no surprise that one of the tactics used again and again by the Mongols, famed hunters, was this feigned retreat followed by the encirclement and destruction of the enemy.

The Battle of Manzikert, as alluded to in Chapter One, was the direct cause of the First Crusade, the crusading movement that grew up from it and ultimately of the Mamluk Sultanate and its military machine that finally cleared Syria of Christian states. It was the central reason for Byzantium's call for assistance from the Papacy and thereby from the military men of the West. What this meant for Islam was that a new enemy had emerged at its western border at a time when the *Dar al-Islam* was already undergoing another process of internal collapse and facing grave danger from the East. The question posed by Fulcher of Chartres at the head of this chapter is certainly a valid one and perhaps masks a feeling of disbelief at the achievements of the pilgrim soldiers of the *expeditio* and the failure of the Islamic powers to arrest the progress and settlement of an exposed and isolated army that had come so close to perishing at the walls of Antioch. Fulcher would have been unaware of the fact that the timing of the First Crusade was extremely opportune. In the 1090s there had been a loss of all the major political leaders in the Saljuq world. The year 1092 saw the murder of Nizam al-Mulk, the powerful chief minister of the Saljuq Sultanate, very possibly by the Assassins of the Ismaili Shiite sect known as the 'New Preaching'.* Sultan Malik-Shah, his wife, grandson and several other senior politicians all died soon after. The centripetal force of Nizam al-Mulk's government was lost and the Saljuq Empire was splintered into a group of discrete polities. Powerful emirs used their forces to their own advantage and formed unstable allegiances to candidates for the Sultanate; in this chaotic period leaders of these new principalities became mutually suspicious of each other and the unity of the state disappeared. Syria was forgotten as Malik-Shah's family fought over Iraq, the contest between his sons Muhammad and Barkyaruq for Iraq exhausting the Sultanate and draining the treasury. Al-Bundari describes how Muhammad lacked funds even to provide for his Mamluks' daily beer allowance. The eastern part of the Saljuq sultanate was embroiled in Transoxanian affairs from 1100 onwards. The Khitans who had set in motion the original movement of the steppe peoples that had been a primary cause of the Saljuq Sultanate had now themselves been pushed from China and towards the west by the Jurchen, who went on to form the Jin Dynasty, the second of a succession of three alien dynasties that were to rule China. This displacement further increased the pressure on Islam's eastern border as the Ghuzz Turks were, in turn, pushed west by the Khitans. The Sultanate's panicked response to all this was to settle a new capital at Marv to stiffen the border, but Sultan Sanjar was totally defeated by the Khitans in 1141. This event gave rise in the Crusader lands and later in Europe to the myth of Prester John, the Christian king who lived on Islam's eastern border and who would save Outremer from the Muslims. It also alarmed many of the Saljuqs who hadn't already deserted Syria for the lucrative business of the Saljuq civil wars into returning to Iran. Many of them held Iranian *iqtas* and the depleted revenues of their Syrian possessions were of little importance to them compared to those they held in eastern Persia with its flourishing agrarian economy.

---

* The Ismailis, of which the Assassins were a faction, still exist, their imam being the Aga Khan.

The Crusaders therefore never faced the full power of the Saljuq Empire. And yet the pilgrim army of which Anna Comnena wrote that, 'one might have likened them to the stars of heaven or the sand poured along the edge of the sea'* was halted and nearly destroyed at Dorylaeum, where Fulcher of Chartres was both horrified and impressed by the 'clouds of arrows' fired at the Crusaders by their assailants. And then in 1119 the decidedly local forces of a minor Turkish ruler, Il-Ghazi of Mardin, inflicted such a resounding defeat on Roger of Antioch that the Crusaders named the battle Ager Sanguinis, the Field of Blood. So what does this failure to win the war but success in battle mean? A clue is given by Ibn al-Qalanasi's description of the scene of the Field of Blood at the battle's conclusion:

> The Franks were on the ground, one prostrate mass, horsemen and footmen alike, with their horses and their weapons, so that not one man of them escaped to tell the tale, and their leader Roger was found stretched out among the dead, the horses too were stretched out on the ground like hedgehogs because of the quantities of arrows sticking into them . . .†

Dorylaeum and Ager Sanguinis are both evidence that the Saljuq Mamluk trooper of this period was an exceptional soldier and that the weapons technology of the Saljuq forces proper was at least the equal of and probably superior to that of the European forces. A Mamluk trooper's composite bow or *qaws* gave exceptional penetration, he also had well-developed heavy armour and was adept with both lance and sword. The problem was that there just were not enough Mamluks in the Saljuq forces. Whilst the size of the Saljuq forces in Syria in this period is hard to estimate, we can be certain it was small. Aleppo and

---

* A figure of between fifty and sixty thousand persons has been suggested at the Crusade's outset. Cf. J. France, 'Technology and Success in the First Crusade', in V. Parry and M. Yapp (eds), *War, Technology and Society in the Middle East*, London: Oxford University Press, 1975.

† In C. Hillenbrand, *The Crusades: Islamic Perspectives*, Edinburgh: Edinburgh University Press, 1999, p. 81.

Damascus both certainly held no more than a thousand soldiers each and Nizam al-Mulk's *Book of Government* gives the standing army or bodyguard of the Saljuq Sultan himself as being just over four thousand men, mostly unmounted. This meant there was a reliance on confederate armies that were both difficult to assemble from leaders of independent cities who had little or no trust and love for one another and even more difficult to maintain for a long enough period to achieve anything of value. Ibn al-Athir wrote that Kerbogha of Mosul failed at Antioch because he alienated other army leaders in his confederation by his 'pride and ill treatment' of them and in 1111 the Crusader Joscelin of Tal Bashir was able to bribe leaders of the Sultan's army into leaving him and his lands in peace. The lesson here was that a strong unified state was required so that a strong, permanent regular field army could be retained. The task of clearing Syria of Crusaders who were both well fortified and a determined foe required nothing less. This was achieved to some degree by Saladin and his successors through the buying of Mamluks, but the notion of fully harnessing the energies of the state to the needs of the army only became more completely developed under the Mamluk Sultanate.

The shortage of men also meant that the small household forces of Syrian emirs at the time of the First Crusade were heavily supplemented by Turcoman irregulars. These Turcomen were fine fighters, this fact is attested to by their annihilation of the third wave of Crusaders that set off for the Holy Land via Anatolia in 1100. Their earlier destruction of the People's Crusade was described by Albert of Aachen. 'When they had seen the Turks, they began to encourage one another in the name of the Lord. Then Walter the Penniless fell, pierced by seven arrows which had penetrated his coat of mail.' Fulcher of Chartres tells us that the Turks, 'dispersed, confounded and almost totally destroyed the army of the Franks', and Albert's writing indicates that this destruction took place while the armies were at a considerable distance apart, moving quickly from the sighting of the Turkish army to Walter being shot to death. The ambush in which an entire army of Germans, the last of the armies of 1101, under Welf of Bavaria was destroyed near

Eregli was performed on a high plateau with little cover for the ambushing force to be able to wait for close contact with the enemy before delivering their onslaught. The Turcomen could not therefore have maintained the element of surprise vital to a successful ambush without being able to hit the Crusading army at very long range. This means that the bowmen must have been delivering their volleys at a phenomenal distance and yet still have been able to penetrate the double-link chain mail that Usama Ibn Munqidh, an Arab warrior prince of the twelfth century, tells us enabled a Frank to survive what appeared to have been an irresistible lance strike.

The sources seem to indicate that the Crusaders had an advantage over the Turcomen once they were in close contact* and it seems likely that the generally more heavily armoured Franks were able to press their advantage once they were within spear and sword length of their adversaries. The later spread of more heavily armoured Mamluks in the armies of Saladin to meet this challenge is evident, as is the lengthening of the lance that Islamic warriors carried along with shields, swords and clubs during the period of the Crusades. The Mamluks who fought the Crusaders at Damietta in 1250 and then went on to create the Mamluk Sultanate were so well armoured that they were able to meet and repel a force of heavy French cavalry in hand-to-hand street fighting.

The biggest problem of employing Turcomen, however, was not so much that they were lightly armoured but that their lack of discipline meant they dispersed all too easily after victories for booty and at harvest time, as Il-Ghazi's force did after the Battle of the Field of Blood in 1119. An important lesson for the Muslims that could be drawn from this early period of confrontation with the Crusaders was therefore that any regular field army had to be of a size sufficient to make auxiliary or irregular forces *truly* auxiliary and not a mainstay of the army. The Mamluk Sultanate often used auxiliary forces of Turcomen and Bedouin but they were never depended upon in the way that regular Mamluk troopers would be.

---

* Cf. France, p. 77.

So it was possible to defeat the Crusaders in the field and Zangi and Nur al-Din even showed that territorial gains could be made from the Franks, but it was Saladin's overwhelming success at the Battle of Hattin in 1187 that really augured the end of Outremer. The end of a period of reverses for Christendom in the East that finished with the death of Saladin in 1193 still found the Franks obdurately holding the coastal lands of Syria but Jerusalem had been lost and Saladin's army – due to his increasing purchases of Mamluks who would fight all year and without hope of booty simply because they were regularly paid and personally dependent on the Sultan – had fought a gruelling one-year war to frustrate the ambitions of the Third Crusade brought to Syria by Richard the Lionheart. The Turkish forces of Islam had shown that they were now capable of undertaking the kind of determined warfare that was required to push the *Franj* from the *Dar al-Islam*, but what was really significant for the Mamluk Sultanate's later eradication of the Crusaders was that the field army of the Crusaders had been destroyed at Hattin. The Franks of Outremer would put armies in the field again in the next century but they were never able to replace this force adequately enough to ensure the relief of the various fortified cities and castles of the kingdom should the Muslims lay siege to any one of them. The judicious use of the field army of the Kingdom of Jerusalem by its kings to cause Muslim forces to break off sieges was perhaps the most important reason, allied to fortification, for Outremer's relative success until King Guy's reckless sacrifice of the flower of Jerusalem's knighthood on the Horns of Hattin. Outremer, from this point on, could never guarantee relief from siege for any of its isolated settlements. All that was needed for these outposts to fall was a determined, capable foe to apply enough force. Islam would have to wait just a little longer for such a champion to emerge in the form of the Mamluk Sultanate. It was both fully prepared to drive the *jihad* to its end and able to deliver the hammer blows required to dislodge the infidel from his strongholds.

3

TO POWER

THE BIRTH OF THE MAMLUK SULTANATE

We have mingled blood with flowing tears, and there is no room
    left for pity
To shed tears is a man's worst weapon when the swords stir up
    the embers of war.
Sons of Islam, behind you are battles in which heads rolled at
    your feet.
Dare you slumber in the blessed shade of safety, where life is as
    soft as an orchard flower?
How can the eye sleep between the lids at a time of disasters that
    would waken any sleeper?
While your Syrian brothers can only sleep on the backs of their
    chargers or in vulture's bellies!

Abu l-Musaffar al-Abiwardi, poet, twelfth century

SUCH WERE THE CALLS for *jihad* from Syria that had
started early in the twelfth and still continued in the
thirteenth century. But there was a problem, after
the death of Saladin his empire of Syria, the Jazira and most
importantly Egypt was divided among his sons and close
kinsmen. Unfortunately, such distributions never seem to have
had a happy ending and infighting among the beneficiaries of
Saladin's estate soon erupted and then there were new threats
such as the Khwarazmians. These were mercenary troops whose
employers, the Khwarazm-Shahs, had tried to build an empire
in the Transoxanian region before being destroyed by Genghis
Khan and who entered Syria shortly after as wandering war

bands. Therefore the Ayyubids* had rather greater concerns than the continued existence of a group of orientalised Europeans without the threat of a large field army living quietly on the coast. Indeed, it is interesting to speculate whether the Crusader kingdoms could have lasted in perpetuity if the Popes and the European sovereigns hadn't effectively forced Islam's hand by the continuance of further Crusading adventures, particularly by their direct assaults on Egypt in 1218 and 1250.

The early thirteenth century is, however, vitally important to a study of the birth of the Mamluk Sultanate because it is in this period that the son of the Sultan of Egypt, al-Salih Ayyub, started specifically recruiting Qipchaq Turks for his *askari*. He recruited as many as he could as fast as he could and was lucky, as in the first third of the thirteenth century the slave markets of Cairo were full of Qipchaqs. The boys were being sold cheap under the normal market rules of supply and demand. The Mongol invasion of southern Russia had passed through the Caucasus and through the Qipchaq lands that were to the east of the Volga and north of the Caspian Sea in the 1220s. Al-Nuwayri, a writer of the Mamluk Sultanate tells us that, 'The Mongols fell upon the Qipchaqs and brought upon most of them death, slavery and captivity. At this time merchants bought these captives and brought them to other countries and cities. The first who demanded many of them and made them lofty and advanced them in the army was al-Salih Ayyub.'†

Al-Salih became Sultan of Egypt in 1240 and it was in this period that many of the traditions of Mamluk lore began to be formalised and in which the ceremonies that would become the outward display of Mamluk culture began to develop. That al-Salih's importance to the men he created endured even

---

* Despite Saddam Hussein's attempt to claim him as an Arabic-Iraqi hero, Saladin was a Kurd whose father was Najm al-Din Ayyub. This is tragic given Saddam's appalling treatment of the Iraqi Kurds.

† The irony of the Mongols effectively creating their own nemesis in the Middle East has been pointed out by R. Amitai-Preiss, *Mongols and Mamluks: The Mamluk-Ilkhanid War, 1260-1281*, London: Cambridge University Press, 1995, p. 18.

after his death is evident in the fact that in the early Mamluk Sultanate military ceremonials including the manumission of new Mamluks were carried out in his mausoleum.

Al-Salih called his Mamluk regiment the Bahriyya. It was garrisoned on a large fortified island of the *Bahr al-Nil* – the river Nile – near Cairo, from which it drew its name. It had a strength of perhaps only about one thousand men but it would soon prove its worth both in urban fighting and in open country warfare. The regiment was engaged first against the largest army that Outremer had put in the field since Hattin. The Crusaders had had to pull troops from every part of the kingdom to form a force that allied itself with the Ayyubids of Syria and faced the Egyptian army of al-Salih in Gaza in 1244. Tyre, Jaffa, Antioch and Tripoli all contributed troops, as did the Knights of the Temple, Teutonic Order and of the Hospital. Al-Salih's Egyptian Mamluks were partnered by Khwarazmian mercenaries who had been employed by al-Salih to put a check on the progress of the Ayyubids of Syria, but who had also managed to totally sour Muslim–Christian relations by entering Jerusalem, slaying at least two thousand of its Christian residents, destroying the tombs of the Latin kings of Jerusalem and desecrating the holy places. They then moved south to Gaza and joined up with al-Salih's forces on the plain near Harbiyya.*

The Crusader army attacked almost immediately upon sighting the Egyptians. They outnumbered their enemy and there must have been a desire among the Crusaders to take revenge for Jerusalem on the Khwarazmians. The Franks had the right flank of the army, the Ayyubids of Damascus and Homs made up the centre of the advance and the Ayyubids of al-Karak formed the left wing. The Egyptian troops stood firm before the assault of the Franks and whilst the impetus of the advance was arrested the Khwarazmians, from their position out to the right of the Mamluks, swung down upon the Syrian Ayyubids, hitting them both on their flank and in the centre of the army as a whole. The troops of Damascus panicked

---

* The battle was known as La Forbie by the Europeans and as Harbiyya by the Muslims.

and fled, as did the men of al-Karak. The forces from Homs attempted to hold their ground and to protect the Crusaders' left flank but the Khwarazmian drive was irresistible and pushed the Crusaders and the men of Homs into the Egyptian Mamluk army, which proceeded to massacre them with bow, mace and axe. At least five thousand Crusaders were killed and eight hundred taken prisoner. After Hattin the Latins had been reduced to the defence only of the coastal strip, after this battle it was doubtful that they could even defend that.

The Battle of Harbiyya triggered renewed calls for Crusade in Europe and the pious King of France, Louis IX, responded, launching his assault in the summer of 1249. The King had been appalled by the Khwarazmian devastation of Jerusalem but was also fulfilling a vow he had made when gravely ill with malaria that he would fight in the Holy Land. However, no other party in Europe was particularly animated by Louis's calls for an expedition. Eastern Europe was still reeling from the Mongol invasion of 1241 and the Pope and the Holy Roman Emperor were on very unholy terms, leading to papal preaching for a crusade against Frederick.

Louis aimed to wrest Egypt from Islam. Richard the Lionheart had always suggested that Egypt was in fact the key to the Holy Land and he was correct in as much as the economic and agrarian resources of Egypt far outstripped those of Syria; Syria's interior, without Egypt's support, was an exposed region and difficult to defend. Louis was to attempt an amphibious attack on Egypt, which had been tried before in 1218 and had very nearly succeeded, it was only when the Crusaders' advance from al-Mansura had been halted by Nile floods that the Egyptians had been able to encircle them and then cut them off totally by bringing down river dams to flood the area to their rear. Louis landed on 5 June 1249 near to Damietta in the Nile delta with an army of about twenty thousand men. He had prepared well and his force had enough shallow-draught boats to put a large force ashore in one go. The Muslim defenders of the delta were easily defeated and the city of Damietta fell on 6 June. It was the flood season on the Nile, but Louis had known this and with a well-established supply chain that was based on Cyprus he was well prepared to deal with a long wait. The Egyptian army withdrew further up the river, they too knew the floods would gain them a little time. The rapidity of their departure is attested to by de Joinville: 'The Turks made a blunder in leaving Damietta, without cutting the bridge of boats, which would have put us to great inconvenience. They did us much harm, however, when they went away, by setting fire to the bazaar, where all the merchandise and raw goods were.'

Louis started his march on Cairo on 20 November and he should have gained an advantage from the death of al-Salih. The heir to the Ayyubid Sultanate of Egypt was al-Muazzam Turan-Shah and he was far away in the Jazira. The Sultan's death and the Crusaders' advance would have been a recipe for political chaos in Cairo but for the swift actions of the Sultan's widow, Shajar al-Durr, who, in league with the senior Mamluk emir al-Shuyukh, concealed the Sultan's death from his household and troops and forged enough decrees to get al-Shuyukh made commander-in-chief of the army.

Louis reached al-Mansura, the fortified city downstream of Cairo. Despite his age and death early in the conflict, the new Egyptian commander-in-chief's leadership was inspiring and his forces were able to stop the Crusader advance on the bank of the Nile opposite al-Mansura and gain enough time to organise the defences of the city fully. The Christian forces would have cross the river whilst under assault from the siege engines and catapults of the Mamluks. A description of the horrendous nature of the 'light artillery' that the Bahriyya employed was given by the Crusader de Joinville:

> We were all covered with fire-darts. By good luck, I found a thick Saracen's tunic. I made a shield of the tunic, which served me in good stead, for their fire-darts only wounded me in five places and my pony in fifteen . . . There was a patch of ground behind the Templars, the size of a day's work, so covered with the darts that the Saracens had thrown, that the soil could not be seen for the density of them . . . Next came the battalion of Lord Guy Malvoisin, which battalion the Turks were never able to overcome. However, they succeeded by chance in covering Lord

Guy with Greek fire, which his followers had great difficulty in putting out.*

This bombardment completely thwarted the Crusaders' efforts to build a river crossing, despite the King devising protective shelters for his workmen. Things looked bleak for them until they discovered, on 7 February, a ford where they felt they could cross the river in sufficient numbers to make an assault on the city feasible. The King had planned for each detachment, after crossing the ford, to draw up and wait until a sufficient number of units were assembled for the assault. This never happened, though, as the crossing turned out to be a lot more difficult than was envisaged. Then Count Robert of Artois, the king's brother, ignoring orders, charged along the river after crossing and took the Muslim encampment on the river by surprise. If Robert had stopped there, perhaps things would have worked out better for the Crusaders but rather than securing the siege engines that the Muslims had left behind he and his companions stormed on and into the city itself. They were trapped there by the Mamluks, who barricaded the streets to prevent their withdrawal and then killed virtually the entire force in hand-to-hand fighting. The contemporary writer Ibn-Wasil, though he identifies Robert of Artois incorrectly as the King gives an idea of how desperate the situation was for the Muslims:

> The king of the *Franj* entered the city, and even reached the Sultan's palace. His soldiers poured through the streets, while the Muslim soldiers and the inhabitants sought salvation in disordered flight. Islam seemed mortally wounded, and the *Franj* were about to reap the fruit of their victory when the Mamluk Turks arrived. Since the enemy had dispersed through the streets, these horsemen rushed bravely in pursuit. Everywhere the *Franj* were taken by surprise and massacred with sword or mace. At the start of the day, the pigeons had carried a message to Cairo announcing the attack of the *Franj* without breathing a word of the outcome of the battle, so we were all waiting anxiously. Throughout the quarters of the city there was sadness

---

* In Jean de Joinville, *The Memoirs of the Lord of Joinville*, translated by Ethel Wedgwood, New York: Dutton, 1906, p. 136.

until the next day, when new messages told us of the victory of
the Turkish lions. The streets of Cairo became a festival.*

The Bahriyya, under the junior emir Baybars then moved
out of al-Mansura to meet the rest of the King's forces, which
had managed to cross the river in reasonably good order. The
fighting lasted for the rest of the day with the Mamluks pouring
arrows into the Crusaders' position but then having to retire
and regroup as Louis counter-attacked when he judged that
they were running short of arrows. Louis managed to maintain
his position on the riverbank and, through a late but decisive
deployment of his crossbowmen, perhaps even won the day in
that he held the field while the Mamluks were forced to retire
to al-Mansura. But even if Louis had won the battle he had lost
a brother, and the campaign was certainly doomed. Muslim
reinforcements were beginning to arrive at al-Mansura and
Louis could only match this increase in manpower by a further
strengthening of his camp's fortifications.

The Mamluk regiment launched an assault on 11 February.
They overwhelmed many of the Crusaders' positions and
succeeded in recapturing the siege engines that the Count of
Artois's charge had secured for the Crusaders on the 8th, but
they failed to reach the pontoon bridge that Louis had built to
aid supply of his front line. The Mamluks threw glass grenades
filled with *naft* or Greek fire during this assault and then followed
up the confusion that these missiles caused by sudden charges.
Furusiyya manuscripts of the thirteenth century show mounted
specialist troops with *naft* being used on the end of spears and
batons as well as 'Chinese Arrows' or rockets – these could be
the fire-darts that de Joinville was struck with so many times.
The Mamluks also combined infantry and cavalry assaults,
with the horsemen giving archery support to the men on foot.
The mounted archers also fired darts through tubes mounted
on their bows; two or three darts could be loaded into the tube
and fired simultaneously, and whilst their velocity was low,
they made for very effective harassing fire at close quarters.

---

* In A. Maalouf, *The Crusades through Arab Eyes*, translated by J.
Rothschild, London: Al-Saqi Books, 1984, p. 239.

The Crusaders' defence was desperate but they still managed to hold the Mamluks off. The Muslims retired to the city; time was on their side now and they were awaiting the arrival of the new Sultan. Al-Salih's son, Turan-Shah, entered the Mamluk camp on 28 February and the Muslims then managed to transport a mini-navy on the backs of camels downstream of the Crusaders. These light boats, when launched, effectively cut the Crusaders off from their supplies in Damietta. The river was by now also choked with corpses and it wasn't long before a 'camp sickness' hit, which de Joinville tells us, 'none escaped from save through the jaws of death'.

The Battle of al-Mansura, with its close-quarters fighting, required that the Mamluks close with their opponents, especially in the street fighting with the men of Robert of Artois's detachment. It has been a long-accepted truth of Crusading history that Turkish troops were lightly armoured and relied on their composite bows, speedy horses and the 'Parthian shot' to destroy Crusader forces that – if they could organise a charge – would clear the field of their Muslim adversaries by virtue of their heavy horses and the shock of their couched lance. This is, however, true only as far as the Turcomen were concerned, in terms of the Mamluk bodyguard that was the core of every Turkish prince's army it is very far from correct. The *Gesta Francorum* tells us about Persian heavy horse as early as the First Crusade, the writer calls them *agulari*, and comments on the fact that these horses carried their own armour; this was unheard of in the West at this time.* Furthermore, whilst throughout the Crusading period the Western horse was larger than the steppe ponies that many Turcomen rode, the Mamluks rode stabled horses that were conditioned in the arena and just as likely to be fourteen hands high, as was the average European war horse of the time.† Also, whilst the composite bow was a hugely impressive weapon, it alone was not enough to close a battle. It was used by the Mamluks to wear an enemy down

---

* Cf. France, p. 166.
† Cf. France, p. 166.

both mentally and physically and to create weaknesses in the line that could then be exploited by a charge of heavy cavalry.

The trooper was protected by a knee-length chain-mail shirt that extended up to the neck as a coif; Saladin was once saved from an Assassin's knife stroke by his coif as he sat watching a siege near Aleppo. The *hazagand*, a jerkin of leather and mail that was commonly worn by Islamic troops in Syria is definitely not light in terms of the protection it affords but it is light in terms of the Syrian summer. It was taken up by the Latins of Outremer and spread to Europe as the hauberk jaseran.* Turkish and Islamic armour was designed this way for mobility and because of the climate in which men fought. There was, however, another reason why the armour of the East never moved toward the total body coverage with plate that was a feature of the Western knight in the later medieval age – the technology and techniques of Islamic metalworking. Ibn Sina (d. 1037) describes three types of iron being produced within the Islamic lands but al-Biruni (d. 1048) tells us that the crucible steel or 'wootz' used to create weapons was imported from India. This steel was perfect for blades but it could not be formed into plates any larger than twenty-five centimetres,† which meant that even into the Ottoman age Islamic troops would have been wearing lamellar armour. It is this that has perhaps worked on historians' minds and created the myth of the heavy Western knight bearing down on unprotected Turkish bowmen.

The Mamluk trooper also carried a sword, dagger, axe or mace, lance and shield. These weapons and mounted archery will be discussed further later, but it is worthwhile to consider at this juncture that the mace was a weapon unknown in either Byzantium or the Arab lands in the early medieval period but was in common use in Eastern Iran and Turkish lands, ‡ and

---

* Cf. D. Nicolle, 'Arms of the Umayyad Era: Military Technology in a Time of Change', in Y. Lev (ed.), *War and Society in the Eastern Mediterranean, 7th to 15th Century*, Leiden: EJ Brill, 1997, p. 35.

† Cf. A. Williams, 'Ottoman Military Technology: The Metallurgy of Turkish Armour', in Lev, p. 370.

‡ Cf. Nicolle, p. 32.

that the Mamluks later developed a regiment of axemen called the *Tabardariyya*. Both the axe and the mace are close-quarters weapons and so this shows that Turkish troops in general and Mamluks in particular were confident exponents of close-quarters fighting and had enough body protection to undertake such encounters.

The game was up for poor Louis and his men. His offers to exchange Damietta for Jerusalem were rejected and he started his retreat on 5 April 1250 but the Mamluks pursued the Crusader army and, catching up with it, killed several thousand more of his men. The rest of the army, including a gravely ill Louis, surrendered. The Mamluks also captured all the boats of sick and injured troops that Louis had dispatched down the river before his retreat began. A reasonably wholesale slaughter ensued; the Mamluks started with the sick on the boats, putting all of them to the sword. De Joinville reports that:

> All the time they were bringing ashore the rest of the sick from the galleys where they had been imprisoned, there were men of the Saracens standing ready with drawn swords, and all those who fell they slew, and cast into the river. I told them through my Saracen, that methought it was ill done; inasmuch as it was contrary to the teaching of Saladin, who said that one ought not to slay any man who has once tasted our bread and salt. He replied that they were not to be accounted men, who were good for nothing, being disabled by disease.*

Mamluks were, without doubt, brutal. They were men who had been taken by slavers as children from unforgiving lands, who had no family apart from their master and whose sine qua non was war and killing. What the psychiatrist's couch would make of them now can only be guessed at. In mitigation of their actions here, one might say that there were just so many sick prisoners that the Egyptians' resources were simply overwhelmed. Disease killed more men than combat in every war up until the age of Napoleon and Mamluks were particularly fearful of disease; as outsiders they almost always

---

* In De Joinville, p. 163.

suffered a higher mortality than the indigenous population during epidemics in Egypt and Syria. One might also say that appealing to chivalry as de Joinville did was meaningless; both Richard the Lionheart and Saladin had executed prisoners. Richard had executed the 2,500 men of the garrison of Acre because he couldn't wait for the ransom to free them before starting his march on Jerusalem, and Saladin had taken the lives of the Templars and Hospitallers after Hattin in rage and in fear of releasing such implacable enemies. All these reasons – revenge, inconvenience and the possible return of a dangerous foe – applied at al-Mansura. Furthermore, the chivalric myth of Saladin is largely a Western construction. Saladin used clemency as Caesar did, as a weapon to encourage surrender, and the Crusaders at Damietta had nothing more to surrender. Louis was ransomed in return for Damietta and 400,000 livres. The negotiations for the King's release were interrupted, however, by Mamluks of the Bahriyya regiment revolting against Turan-Shah and murdering him on 2 May. The young emir Baybars broke into Turan-Shah's tent during dinner with a sword in his hand and aimed a blow at his head, which the Sultan was able to ward off. Turan-Shah screamed for help and ran to a wooden siege tower but Baybars's men surrounded and fired it. The Sultan and his emirs bolted into the river but Baybars waded in and killed him.

Looked at in its simplest terms the reasons for the mutiny were simply that some of the Bahriyya feared loss of their power to the established emirs of the new Sultan's household; the Sultan had already appointed several of his own men over Bahriyya officers. The Mamluk historians of later periods give the impression that Turan-Shah was also a little unhinged, there is a tale of the Sultan wandering around his palace at night slashing at candles with his sabre and muttering, 'so I shall deal with the Bahris!'* A slightly deeper investigation of the coup also makes the whole event look somewhat inevitable. Al-Shuyukh was the last emir who was not a Qipchaq Mamluk

---

* In R. Irwin, *The Middle East in the Middle Ages: The Early Mamluk Sultanate*, London: Croom Helm, 1986, p. 21.

and he had died fighting the Crusaders on 9 February 1250. This left a Qipchaq hegemony with ethnic bonds to each other that superseded their bonds to the Egyptian state and of course their master, al-Salih, was now dead. The loyalty of a Mamluk traditionally stopped at his master or *ustadh*; he owed nothing to the sons of the lord. The finite nature of this allegiance was to set the pattern of murder and intrigue that followed the death of almost every Mamluk Sultan.

Of course, their defeat of the Crusaders, who finally left Egypt later in the same month, and the fact that, for a short period of time these slave soldiers had effectively had control of the state could just simply have suggested to them that their time was at hand. What was curious was that after the coup the Mamluks elected Shajar al-Durr to rule as Queen of the Muslims using the authority of a deceased son. Chaos immediately ensued, evidently the medieval Islamic world wasn't quite ready for such a thing, and a woman could most definitely not lead the army. Moreover, the coup had not actually had the full support of the army. Indeed, some Bahriyya Mamluks had attempted to kill Baybars after his murder of Turan-Shah. The Mamluks then put up as the new commander-in-chief the senior emir al-Muizz Aybeg, who, despite being a Bahriyya Mamluk, also had a support base independent of the Bahriyya in the shape of his own bodyguard of Mamluks, named the Muizziyya.

The Mamluks then forced the Sultana to abdicate in favour of Aybeg in July 1250 as a reaction to the loss of Damascus to the Ayyubid Prince, al-Nasir Yusuf, of Aleppo. The Mamluks were showing themselves to be novices in the exercise of power and their panicked response continued five days later when the leading emirs of the Bahriyya led by the emir Aktay al-Jamamdir and Baybars forced Aybeg to stand down in favour of al-Ashraf Musa, a ten-year-old great nephew of al-Salih. They obviously hoped that re-establishing the Ayyubid line in Egypt would placate the Ayyubids of Syria but it did not. Aybeg married Shajar al-Durr; it is uncertain if there was any love involved in the union but it allowed Aybeg to consolidate his position in what was fast becoming a state split into factions following either himself and the Muizziyya or Aktay, Baybars and the emirs of the Bahriyya. Aybeg also obtained the title of *atabeg* or guardian to the new child Sultan and this, effectively, made him the real power in the state. He also managed to unite all the Mamluks under his command to repulse al-Nasir Yusuf's Ayyubid army from its march on Cairo. It was defeated in February 1251 but there was to be no peace with the Syrian Ayyubids until the Caliph of Baghdad's intervention in 1253, which tried to ensure a united Muslim front against the Mongols. The presence of Mongols in the Caucasus region as a part of their occupation of southern Russia and in Anatolia as the overlords of its Saljuq Sultans had been an unpleasant fact of life since the 1240s and the north Syrian Ayyubids even paid tribute to them, but now the hooves of a vast Mongol army readying itself for the complete subjugation of Islam could be heard pounding in the distant East.

The enforced unity of these few years allowed Aybeg to strengthen his position, and his right-hand man, Kutuz, carried out the murder of Aktay in September 1254. Baybars and other senior officers of the Bahriyya fled with about seven hundred Bahri troopers to Ayyubid Syria and to Anatolia, where they acted very much like one of the free companies in the Hundred Years War, making trouble for the rulers and populace of both Syria and Egypt. Aybeg, heady with success, overreached himself, formally deposing the puppet Sultan and seeking a new political marriage. It is fairly certain that it was fear for her own position rather than jealousy that caused Shajar al-Durr to arrange her husband's death, and he was slain in his bath in April 1257. Shajar herself was killed within the same month, her body was found just outside Cairo's citadel, doubtless the victim of a new faction that used a son of Aybeg by another of his wives as a pawn to oppose the Sultana's ambitions. The infighting continued with Kutuz as kingmaker and at this point in its history the Mamluk Sultanate never looked likely to create a stable polity.

The refugee Bahriyya made an abortive attempt on Cairo in 1258 and Kutuz executed all of the leaders that he captured. The Bahriyya vowed vengeance, but any revenge would have to wait, however, as the Mongols were now very much at hand.

4

PRESTER JOHN COMETH

THE MONGOL WAR BEGINS

When I lead my army against Baghdad in anger, whether you
hide in heaven or on earth.
I will bring you down from the spinning spheres; I will toss you
in the air like a lion.
I will leave no one alive in your realm; I will burn your city, your
land, your self.

From Hulegu's letter to the Caliph Al Mustasim, 1258

THE WHOLE WORLD WAS the rightful possession of the
people of Genghis Khan. Whether this belief was
what started Genghis Khan on his career of conquest
or whether it developed once the successes started rolling in
is a question that has perplexed Mongolists for some time.
For the peoples in the Islamic lands lying to the west of the
Mongols it was academic. They were in the way of the Mongol
project and that could only bring war and devastation. Sultan
Sanjar's death in 1157 had caused the dissolution of the Saljuq
Sultanate in eastern Persia and Transoxania. As mentioned
earlier the Khwarazmians, a Turkish dynasty from the Aral
Sea area had carved out an extensive empire in former Saljuq
lands and its Shah took Samarqand as his capital in 1210. He
was not to be allowed too long to enjoy it. In 1219 the entire
empire was rolled up in a three-pronged Mongol assault. The
Shah fled and died on a Caspian Sea island; Transoxania and
Khurasan were virtually destroyed as viable provinces by the
Mongols as they rounded up the Shah's leaderless armies and

undertook wholesale slaughter on the populace. It would seem that Genghis had been greatly concerned about this power to his west and, like Rome with Carthage after the Third Punic War, had decided that total destruction rather than conquest was the safest option to prevent any rebirth of the Khwarazm Empire. Perhaps his policy was wise: the Shah's son, Jalal al-Din did maintain a resistance, albeit somewhat patchy, against the Mongols in his father's former dominions.

Under Ogedei and Guyuk, Genghis's successors, the conquest of southern Russia was completed and the Saljuqs of Anatolia were comprehensively beaten at the Battle of Kose Dagh and the region became a Mongol protectorate in 1243. But even at this point the Mongols had yet to turn their full attention to the reduction of the Middle East and its addition to their realm. The Great Khan Mongke took the throne in 1251 and it was he who sent his brother Hulegu forth on a mission of conquest to the West.

Ostensively, the mission Hulegu was charged with was the destruction of the Assassin sect, the Syrian branch of which we met earlier trying to assassinate Saladin. The Persian branch of the sect had managed to upset the Great Khan by sending four hundred of its followers in disguise to kill him. Hulegu was also instructed to bring the Abbasid Caliph to submission and to bring Mongol dominion over Syria and Egypt. This is at least what the pro-Hulegu sources tell us. The problem is that this may be a later invention created to justify Hulegu's establishment of a state under his control in Iran and Iraq – the Ilkhanate. But to whom was it to justify his actions? The Golden Horde, the Mongols that had conquered southern Russia, were led by Batu, the cousin of Mongke, and Batu's branch of the Genghisid family tree may have had, or at least felt they had, rights of conquest over Persia. This was to be of huge significance later in the struggle between Hulegu's Ilkhanate and the Mamluk Sultanate. It is perhaps significant too that the Saljuq Sultanate of Anatolia had been brought to submission by Batu in 1243 and yet later this area was to come very much under the control of Hulegu's Ilkhanate. The Horde also kept forces stationed south of the Caucasus Mountains in what is today Azerbaijan; this area would later become a contested border land separating the two Mongol states.

Hulegu's forces began their invasion in 1253. It is difficult to be exact about the size of his army. A Mongol *tumen* comprised 10,000 men and from the number of *tumen* commanders mentioned in the sources as having accompanied Hulegu it has been suggested that Hulegu had about 170,000 troopers under his command and with the additional forces of Turkic auxiliaries that we know accompanied Mongol movements to the west a total figure of 300,000 men is arrived at. However, it was common for a *tumen* to carry far less than 10,000 men so these figures must be approached with caution. Fifteenth-century writers, who were far closer to the events than we are, give a figure of 120,000 troopers plus additional forces. An impressive logistics system was put in place to meet this army's needs, ahead of the force's move across Mongol-controlled territory. Pastureland was reserved, bridges were repaired and roads were cleared.

The leaders of the western Islamic lands certainly knew early on of Hulegu's intentions, they had all received letters requiring their submission as early as 1253. But Hulegu's campaign was not exactly a blitzkrieg, by 1256 he was just beginning to face the Assassins in their Persian strongholds and although he finally achieved their virtual extinction in Persia it took a considerable amount of time. He arrived just northeast of Baghdad in 1258, and Mongol forces that had been stationed to the east of Anatolia since the 1240s moved down the Tigris and defeated the Caliph's small army about thirty miles from Baghdad, with the trusty feigned-retreat strategy once again working its magic. This time the enemy was lured into marshy land that inhibited both its manoeuvres and then its attempts to escape the subsequent massacre. The Caliph initially refused to submit, this was certainly unwise as he had little military power left and there was no likelihood of relief from any of the other powers in the region. Once the city was surrounded by the Mongol army and their Chinese-manned siege engines had begun to batter at the walls, however, his mind was changed for him and he surrendered.

Ibn Kathir tells us a little of the closing stages of the siege:

> The Tatars surrounded the seat of the Caliphate and rained arrows on it from every side until a slave girl was hit while she was playing before the Caliph and amusing him. She was one of his concubines, a mulatto called Urfa, and an arrow came through one of the windows and killed her while she was dancing before the Caliph. The Caliph was alarmed and very frightened. The arrow which had hit her was brought to him, and on it was written, 'When God wishes to accomplish His decree, He deprives men of reason of their reason'.
>
> Hulegu Khan came to Baghdad with his numerous infidel, profligate, tyrannical, brutal armies of men who believed in neither God nor in the Last Day ... The armies of Baghdad were very few and utterly wretched, not reaching ten thousand horsemen ...*

The city capitulated on 12 February 1258. The Mongols undertook a wholesale massacre that, due to the intercession of Hulegu's Christian wife, spared the Nestorians of the city. By Hulegu's own admission in a letter to King Louis IX of France in 1262 at least two hundred thousand people were killed. Mongol troopers kicked the unfortunate Caliph to death after having rolled him in a carpet – the Mongols apparently did not wish to spill royal blood directly.

Hulegu moved north from Baghdad and accepted envoys from the Jazira and Syria at the city of Maragha in what is today the very northwest of Iran. The Christian states of Armenia and Georgia aligned themselves as full allies of the Mongols. The Muslim leader of Mosul, Badr al-Din Lu Lu, made obeisance and the Saljuq Sultans of Anatolia offered their forces to Hulegu's Syrian ambitions. Al-Nasir, the Ayyubid Prince of Aleppo and Damascus, sent his son to Hulegu's court to appeal for clemency. It did him no good; Aleppo fell bloodily on 25 January 1260. It is perhaps an historical topos that the Mongols offered to let the city capitulate without bloodshed provided that the inhabitants gave all their cats to the besiegers. The

---

* In B. Lewis, *Islam from the Prophet Muhammad to the Capture of Constantinople*, New York: Harper & Row, 1974.

story goes that the Mongols then set fire to the cats' tails and set them free and the terrified cats, as cats would do, ran back into the city and started an enormous fire that hastened the siege's end. An unlikely tale, but what is certain is that the city's fate was just as awful as Baghdad's. Al-Nasir, who had been in Damascus attempting to raise an army and the courage to lead it as well as entreating Kutuz for help, met swarms of refugees as he headed north to relieve Aleppo. He quickly turned back, his army deserted and he was captured by Hulegu.

Hulegu also took al-Bira on the Euphrates, and Damascus, Syria's major city, capitulated rapidly and possibly wisely upon his approach. The Mongols then proceeded to disestablish Islam as the official religion of the area. The Christians of Damascus drank openly during Ramadan and Muslims were made to stand for each procession of the Cross through the city. Doubtless many processions were hurriedly arranged. Bohemond VI, the Crusader Prince of Antioch, made submission to Hulegu but his policy was viewed with distaste by the Crusaders and merchants of Acre; it earned him an excommunication from the city's Papal legate. The Venetians in particular were concerned about a diversion of the trade of the Levant, which normally flowed from the Persian Gulf and Red Sea areas up to Acre and then onto Europe. Already the Mongols were beginning to move trade away to the north to the Black Sea ports where the Genoese, who had strong alliances with the Byzantines, operated.

Only Egypt, a few isolated cities in Syria and the Arabian Peninsula were left to Islam in its historic heartland and now Hulegu sent envoys to Kutuz, the Mamluk Sultan, in Cairo demanding his surrender. Kutuz killed the envoys, cutting them in half in the horse market, and placed their heads on the gates of the city. Kutuz's action, at first glance, seems reckless. He was the Sultan of a dynasty that hadn't managed any degree of stability since its inception and had shown a tendency, like so many other revolutionary regimes, to devour its children. Furthermore he had not been Sultan very long, having deposed his puppet, the son of Aybeg, in November 1259. It may be that he felt he really had no choice but to face up to Hulegu. Any kind of treaty that fell short of total submission to the Mongols was impossible; Hulegu's letter to him carried the following explicit message:

> From the King of Kings in the East and the West, the mighty Khan:
>
> In your name O God, You who laid out the earth and raised up the skies.
>
> Let al-Malik al-Muzaffar Kutuz, who is of the race of Mamluks who fled before our swords into this country, who enjoyed its comforts and then killed its rulers,
>
> Let al-Malik al-Muzaffar Kutuz know, as well as the emirs of his state and the people of his realms, in Egypt and in the adjoining countries, that we are the army of God on His Earth.
>
> He created us from His wrath and urged us against those who incurred His anger. In all lands there are examples to admonish you and to deter you from challenging our resolve. Be warned by the fate of others and hand over your power to us before the veil is torn and you are sorry and your errors rebound upon you.
>
> For we do not pity those who weep, nor are we tender to those who complain. You have heard that we have conquered the lands and cleansed the earth of corruption and killed most of the people. Yours to flee, ours to pursue.
>
> And what land will shelter you, what road save you, what country protect you? You have no deliverance from our swords, no escape from the terror of our arms. Our horses are swift in pursuit, our arrows piercing, our swords like thunderbolts, our hearts like rock, our numbers like sand. Fortresses cannot withstand us, armies are of no avail in fighting us. Your prayers against us will not be heard . . .
>
> . . . those who make war against us are sorry, those who seek our protection are safe. If you submit to our orders and conditions, then your rights and duties are the same as ours. If you resist you will be destroyed. Do not therefore destroy yourself with your own hands. He who is warned should be on his guard. You are convinced that we are infidels and we are convinced that you are evil-doers.
>
> God, who determines all, has urged us against you. Before us, your many are few and your mighty ones are lowly, and your kings have no way to us but that of shame. Do not debate long, and hasten to give us an answer before the fires of war flare up

and throw their sparks upon you. Then you will find no dignity, no comfort, no protector, no sanctuary. You will suffer at our hands the most fearful calamity, and your land will be empty of you. By writing to you we have dealt equitably with you and have awakened you by warning you.

Now we have no other purpose but you.

Peace be with us, with you, and with all those who follow the divine guidance, who fear the consequences of evil, and who obey the Supreme King.

Say to Egypt, Hulegu has come,
With swords unsheathed and sharp.
The mightiest of her children will become humble,
He will send their children to join the aged.*

Another factor in favour of making a stand was the reappearance of Baybars and his refugee Bahriyya in March 1260 under an oath of safety from Kutuz. Baybars had been serving with al-Nasir and had been urging a stronger anti-Mongol policy of his employer, even to the extent of beating al-Nasir's chief adviser in the royal tent when he spoke of appeasement, and offering to lead attacks on the Mongols despite having only three thousand men. Al-Nasir's failure to mobilise after the fall of Aleppo had been the last straw for Baybars. Of course, an oath of safety meant little coming from Kutuz, the slayer of Baybars's old commandant, but it must have been obvious to both men that Baybars and his troops, reduced in number though they were after years of mercenary work, were an invaluable asset at this desperate time and that standing together gave them their only chance of survival. Every man counted now; there were only twenty-four thousand cavalrymen in Egypt and perhaps thirty thousand more in Syria in total at this time.†

More important than the return of Kutuz's favourite enemy, however, was that his other foe Hulegu had retired from Syria with a very large part of his forces in the summer of 1259. It has

---

* In Lewis, *Islam from the Prophet Muhammad to the Capture of Constantinople*, pp 84–5.

† Cf. D. Ayalon, 'Studies on the Structure of the Mamluk Army – III', *Bulletin of the School of Oriental and African Studies*, 1954.

been suggested by some historians that the logistical limitations of Syria were so severe in terms of water and pasture that the region could not support a Mongol army any longer than one campaign season* and of course Hulegu's army was vast. Each Mongol trooper had five ponies and the army moved with a supply of meat on the hoof – goats and sheep sufficient for its needs – so the grazing requirements must have been enormous. Furthermore the available river water is greatly reduced during Syria's summers. Even the Orontes falls tenfold from its winter flow rate. However, Hulegu could certainly have managed to keep his army in Syria for one campaign season at least by the simple expedient of plundering grain supplies and by displacing nomadic herders.

What was certainly more significant was the death of Mongke, the Great Khan who had sent Hulegu to the west, in August 1259. Hulegu was certainly distracted by this event and its sequelae far to his east. His brothers Qubilai and Ariq Boke were both prepared to undertake war on each other for the succession. Hulegu never really seems to have counted himself as a candidate; if he had he would have had to go much further east than he did and submit to a *quriltai* or tribe meeting,† but he did have concerns about the outcome of the contest. Ariq Boke was backed by most of the Genghisid family in Mongolia and by the Golden Horde's Khan, Berke, whilst Qubilai held the support of most of the generals of the Mongol army and, what was more, he held China, the Mongols' most prized possession. Indeed Mongke had died whilst campaigning with Qubilai in China.

What would really have concerned Hulegu was that Berke's forces lay directly to his north in the Caucasus region. As was discussed earlier there was already the potential for antipathy between these junior Khans over rights of conquest in Persia but since that time the situation had been worsened by Berke's

---

* Cf. D. Morgan, 'The Mongols in Syria 1260–1300', in P. Edbury (ed), *Crusade and Settlement,* Cardiff: Cardiff University Press, 1985.

† Both Qubilai and Ariq Boke held *quriltai* – both were technically illegal as each excluded family members and commanders.

conversion to Islam and Hulegu's persecutions of that same religion since his arrival in the Middle East. Hulegu never really committed himself to the support of either candidate for the throne but he was viewed very much by members of the Ariq Boke faction as pro-Qubilai. Hulegu therefore went to Maragha to be in a good position to meet any invasion of the Golden Horde. For the Mamluks he was far enough away to give them at least a chance against the remainder of his force that he had left behind under Kit Buqa, one of his most experienced and trusted lieutenants, to mop up Syria. In the spring of 1260 Kit Buqa sent detachments to Gaza and Nablus and there were Mongol raids on Hebron, Ascalon and Jerusalem. He wanted to have forces far enough south to be able to watch developments in Egypt. These actions also effectively surrounded the Frankish kingdoms on the coast, and it rapidly became obvious to the Crusaders that the Mongols' arrival in Syria would not herald any immediate change in their fortunes. When Julian of Sidon raided the Biqa Valley he was punished by Mongol raids on his kingdom. John II of Beirut suffered similar reprisals when he raided with the Templars in Galilee.

On 26 July 1260 Kutuz left Cairo. Al-Yunini states that the last Ayyubid Prince of Egypt had between ten and twelve thousand horsemen, but Kutuz had also accrued contingents of left-over Khwarazmians as well as Ayyubid soldiers, Kurds, Bedouins and Turcomen, all refugees from the Mongols, and the army may have had many as twenty thousand men. Kutuz decided to meet the Mongols in Syria rather than to wait for them in Egypt. He had to seize the moment, the auxiliaries he had acquired could simply melt away or go over to the Mongols and even the Mamluk emirs might lose the will to fight; the Mongol numbers in Syria were reduced at this moment and defeat in Syria still gave the chance of forming a second front whilst defeat in Egypt meant the end of the war. There was also the consideration that an early victory over the Mongols would be psychologically important – it would boost the army's morale and tighten Kutuz's grip on the Sultanate. The problem was that the very fear he wanted to counter by bold action was already creeping into the army. He used religious propaganda, invoking *jihad* and both he and Baybars used shame, guilt and ridicule as motivators. Al-Maqrizi gives Kutuz this speech:

> Emirs of the Muslims! For a long time you have been eating the money of the treasury and now you don't want to fight. I, myself will set out. He who chooses the Holy War will accompany me; he who doesn't can go home. God observes him, and the guilt of those who violate the women of the Muslims will be on the heads of the laggards. . .

The emirs were made to swear their agreement to the expedition, but it was only when Kutuz made his preparations to leave and said, 'I am going to fight the Mongols alone', that they followed him out of Cairo's citadel.

On the 26 August Baybars, leading the vanguard of the Egyptian army, met a forward detachment of the Mongol force under Kit Buqa's second in command, Baydar at Gaza. The Mongols fled and sent word of the approach of the Egyptian army to Kit Buqa, who was at this time in Baalbak. The Mongol commander sent word back that Baydar was to hold firm until he could arrive with the main force, Baybars, however, acted quickly and he pushed Baydar's forces away from Gaza and pursued them as far as the Asi River. Kutuz expected this action to draw the main Mongol force down to meet him in battle but Kit Buqa was held up suppressing an anti-Christian revolt in Damascus. Kutuz was reunited with Baybars at Gaza and the Mamluk command decided, in the absence of an enemy to fight, to march north along the coast so that they would be able to then move inland sharply to cut the Mongol lines of communication if Kit Buqa should decide to try to strike south towards Egypt.

The army therefore had to march through Frankish lands and Kutuz sent an embassy to the Franks of Acre to ensure safe passage for his forces through the Crusader kingdom. Christian writers of the time tell us that the Mamluks requested safe passage, supplies and military alliance against the Mongols from the Crusaders and that only the latter was refused on the counsel of Anno of Sangerhausen, Lord of the Teutonic Order, who warned the leaders of Acre that in the flush of victory over the Mongols the Muslims could very well turn on their other enemies in Palestine. This was prophetic and it is at first glance a little surprising that the Franks chose the Mamluks over the Mongols, but perhaps they felt that there was really no other choice. The Mamluk army was already in the Frankish zone and if relations became unfriendly they were certainly able to inflict considerable damage to the Kingdom of Acre. They, then, were unwelcome guests, but were the Mongols really anymore welcome? The loss of trade revenue experienced by Outremer's ports since the Mongols arrival in the Levant has already been discussed and the recent Mongol raids on Sidon certainly hadn't improved relations.

Frankish policy towards the Mongols had been one of appeasement thus far, the Franks of the coastal cities had sent gifts to Kit Buqa after the fall of Damascus and the Franks of Safad had built a giant tent for the Mongols during their campaign in the Golan but Kit Buqa's activities of the last few months, especially his reduction and destruction of fortified centres in both Syria and the Trans-Jordan, made it obvious that Syria was, to the Mongols, just another colony to be pacified without reference to any of its inhabitants. The *Gestes de Chiprois* also tells us that the Franks were offered the horses of the Mongols should the Mamluks defeat them. Perhaps this swung them in favour of the Egyptians, after all, business is business.

The Mamluks encamped in the orchards surrounding Acre. Kutuz spent his time attempting to maintain morale and to get the emirs and men ready for the coming combat. His reported speeches, exhorting the Mamluks to fight for home and hearth and to defend Islam read very much like the standard pre-battle speeches put into the mouths of generals by chroniclers throughout the ages. They perhaps sound slightly ironic given that the Mamluks, natives of the steppe were going to war against another steppe army to maintain their possession of a state in which they were aliens, but it apparently worked; the men wept at his words and made personal oaths to each other to push the Mongols from Syria and to protect Egypt. Baybars used his time differently, after being received honourably in the city he is reported as having said that the city would be easy to take. His mind, ever active, like that of all true leaders, was already looking to future opportunities. Al-Ansari's war manual gives the following counsel: 'The commander of the army should know the conditions of the fortress, the inaccessible places and those with ease of access, the impossible and possible places for military action. Further he should know the positions for mining the walls and for scaling ropes, siege ladders and grappling irons.'

Kutuz learnt that Kit Buqa had crossed the Jordan and entered Galilee and was now moving south, encamping at Ayn Jalut, the Spring of Goliath, at the foot of Mount Gilboa. The Mongols were definitely looking for a place to meet the Egyptian army and to offer battle and Ayn Jalut had pasture for horses, good water supplies and terrain suitable for cavalry operations, with the mountain securing the Mongols' southern flank. So whilst Kit Buqa's army was smaller than that of the Mamluks he must have felt that his chances were good. His army probably numbered somewhere around twelve thousand men, but a sizeable portion of it was not Mongol – he was employing Georgian and Armenian auxiliaries and troopers from the now dissolved Ayyubid armies of north Syria.

Kutuz departed Acre on 2 September 1260. The Mamluks marched through Nazareth and arrived at Ayn Jalut shortly after the Mongols. Baybars, however, had gone ahead again with a detached vanguard. From the Hill of Moreh he spied the Mongols' position in the valley below and sent word to Kutuz, who was one day's march away. Baybars also destroyed a Mongol reconnaissance unit in a small skirmish, which might explain Kit Buqa's subsequent failure to realise the size of the main strength of the Mamluk army just prior to the battle. Baybars's force on the hill was spotted and the Mongols attempted to encircle him, but he was able, by precipitate flight, to avoid the manoeuvre and to join with Kutuz's force riding in from the northwest along the Jezreel Valley.

The battle proper began on 3 September. The Mongols took up position on the plain near the spring and the vanguard of the Mamluks rode forward to meet them. The Mongol line ran north to south across the valley and was anchored on its left by Mount Gilboa; its Ayyubid troops were positioned on its extreme left wing ready to form the second assault rather than the first. The Mongol right very quickly defeated the Mamluk left under Baybars, perhaps too quickly, as the Mongols then found themselves under heavy assault by the troopers of Kutuz's bodyguard. Kutuz led his men into the fray in person and this counter-attack sent the Mongol right into disorder. Perhaps a feigned retreat was being used here by the Mamluks – the Qipchaq Turks knew just as well as the Mongols how to use provocation to draw the enemy on. Kit Buqa, however, was far from beaten and it is a credit to his generalship that he reorganised his forces so quickly that he was nearly able, within only a short time, to turn the battle around again. Again, Kutuz's intervention was crucial to the saving of the day. He threw off his helmet so that his troops could see him clearly and led a frontal charge as he called out the battle cry, 'Oh Islam! Allah! Help your servant Kutuz!' This sent the Mongols into disarray, and then the Ayyubids of Homs chose this most inconvenient moment to desert them.

The bloody battle lasted from dawn until midday and changed from combat to slaughter. One detachment of Mongols fled the battle but were pursued by Baybars and slaughtered at the top of a hill just clear of the main battlefield. The Mamluks set fire to reed beds near the small river that runs through the valley to flush out Mongols who were either hiding in them or trying to escape across the river. Lone Mongols who fled the field were set upon by local villagers and killed. The debacle was completed by either the death or capture of Kit Buqa. It seems most likely that he was killed during Kutuz's final charge but the chroniclers have him being beheaded by Kutuz after Kit Buqa claimed that the gates of Egypt would shake with the thunder of Mongol cavalry horses. The writers even gave him the power of prophesying Kutuz's murder by his own comrades.

The immediate results of the battle for the Mongols were the loss of a sizeable portion of their army and the flight of the remainder to the north to find sanctuary with Hetum, the King of Armenia. Damascus was abandoned by its Mongol authorities, as was Hama and Aleppo. The Mamluks sent a flying detachment to capture Kit Buqa's camp in the Biqa Valley and Baybars was dispatched with another force to chase the Mongols up through the north of the country. He caught up with one group, along with their women and children, at Homs and liquidated them. He got as far as Harim and Afamiya, where he defeated a contingent of two thosand Mongol troopers that Hulegu had belatedly sent to Kit Buqa's aid, before turning back to meet with Kutuz at Damascus. At news of Baybars's follow-up victory Kutuz dismounted, rubbed his face in the dust and made thanksgiving prayers.

The importance of the battle of Ayn Jalut cannot be overstated. It is true that the Mamluks engaged only a small proportion of the forces of Hulegu and that events far in the east had hampered the Mongols' efforts in Syria just as the death of Ogedei Khan had distracted them from further conquests in Europe after their crushing defeat of the Poles and Teutonic Knights at the Battle of Leignitz in 1241. It is also true that the Mongols would come again, several times, into Syria and even enjoy some success against its Mamluk defenders, but Ayn Jalut stopped a run of Mongol success and it gave the Mamluks and other smaller powers in the region a degree of belief. It had seemed before the battle that the age of Islam was at an end, there had been invasions before but previous invaders from the East had either already converted to Islam or did so shortly after their arrival in the Islamic lands, and the Crusaders had never had the manpower to be a truly deadly threat. The Mongols were different – they were numerous and antagonistic. Their destruction of the Caliphate and their wholesale slaughter of cities gave the appearance of a direct assault on Muslims. The long view that history offers suggests that the Mongols were no more intolerant of or indifferent to Islam than any other of the faiths they encountered – the Caliph would have been put to death for his, albeit limited, political significance not as an act of religious zealotry – but that wasn't how it seemed at the time. Kutuz's call on his army and to the populace of Egypt and Syria for *jihad* and the success of his Holy War against the greatest enemy the *Dar al-Islam* had ever faced also effectively made the Mamluks the champions of Islam and cemented their grip on power. A passage from a Mamluk war manual captures nicely how successful *jihad* justified military government:

> An arrow from a warrior
> Shot at an unbeliever
> Counts more than the endless prayers
> Said by a pious hermit

In terms of how the battle was won and lost, the desertion of the Ayyubids was very significant. Classic Mongol battle plans used wings made up of auxiliaries late in the battle after the enemy had been engaged by the principal force of Mongol troops. A first wave of Mongol troops would attack the enemy's main force with volleys of arrows and then turn before close contact was made. They would then ride to the rear between the flank forces and the next wave of the army's centre, which moved forward at speed to meet an enemy that was now disordered both from the initial shock of attack and from pursuit of the retreating first wave. This first wave would now be rearming itself with arrows and changing horses in the army's rear and readying itself to re-enter the fight. The Mongol second wave would extend into a half-moon shape with its points facing toward the enemy, these points would also maintain contact with the wings, who – thanks to the loss of cohesion in the enemy force – were now able to mount flank attacks that pushed past the enemy's rear and would at the battle's conclusion lead to encirclement of the enemy forces. The re-supplied first wave either added to the final destruction of the opposing army or if resistance was proving to be more stubborn it could form a third wave behind which the second detachment could retire for rearming and a change of mount. The waves, could, in theory, be mounted again and again until the enemy was degraded enough to allow encirclement. What went wrong for the Mongols at Ayn Jalut was that their allies on the flank deserted them at a key juncture when the Mamluks had committed to a frontal assault and that they were simply outclassed by the Mamluks.

A Mamluk who was present at the battle, fighting with the Ayyubid princes of al-Ashraf of Homs, Sarim al-Din Uzbek ibn

Abdallah, states in his account of the battle that this desertion was pre-arranged and that al-Ashraf had sent his page to Kutuz's camp the night before the battle to make the arrangements and also to inform the Sultan of the size of the Mongol army. The Sultan was also advised to reinforce the left side of his force. Sarim also gives us a few other details left out of the later chronicles. He tells us that the sun was in the Mongols' eyes, whilst the Mamluks came out from under some trees at the far end of the valley and were in the shadow of the mountain. Furthermore, he was called over by Kit Buqa and was asked to identify each of the Mamluk banners as they came into view. Many later pro-Mongol sources describe the Mongol defeat as a Mamluk ambush but Sarim's testimony makes such a claim impossible. Muhammad Ibn Isa's *Manual of War for Superior Military Leadership*, a standard text of the day, tells us to 'find an appropriate place and draw the enemy into an unfavourable position'. And this is in fact what happened; Baybars's retreat drew the Mongols in and then Kutuz crashed into their flank. There was no ambush, just superior strategy.*

Even with the desertion Kit Buqa could, ordinarily, have won the battle. What was more significant was that his opponents were highly skilled mounted archers. The Mamluks were able to outdo the Mongols' archery assault in terms of rate of fire, accuracy and power. The Mongols' first charge would have been at least as damaging to them, in terms of body count, as it was to the Mamluks they were assaulting. William of Rubruck's observation on the Mongols, 'they make war without combat',† could not apply in this battle. The Mongols used light arrows during the first stage of their charges because they needed to be able to engage their enemies at a distance, Mamluk armour was certainly able to withstand these arrows. As they closed they would switch to heavy arrows to aid penetration. The Mamluks,

---

* Cf. P. Thorau, 'The Battle of Ayn Jalut: A Re-examination', in Edbury.

† 'Ils font la guerre mais le combattent', J. Guillaume de Dauvillier, 'Roubrock et les Communautes Chaldéenes d'Asie', in *Histoire et Institutions des Eglises Orientales*, London: Variorum Reprints, 1983.

with their crafted bows, were able to engage the Mongols at a greater distance than the Mongol bow would allow and would likewise switch arrows to shoot for penetration at close range. They also moved forward during firing and a Mamluk unit moved as one and held together under fire. The Mongols, certainly in their campaigns in Russia, Persia and Anatolia, had met confederate armies. Even the knights that faced them at Leignitz were not used to fighting with and for each other; the first Mongol assault wave was usually enough to reduce such forces to disorder. The Mamluk core of Kutuz's army, however, was a disciplined body of troops who drilled together almost daily and who were firmly established as regiments. The Mamluk word *khushdashiyya* implies loyalty between men who shared the same *ustadh* but it also meant that these men lived almost in one another's pockets. So after the Mamluks had provoked and drawn in the first Mongol wave they were able to move to a coordinated attack that placed incredible pressure on the Mongols' cyclical pattern of battle. Kutuz's frontal assault on the Mongol first wave required Kit Buqa to launch his second wave before the first group had done its job. This precluded the resupply and introduction of a remounted Mongol third wave of archery assault and effectively drew the Mongols into a type of battle – one of charges with lances and sword – that they were not able to win.

The Mongols and Mamluks used the same compound bow, but the Mamluk version was of a better quality. The compound bow of central Asia is an ancient design that was found over a wide area. It was made out of horn and sinew and it took many months to fashion the materials into the complex shape required to give maximum power and consistency of shot. It was stable and reliable but, like all bows, it aged and was also fragile and prone to weakening from the effects of both humidity and drying out. Both the Mongols and Mamluks usually carried two bows because of this fragility and because of string breakage. The bow could be shot left or right handed, or more importantly for a mounted archer, arrows could be shot off the 'wrong side' of the bow by using the thumb as a rest for the arrow rather than the top of the fist. The bow was drawn to the ear rather than to the eye in order to maximise its power and the string was pulled with the thumb as the pull required, some 30kg, was too much for a finger pull. Thumb rings, used to prevent the string cutting the thumb, were made of bone, stone or jade. The effective range was about two hundred metres but at this distance it generally could not kill an armoured man. The weapon became distinctly deadly, even to troops wearing mail, at seventy-five metres. Mamluks carried about sixty arrows in a splayed quiver or *jabah* that gave easy access to the weapons, the quiver was carried on the hip with its mouth sitting forward to aid rapid reloading and firing. The arrows themselves were of considerable quality considering that such volumes were used, their heads were made of hardened iron that, during manufacture, was quenched in salt water after heating to harden its cutting edge. A selection of different headed arrows was carried. Those with triangular or square section heads were best suited for armour piercing, whilst the arrows described in Middle Eastern archery manuals for 'shower shooting', the longer-range archery designed to 'let arrows fall like thunder upon the enemy', were much lighter and their fletching was longer and higher. The feathers were also only taken from the right side of the bird – vultures' and eagles' feathers were used. Arrows with three feathers were used for long-range shooting whilst four feathered arrows were used for accurate shooting. There were also heavier heads for felling horses.

Looking at Mongol successes up to Ayn Jalut it is obvious that only an army composed of mounted archers and capable of surpassing their rate of fire and mobility would ever have had a chance of defeating them, and this is precisely what the Mamluks were, they used almost the same weapon and possessed the same archery skills but to a higher level. The key to their victory over the Mongols in this battle, however, lay in their discipline. The Mamluks' qualities as close-quarter fighters on foot and in close cavalry support were discussed earlier as part of their contribution to the defence of al-Mansura against the Crusaders. At Ayn Jalut there were two charges by the Mamluks under Kutuz but these were not planned and launched from a defensive position with a mix of infantry support as at al-Mansura, these were made in the heat of a fluid, fast-moving cavalry battle. To organise such a charge was, in the medieval age, extremely difficult. The charge is only effective if it is timed to strike the enemy at a point where his formation is already breaking up; charging against well-organised ranks, especially of mounted archers, was a recipe for disaster. Kutuz's first charge was against a Mongol contingent that was flushed with its success in defeating the Mamluk left wing and was therefore vulnerable to a charge; his second charge was against Kit Buqa's hastily formed counter-attack. Mamluk battlefield communications must have been impressive for the period and Kutuz's abilities as a commander were obviously equally outstanding.

So much for timing, but what of delivery? The charge is a mass movement, requiring men moving as one – the shock is dissipated if members of the unit arrive piecemeal. The Normans, famous for their discipline and mobility, overcame this problem by withdrawing their knights slightly from the front line, usually behind their infantry, to line up before sallying forward. Even this manoeuvre was difficult if the knights were unused to fighting together, indeed it has been suggested that the European charge was a development of the First Crusade that was only possible because the Crusaders fought together over such a protracted period.* The Mamluks at Ayn Jalut had no close support infantry to cover them while they organised and certainly there was very little time for them to form up methodically. Their charges were organised literally on the hoof and yet they were timed and delivered to maximum effect. The battle was won by what had been instilled on the training ground.

Syria had fallen by the outcome of one battle under Mamluk dominion. Kutuz returned some of the cities to Ayyubid control as Mamluk resources were stretched thin by the acquisition of their new principality, but it was obvious who the new masters of the region really were. He rewarded al-Ashraf Musa, the Ayyubid Prince who had deserted the Mongols during the

---

* France, pp. 34–8.

battle, by returning him to Homs. The Ayyubid al-Said Hasan of Banias had also fought with the Mongols but had fought fiercely against the Mamluks right to the battle's end; he was beheaded. Al-Mansur Muhammad of Hama, who had been allied with the Mamluks from the first, was rewarded by the return of his city and an enhancement of its lands. Kutuz appointed Ala al-Din, a Prince of the Jazira as governor of Aleppo. The governorship was a reward for loyalty but it also made use of Ala al-Din's family connections with the Jazira. His brother controlled Mosul, which was now on the newly redrawn border of Mongol controlled territory. Kutuz therefore effectively linked the Jazira to Syria, and he evidently hoped that it would make Mosul into an advance warning post for Mongol activity much as Edessa had been in the past for the Crusader states against the Turks. Baybars had hoped to be made governor of Aleppo but Kutuz could not place such a dangerous 'friend' so far from him, he chose to keep Baybars close to him, but that was dangerous too. Damascus was given over to a Mamluk governor, Sanjar al-Halabi, and Kutuz's business was concluded by the granting of an *iqta* to the leading family of the Bedouin of North Syria.

The Bedouin had done nothing to assist the Mamluks against the Mongols but Kutuz knew his control over Syria was far from absolute: the Crusaders were still at the rear of any front he formed against the Mongols and his lines of defence stretched right along the Euphrates up to Anatolia. He needed the Bedouins pacified at the very least and at best antagonistic to the Mongols. The nomadic Arabs were still strong in Syria although in Egypt their power had been broken in the 1250s when Aybeg had invited the chieftains to a parley and then had every one of them, nearly three thousand men, hung and left to rot on the road between Cairo and Bilbays.

Kutuz didn't stay in Syria long. He wanted to return to Cairo, his political stronghold, as he was becoming increasingly nervous of Baybars's growing support base among the emirs. His fears were not misplaced and he was murdered on 24 October in the desert by emirs who had joined his hunting party. Baybars orchestrated the killing and struck the fatal blow himself, stabbing Kutuz in the back whilst the Sultan was distracted by an accomplice making obeisance and kissing his hand. Baybars rode back to the Mamluk camp with his co-conspirators. Entering the royal tent he blithely announced the murder to Kutuz's chief of staff and claimed the Sultanate for himself. The only other contender was Balaban al-Rashidi, but he lacked supporters.

Kutuz was eulogised by Islamic chroniclers but then it could not be otherwise. He had saved Islam. Abu Shama, who died in 1267 and was therefore directly affected and imperilled by the Mongols, wrote the most telling words both on Kutuz's achievement and death and on the fact that the Mongols were undone by men who were so much akin to themselves:

> The Mongols conquered the land and there came to them
> From Egypt a Turk, who sacrificed his life.
> In Syria he destroyed and scattered them.
> To everything there is a pest of its own kind.*

There is no gravesite or mausoleum for the victor of Ayn Jalut. Baybars had Kutuz secretly buried to avoid any tomb becoming a focus of resistance to the new rule.

Baybars's usurpation seemed, initially, to be a complete success. He rode into Cairo well ahead of the main army in order to secure the treasury and to ensure that his coronation took place before any dissenting voices could return from Syria. He was formally enthroned on 25 November 1260 but waited for several weeks before he made his procession through the streets of Cairo with the royal insignia. His murder of Kutuz had delivered him the Sultanate but what had he taken on by his bloody act?

It was only a question of time before the Mongols would come again into Syria both for revenge and as a prelude to the conquest of Egypt. The Mamluks, by virtue of their victory and by their presentation of themselves as a dangerously viable opponent, had made another major confrontation inevitable. Raiding parties were already being reported in northern Syria

---

* In Amitai-Preiss, *Mongols and Mamluks*, p. 1.

and it was just a question of how many times larger than Kit Buqa's army the next Mongol force would be.

Baybars had problems inside his borders too. Kutuz's Syrian solutions soon began to crumble. Sanjar al-Halabi declared Damascus an independent Sultanate in November 1260 and, not surprisingly, appointed himself its first Sultan. Almost at the same time al-Said, Kutuz's choice for governor of Aleppo, was ousted by a group of Mamluks of the now defunct Ayyubid regiments of Syria, and they also looked to go their own way.

Al-Halabi's rebellion was short lived. Baybars acted quickly, resolutely and, for probably the first and last time in his reign, mercifully. A faction was formed in Damascus among the Kurdish troops of the city under the leadership of Aydigin al-Bunduqdar and supported by secret payments from Baybars's Egyptian treasury. Al-Bunduqdar was a senior Mamluk who, whilst serving under the Ayyubid Sultan al-Salih, had bought the fourteen-year-old Baybars in Damascus's slave market in 1242 and then given him to al-Salih in 1246. Such a beginning to a relationship does not, at first, seem like a strong basis for a friendship or an enduring bond between two men but Mamluk society was essentially made up of such associations – Mamluks even took their first master's name as a 'family' title, hence Baybars al-Bunduqdari and, of course, Baybars was now Sultan and al-Bunduqdar could expect reward from his former novice. His faction deposed al-Halabi, who fled but was soon captured and sent to Baybars. The Sultan briefly imprisoned the rebel and then restored him to favour. Again this odd phenomenon of ties that were stronger than blood binding Mamluks together applied here too. Al-Halabi was one of Baybars's *khushdash*, having been a fellow novice of the new Sultan.

The Mongols sent a six thousand trooper strong raiding and reconnoitring party into northern Syria in December 1260 under Baydar, Kit Buqa's second in command at Ayn Jalut. This put a stop to any further plans the new Mamluk rulers of Aleppo may have had for total independence since they had to look very quickly for allies as the Mongol force raided around their city. They made the unusual move of leaving Aleppo virtually undefended and taking the army south to ask for an alliance against the invaders with al-Mansur Muhammad, the Prince of Hama whom Kutuz had appointed after Ayn Jalut. Al-Mansur agreed and the allies marched on to Homs to make a further partnership with al-Ashraf. Even after this grand alliance was formed the combined strength of the army was only fourteen hundred men, with Al-Ashraf in overall command. The Mongols quickly took Aleppo and moved on, they headed south towards the Ayyubid–Mamluk army, bypassing Hama despite the fact that it was only thinly manned and would have been easy to take. Perhaps Baydar was truly hungry for revenge and only confrontation with al-Ashraf, the traitor, could satisfy him.

Battle was joined on the plain just north of the citadel of Homs. The Mongols took up an unusual formation: they mustered into eight squadrons one behind the other, whilst al-Ashraf arranged his force into one body. He commanded the centre or *qalb* and his line was extended to the left by the Mamluks of Aleppo and on the right by al-Mansur's troopers. The day was foggy so perhaps the far inferior size of the Ayyubid–Mamluk army was not such a handicap; reduced visibility might also explain the Mongols' abandonment of flanking and envelopment manoeuvres, which would have been the logical way to destroy an enemy outnumbered some three to one. There may have been a fear of losing touch with extended wings and the Mongols may also have feared an ambush from detached forces. They would have been aware of the threat of a Bedouin force in the area under Zamil ibn Ali as Kutuz's settlement had brought the Bedouins over – if such a thing can ever really be said of the Bedouins – to the Syrian alliance.

Al-Yunini, in his description of the battle, claims that birds flew in the Mongols' faces but it has to be wondered if he was just trying to show God's part in a victory that seemed so unlikely that a miracle was the easiest way to explain it. What seems more likely is that sun glare on the fog reduced visibility to such a degree that the Mongols were unable to fix their targets in a Muslim force that was approaching them at speed. The plain on which the battle was fought is, at its longest point, only 1,500 metres long and Al-Ashraf had obviously concluded that, given the weather conditions and the fact that he was already within reasonable proximity of the enemy, his best chance would be to close quickly on the Mongols and hope that his force would, given the shortness of the Mongol lines, be able to enfilade the first squadron's line with arrows whilst moving forward rapidly and then make a charge with the lance. It was to be hoped that this, plus what might literally be called the fog of war, would be enough to cause chaos in the Mongol ranks. The stratagem worked, but equally important was the arrival of the Bedouin in the Mongol rear. Baydar fell during the combat and the battle may have taken even more Mongol lives than Ayn Jalut had. The surviving Mongols fled the scene and rode on to Aleppo. They revenged themselves on its populace for four months before quitting Syria. The government they had hurriedly constructed in the city was equally hastily dismantled on intelligence of the approach of a Mamluk army from the south.

The Princes of Hama and Homs returned to their cities but the Mamluks of Aleppo decided to take service with Baybars rather than to return to their city and they headed south. There they were well received by a Sultan who could certainly be confident of their ability to fight Mongols. They were integrated into the Mamluk army that the Sultan was building up in Syria. Aleppo's power vacuum was filled by a junior Mamluk emir, al-Barli, who seems just to have wanted to try his luck as a petty ruler. Baybars sent the rehabilitated al-Halabi to retake the city from this new rebel and the irony of the situation could not have been lost on any of the parties involved. Al-Barli was deposed but returned as soon as al-Halabi had moved on. The city was finally retaken by Baybars's old patron and right-hand man in Damascus, Aydigin, in October 1261. Al-Barli and his men moved on to al-Bira which, positioned as it was in the no man's land between the Mongol and Mamluk occupied territories, wasn't such a bad place for him to be from Baybars's point of view.

This was the first of two battles that the Muslims and the Mongols would contest around Homs and the significance of this first success was that once again the aura of invincibility that had surrounded the Mongols was dimmed. This time they had been defeated by forces markedly inferior in size to their own. The victory was achieved under Ayyubid command but the mainstay of their force had been Mamluks, so once again the Mongols had been defeated by fighting men who outdid them in the arts of war in which they themselves had always excelled and who went far beyond them in their proficiency with the lance, sword and club. A further effect of the battle was that from this point *wafidiyya* started entering the Mamluk lands. These men were Mongols or perhaps more correctly Turks from Mongol-controlled lands that had joined the Mongols as auxiliaries or freebooters as the Mongols had moved west, but who then deserted to the Mamluk side. The Mamluks were obviously now being viewed as a viable alternative employer to the Mongols. Many of the prisoners taken at the Battle of Homs were also of this same Turco-Mongolic group. Many were sold into military slavery and became Mamluks, one youth, Kitbogha, a captive at Homs, was later to become Sultan of the Mamluks.

To the Franks of Outremer, looking out from their castles and fortified towns, all this political turmoil was too good an opportunity to miss. The forces of Acre were mustered for an assault on Turcoman *wafidiyya* who had been stationed by Baybars in the Golan Highlands in February 1261. Nine hundred knights, three thousand infantry and fifteen hundred Turcopoles* were sent to make the attack, but it was severely mauled by the Turcoman force and returned defeated to Acre. A different tack was tried. The Crusaders warned by letter the Mongols who had been defeated at Homs and had now retired to Aleppo of the approach of the relief army that Baybars had sent north. This was the intelligence that caused their flight from the city in April 1261. Such interference from the Franks in the Sultan's confrontation with the Mongols could not be tolerated. Baybars was starting to build a war machine in Egypt to meet the Mongol threat but it would be the Crusaders who would be the first to suffer from it.

---

* Turcopoles were Turcoman mercenaries.

5

BLOODLESS BATTLES AND BLOODY DRILLS

BUILDING THE WAR MACHINE

Attacked by the Mongols in the East and by the *Franj* in the West. The Muslims had never been in such a critical position. God alone could still rescue them . . .

Ibn al-Athir (d. 1233)

BAYBARS RELIED HEAVILY IN the early years of his reign on the Mamluks of the Bahriyya. His biographer Ibn Abd al-Zahir tells us of his *khushdashiyya*. 'He gathered the fugitives . . . he promoted those who lacked advancement and gave office to those who had been set aside. He appointed the deserving to emirates, and promoted the competent . . . they formed his immediate entourage, who guarded his citadel, whether he was absent or present'.* Also, as a senior emir in al-Salih's army, Baybars had been able to buy Mamluks of his own, these men were now known as the Zahiriyya, taking their name from al-Zahir Baybars – the Sultan's throne name. Baybars pushed these men forward into government posts and into higher positions in the army. Even at this early stage he was aiming at the succession of his son Baraka and he hoped therefore to place close associates in all areas of the state in order to ensure a smooth transition of power through his bloodline.

---

* Maalouf, *The Crusades through Arab Eyes.*

So Baybars had loyal men around him but he needed to bring the state as a whole under his control. In January 1261 he had made an inaugural procession through the streets of Cairo with the emblems of royalty; there was a golden saddlecloth set on a riderless horse ahead of him and over his head a parasol topped with a golden bird, the emblem of the Fatimid Caliphs. He wore a black turban – usurping the traditional costume of the Abbasid Caliphs – and on his hip he wore the ancient sword that Umar the second Caliph had carried. The propaganda value of this regalia was huge to a man who was, at the end of the day, an alien, but Baybars knew he needed much more than ceremony to tighten his hold on power. Even the Mongol threat had not been enough to keep Kutuz safe and almost immediately after his coronation Baybars had faced a revolt of the black slave troops of Cairo and a conspiracy among the Muizziyya. Baybars was able to suppress the revolt without too much trouble and the conspiracy was quashed, but a revolt among Cairo's black troops had nearly toppled Saladin early in his career and the first ten years of the Mamluk Sultanate had been riven by conspiracies. What could the Sultan do to bind the factions together under his control?

Abolishing taxes worked to a degree with Cairo's populace but a more immediate and effective solution was the taking up of *jihad* against the Crusaders. The state needed an enemy or, as Mencius succinctly put it over a thousand years earlier in his advice to Chinese princes, 'without foes and external threats, a state will surely perish'. War with the Crusaders would legitimatise Baybars's reign by making him a *Mujahid*, a fighter of the Holy War. *Jihad* had been an effective stalking horse for the dynastic ambitions of princes in Syria throughout the Crusades period right from Zangi's conquest of Edessa in 1144 through to Saladin's taking of Jerusalem. *Jihad* gave usurping rulers legal and moral authority. The leader who took up *jihad* could expect the support of the clerics and the service of their religious propaganda even if his ventures were self-aggrandising. Furthermore, individual soldiers who died during *jihad* were guaranteed paradise, a further impetus for Baybars's army to fight fervently for him. This is not to suggest that Baybars was

devoid of passion for *jihad*. He certainly showed an extreme
hatred for the Crusaders and he led his armies personally in his
assaults on the Franks, even through sometimes fruitless sieges
of their castles and fortified towns. *Jihad* also requires a leader
to maintain a just regime during Holy War and whilst it is true
that the Mamluks' loyalty was more to 'Mamlukdom' than to
the state, Baybars fulfilled his role of protector of the people. For
example, in 1263 the Nile failed to rise and government grain
was released to be sold at a fixed price and when this wasn't
enough to stave off shortages Baybars ordered the emirs to feed
numbers of the poor at their own expense.

Baybars was assisted in his efforts to present himself as
the leader of the Holy War by his restoration of the Abbasid
Caliphate. He had been fortunate enough to be presented
with a man who claimed to be a survivor from the Mongol
extermination of the Caliph's family in 1258. Whether this
individual really hailed from the Abbasid line we shall never
know but he passed the investigation of a panel of Egyptian
Islamic jurists. He was installed as the Caliph al-Muntasir in
June 1261. Baybars swore allegiance to the head of the Islamic
faith and in return the Caliph gave him a diploma of investiture
that made Baybars the universal Sultan of Islam, the ruler of
Egypt and Syria and the protector of the Holy Places of Mecca
and Medina. The value of the Caliph in the battle for the hearts
and minds of the Egyptians and Syrians was huge, the Caliph's
Friday *khutba*, or sermon, recorded by the writer of the *Sirat
Baybars* has the following:

> This Sultan al-Malik al-Zahir, the most illustrious lord, the learned,
> the just, the fighter of the holy war, the warrior at the frontier, pillar
> of the world and of the faith, has undertaken to secure the victory
> of the Imamate with a small number of helpers, having dispersed
> the armies of the infidels who had already penetrated into the
> heart of the lands . . . O servants of God! Hasten to give thanks for
> such a benefit; purify your intentions and you will be victorious,
> fight the followers of the Devil and you will gain victory!*

---

* The *Sirat Baybars* is an anonymous chronicle that is still popular in
the Arab-speaking world.

Baybars's Caliphal diploma called upon him to make Holy War, an article that he would be only to pleased to comply with, indeed he even sent the Caliph off to the Mongol lands to make *jihad* himself. Al-Muntasir was given a small force for the projected enterprise of retaking Baghdad from the Mongols and dispatched east. Oddly enough he met another Caliph on the way, another refugee of the Abbasid family who had been created Caliph by the good offices of al-Barli, the usurper of al-Bira. This Caliph, al-Hakim, had just returned from the Mongol territories, where he had enjoyed some success against the invaders of his historic homeland with the support of al-Barli's forces, although he had failed to get to Baghdad. The two Caliphs decided to join forces and marched down the Euphrates towards Baghdad. They were roundly defeated several miles from Baghdad on 18 December 1261 by a Mongol force. Al-Muntasir was killed and his head was paraded around Baghdad. Al-Hakim escaped and fled to Cairo, where Baybars received him cordially and then ignored him while he got on with other things. The two Caliphs' campaign in Iraq seems somewhat ridiculous now but at the time it was launched there may have been reasonable hope for success from the venture. Reports had been received that the Mongols, post Ayn Jalut, had gone as far as to evacuate Baghdad. There were certainly still a great many bands of Islamic soldiers of fortune drifting around Iraq and Iran, remnants of the forces that had been broken by the Mongols in 1258, and at this time the Mongols were also struggling to deal with the Khafaji, Arab nomads who constantly raided around both Baghdad and Basra. Perhaps the Caliphs hoped to join up with these forces to retake Baghdad. Of course, the venture had also cost Baybars virtually nothing in resources.

Baybars's own Holy War began first against Antioch. Bohemond VI's support of the Mongols and his close ties to Armenia, the Mongols' ally in the north, required that he be brought to heel. Baybars started a series of raids designed to weaken Antioch's military capability and to reduce its ability to assist the Mongols during any invasions they might plan for northern Syria. Eventually the attacks would erode Antioch's power to a point where it could be taken by siege. They started in 1261 and continued unabated year on year; it was only an appeal to Hulegu by Bohemond's father-in-law King Hetum of Armenia and the subsequent support of Mongol troopers that prevented the city's fall in 1261. In 1262 Antioch's port, Saint Symeon, was looted. Baybars moved more slowly against the Crusaders of Acre, the Mongols were still more of a concern, especially as the border lands along the Euphrates and in the Jazira were not settled to his satisfaction, but he signalled his intentions towards the Crusaders of the coast late in 1261 when John of Jaffa and John of Beirut came to parley with him to request a prisoner exchange. He refused and promptly ensured that all the Frankish prisoners under discussion were sent to labour camps, which was tantamount to a slow death sentence.

With the Crusaders made suitably fearful and unlikely to disturb the peace, Baybars turned to the other front. He knew that he needed to act quickly to tighten up the borders of Syria; Hulegu's preoccupation with the Great Khan succession struggle couldn't last forever. He obtained two key border towns without having to even fight for them, one through opportunism and one through simple deceit. In July 1261, our old friend al-Barli, the adventurer, attempted to relieve Mosul while it was under attack from the Mongols, he went to the city's aid – perhaps he wanted to become lord of that place too – but he was roundly beaten by the Mongols and he fled back to al-Bira and locked the gates. Hulegu offered him al-Bira under Mongol suzerainty but al-Barli sought Baybars's protection instead. Baybars agreed and flattered al-Barli by receiving him with full honour at Cairo, then after a few months he was thrown into prison. Thus Baybars took full possession of a castle and town that pushed hard into Mongol territory and would be the scene of many of the confrontations between the two sides over the next sixty years. The second fortress was in the possession of an Ayyubid Prince, al-Mughith. Al-Karak was out to the east of the Dead Sea. It dominated the lines of communication from Damascus to Egypt and to the Arabian Peninsula. Al-Mughith was politely invited to Baybars's camp at the base of Mount Tabor but when he arrived he found a court in session. The chief judge of Damascus had been brought out to the Sultan's camp to hear allegations that al-Mughith had been corresponding with the Mongols. Of course al-Mughith was guilty, the letters he had sent were conveniently provided by Baybars's agents to prove it. The Prince was sent off to a Cairo jail and his sons panicked and offered the fortress to the Sultan. Baybars later paid 1,000 dirhams to have al-Mughith murdered, but the murderer, after drinking away the money, started bragging of his deed – he soon disappeared.

So Baybars was unscrupulous, merciless and untrustworthy, but he was also a superb tactician of grand-scale warfare. It is clear that early on in his reign Baybars was setting the pattern for the conflict with the Mongols. He concentrated on ensuring that his internal lines of communication were solid and this required as its most basic element the formation of a strong border. The Mongol forces surrounded Syria on both its eastern and northern edges but in many ways this was a disadvantage to them as Baybars and the later Sultans could move troops inside the region on safe, protected interior lines of communication quickly to plug gaps or to meet Mongol incursions, simply because the distances covered were, if not short, at least much less than those the Mongols had to contend with as they moved forces around Syria's fortified frontier. This was vital as the main Mamluk army and certainly all of the Sultan's Royal Mamluks resided in Cairo during periods of inactivity. Baybars also utilised an offensive scorched-earth policy, launched from fortified towns and castles. Much of the border skirmishing between the two sides took place on the Mongol side of the line, with Al-Bira being particularly important in this respect as it jutted out into Mongol territory. During sorties from their lines into Mongol lands the Mamluks effectively made it almost impossible for the Mongols to mass troops on the border as they set fire to pastureland, destroyed villages and farms likely to offer supplies to the Mongols and spoilt water sources that the Mongol cavalry would need during muster. This destruction was carried out to a distance of ten days' march on the Mongol side of the line.

Hulegu wasn't the only junior Mongol Khan to have his plans upset by the struggle in Mongolia and China. Berke, the Jochid Khan of the Golden Horde was also worried over the result of the Qubilai–Ariq Boke power struggle. He had declared himself in favour of Ariq Boke early in the conflict and now found himself at loggerheads with Hulegu, which involved him in protracted struggles over pasturelands and the silver trade routes in Azerbaijan, and isolated from the Mongol Khanate of the Chaghatay Horde to his east by his conversion to Islam. He needed an ally and Baybars sent emissaries to him to present the case for alliance with the only Muslim power that had been able to stand up to Hulegu and that could continue to do him harm. When Berke's ambassadors made a return trip to Cairo in May 1263 to start the process of cementing relations between the two states, they were received with full splendour and Baybars used his new Caliph, al-Hakim – whom he had suddenly remembered and had installed in office after rather less than rigorous scrutiny of his credentials – to good effect to give the negotiations the sanctity of a religious concord between brothers in faith. Baybars's letters to Berke before this summit expound again and again the obligation of Berke as a Muslim to maintain hostility against the unbelievers of the Ilkhanate, the Caliph was instructed to return to this message repeatedly in his meetings with the emissaries. Berke's name was placed alongside Baybars's in the Friday prayers in Cairo's main mosque and his ambassadors were also enrolled in the *futuwwa*, an honourable court circle of young men that had its origin in the Abbasid Caliphate of old.

Baybars was never able to realise joint operations against the Ilkhanate with Berke Khan – the distance between their realms precluded anything so complex – but there were immediate benefits to the agreement in that Berke ordered all tribal confederations who were by clan affiliation part of the Golden Horde but who were in the employment of Hulegu to depart the lands of the Ilkhanate immediately. Many Mongols of the Jochid clan had been fighting with Hulegu during the early stages of his Middle Eastern campaign but Hulegu, suspicious of their loyalties, had started to turn on them as early as 1262.

Some had fled to the Mamluk Sultanate at this time and Berke's later order brought many more into Baybars's realms or back into the lands of the Golden Horde. In fact many of these men were not Mongols but rather Turks who had joined the Mongols' western expeditions, so a feeling of affinity with the Turkish Mamluks among this group is highly plausible. Berke died in 1267, but whilst his immediate successors were not Muslims, enough Islamisation had taken place among senior members of the court through missionary work sponsored by Baybars to ensure that the Golden Horde remained a staunch ally of the Mamluks. A longer-term benefit of the accord was that the Khan's lands extended over the Qipchaq steppe where Baybars had been born and over the forests of southern Russia. Egypt and Syria were both poorly forested, and so wood from Berke was certainly a vital war supply, but the most essential war supply was the Qipchaq boys who would be harvested by the Horde's slave traders for the growing army of Mamluks that the Sultan was creating.

The Sultan led this growing army against Nazareth in February 1263. The city was severely treated by Baybars and the Church of the Virgin was levelled. By April Baybars's forces were at Acre's doorstep, the walls of the city stymied him but there was fierce fighting around the suburbs. It is possible that the Sultan might have succeeded in breaking into Acre had he had the support he had been pledged from the Genoese, who as discussed earlier had a commercial interest in the disruption of Acre's trade. As an aside to their desire to move more trade away from the ports of the Levant and up to the Black Sea was their other commercial interest, supplying Baybars with military slaves. The Genoese were the middle men who bought the Qipchaqs from the steppe via the Black Sea and down to the Egyptian ports, they continued in this trade over centuries despite uncountable Papal interdictions against them. On this occasion, however, despite promises, they failed to act in favour of their customer and Baybars had to retire from his attack on Acre, but he would return many times. He probably didn't want to actually destroy Acre at this point, but instead to weaken it so that it would be unable to support the other

Crusader possessions he was to seize in this period. At this point there was an economic value to Acre as a trade outlet for his Syrian possessions. Baybars never made a move without careful planning and consideration of its wider consequences and in the great game he was playing against the Mongols; a prosperous Syria was a Syria more able to pay for its own defence. Acre's termination could wait awhile.

Baybars left for Egypt but he had already found a specific use for the *wafidiyya* that were now coming over from the Ilkhanate lands in a steady flow: they were sent to raid up and down the Crusader kingdom for the whole of April. Such was the intensity of this plundering that frontier lords such as Balian of Ibelin found their treasuries exhausted by the cost of paying for the defence of their lands. Balian gave over his lease to the Knight Hospitallers to prevent personal bankruptcy, and the region to the south of the monastery on Mount Carmel was depopulated as farming there became impossible to maintain. Entire Frank villages and the small fortified towns were deserted. Other soldier refugees were also used against the Mongols in a way similar to the way that the Caliph al-Muntasir had been used. They were reorganised, given new weapons and money and sent off to the Mongol lands to attempt to reclaim their towns. More often than not these expeditions failed but they cost the Sultan very little, they tied up Mongol resources and kept the war on the Mongol side of the line. Occasionally there were even successes. Kurds from Cholemirk were sent back to their region in 1262 and gave the Ilkhanate so many problems once they were established in the mountains of Kurdistan that the Mongols had to make terms with them.

The Mongols were distracted by this policy but still their own affairs caused them more political trouble than the Mamluks could ever hope to do. Open warfare had broken out between the Ilkhanate and the Golden Horde in late 1262 and carried on throughout 1263. One of Berke's armies was defeated by Hulegu in a pass of the Caucasus Mountains near the Caspian Sea and was then beaten again after retreating back into the mountains. Hulegu sent an advance force under his son Abagha to pursue the Horde's army and they raided Berke's winter camp. However, Berke was able to organise a counter-attack with a second army and he completely routed Abagha in January 1263. As Abagha's men retreated they staggered into another catastrophe, many of them drowning as the ice of a frozen lake broke under the weight of the army. The year 1263 saw many raids across the border by both sides and the threat of full invasion by the Horde's armies under general Noghai. A direct consequence of this escalation in the war was the Baybars–Berke *entente cordiale*. an indirect effect was the free hand that Baybars enjoyed against the Crusaders in 1263.

The war between Qubilai and Ariq Boke ended in 1264 with Ariq Boke's complete defeat, but there was still a vast amount of dissatisfaction within Mongolia proper with Qubilai, who was now seen by some as having become Sinicised and having forgotten the true Mongol path. This discontent was lead by Qaidu from the line of Ogedei, who managed to maintain a great deal of control over the Central Asian lands and who obtained de facto leadership of the Chaghatay Horde in what is today roughly Uzbekistan. The Chaghatay branch of the family had lost out in the first round of succession disputes after the death of Genghis Khan and retained a vehement hatred for the house of Tolui from which Mongke Khan, Qubilai Khan and Hulegu sprang. From 1264 onwards Hulegu had to endure raids and conflict on his northeastern border as Qaidu used the Chaghatay Horde to strike at Qubilai through Hulegu. Then on 8 February 1265 Hulegu died and it was several months before his son Abagha, who had been watching the border against the Chaghatay Horde, could travel to Tabriz. Doubtless Abagha would have been disappointed to have missed the spectacle of human sacrifices at his father's funeral, and it was not until late in the year that he was fully in control of the Ilkhanate. It was also Mongol custom to close all roads upon the death of a Khan, therefore the business of warfare against the Mamluks could not take place for a protracted period. Then in the spring of 1266 the Golden Horde invaded Abagha's newly acquired lands and the fighting continued into the summer.

All this meant continued freedom of action for Baybars and he was able to concentrate more and more of his energies on the Crusaders. He knew that by his piecemeal destruction of Outremer he might well provoke a Crusade from Europe; equally he knew that Hulegu had been in correspondence not only with the Franks of Syria but also with the court of King Louis IX of France, who ever since Damietta had been the leading voice of the Crusading movement in Europe. There was a possibility of joint operations between the Mongols and Crusaders from Europe and of coordinated assaults on Mamluk Syria by Syrian Crusaders and Hulegu's forces. If he did nothing he would increase the confidence of his adversaries and give them time to prepare the elaborate communication channels essential for any such joint venture to work. If he pushed too hard and got his forces dragged into a long war of attrition with the Crusaders he could very well precipitate the Crusade he wanted to avoid.

Baybars's approach to this thorny problem was like that of an experienced rider on a difficult horse. The *Furusiyya* texts give inexhaustible advice on how to manage horses and we know that Baybars was a gifted horseman and polo player. He pushed the horse of state on into war when he could be sure that there was nothing to trouble it and reined it in when there was any likelihood of danger to his mount, making every effort to see what problems lay ahead in the political landscape. His intelligence gathering from the European courts was superb and was based both on an understanding of the divisions within Christendom and the shifting alliances and antagonisms within European politics and on an extensive network of spies, commonly merchants, who reported back to a central office of intelligence in Cairo. The identity of these agents was kept secret even from each other, Mamluk war manuals suggest this policy because, 'if they know one another they might consult about an affair, arrange it in their own favour and report it. If they submit reports individually the true and the untrue will appear.'* When they visited the Sultan during the day the agents were disguised under a heavy cloth and their salary was not listed in the government accounts. This espionage

---

* R. Amitai-Preiss, 'Mamluk Espionage Among the Mongols and Franks', *Asian and African Studies*, vol 22, 1988, pp. 173–81.

network also extended into the Ilkhanate. In the reign of the Mamluk Sultan Kalavun, the Ilkhan Ahmad taunted Kalavun by sending back a Mamluk spy who had been disguised as a Muslim preacher. The Ilkhan's emissaries told the Sultan that his troops had been killing many preachers as they could not be sure that they weren't spies. The Sultan calmly replied that every preacher killed on the Mamluk side of the border was a Mongol spy. Even in 1335, fifteen years after peace had been signed between the Mamluks and the Mongols, reports were still being filed from agents in Iran and Iraq.

By the middle of 1263 Baybars had again ceased full military operations against Outremer. He had even agreed to a truce and prisoner exchange earlier in the year but the idea had been scuppered by the Hospitallers and Templars; by the end of 1265 the knights of the military orders probably wished that they had taken the peace offer. Baybars was heading north to meet a Mongol threat to al-Bira when he learnt through his intelligence and messaging system that the fortress's garrison had repelled its attackers. He turned the army he had prepared for the Mongols on the Crusaders instead. The Knights of the Temple and of the Hospital, in accord for once, had been raiding down to Ascalon in an attempt to relieve Frankish settlers in the region. The Sultan's army appeared before the great coastal Hospitaller castle of Arsuf in January 1265 and, having given warning of his intent, he proceeded to amuse himself with a great hunt in the surrounding hills. Then suddenly he was gone only to reappear at the walls of Caesarea. The city fell quickly on 27 February after the Mamluks used makeshift rope ladders constructed from their bridles to haul themselves up the walls, and the troops trapped in its citadel surrendered on 5 March. Baybars's razed the citadel and the lower town to the ground. Haifa suffered the same fate only a few days later. The citizens of the city who were unable to flee by boat were massacred. Ibn al-Furat wrote of Baybars's castle policy, 'the Muslim army uproots Frankish fortresses and destroys their castles, while elsewhere we rebuild to withstand the Mongols'. In short, Baybars destroyed Syrian coastal cities and rebuilt inland ones. He wanted to leave no toehold for European Crusading ventures. Saladin's failure to clear Syria of the Franks at the close of the twelfth century had been due to the landing at Acre of Richard the Lionheart's Crusade and the support of his army's march down the coast to Jaffa by a Crusader fleet. The Muslims had not enjoyed naval supremacy in the eastern Mediterranean since the early twelfth century because the new shipbuilding technology allowing much faster construction of vessels that was employed by the Italian maritime republics from the middle of the eleventh century had meant that navies of Venice, Pisa and Genoa could not be matched by the limited resources of Egypt. Baybars's solution was therefore to create a wasteland on the coast that allowed no port for supply or disembarkation.

Baybars moved onto Athlit, the grand Templar castle and town on the coast between Haifa and Caesarea. The villages around the settlement were burned to the ground and its farmlands were laid waste, but the castle stubbornly resisted the Sultan's siege engines. Baybars therefore decamped back to Arsuf castle south of the remains of Caesarea. The fortress was well garrisoned, it boasted 270 knights of the order and it as well stocked with food. Baybars's Mamluks battered their way into the lower town on 26 April after flattening its walls with siege engines and filling in its immense moat. The situation was obviously hopeless for the knights, there could be no relief from Caesarea or Haifa, both were gone and there was no field army worth the name in Outremer anymore. They capitulated on terms of abandoning the castle and going free on 29 April, but Baybars sent them all into captivity once he had taken their surrender. He knew that releasing any of the Knights of the Holy Orders was a sure guarantee of having to meet them again in battle; these men were Syrians now, this was their only home, and they would never leave of their own volition. Baybars then moved again against Acre just as he had in 1263, and again discovered that the city was far from ready to fall. It had just been reinforced by troops from Cyprus. He withdrew from the city but left troops to guard a border that was now within sight of Acre's walls.

So far we have seen the Mamluks as fearsome close-quarters combatants and as horse archers par excellence. They also became consummately skilled in siege warfare. This is not surprising; the Crusaders had built extensively and they had built well because fortification effectively tackled much of their problem of manpower shortage. The Franks fortified the coast with maritime castles, and coastal cities such as Tyre were ringed with defensive walls. As noted above the importance of the possession of the Syrian coast to the survival of the Latin states cannot be overstated. The year 1265 was a catalogue of castles taken and cities' walls crumbling before the Sultan's army. The Mamluks' *manajiq* or mangonels were the mainstay of their siege arsenal. In the mid-twelfth-century sources there are descriptions of machines that could throw missiles of about eighty kilograms over an arrow's distance. Baybars possessed mangonels that hurled 450-kilogram rocks at the walls of Crusader castles. These machines no longer relied on the coordinated pull of a team of men to send the stone flying, as by the end of the twelfth century the swing-beam counterweighted mangonel had been introduced across the Levant. The design had probably come to Syria with the Crusaders but it is interesting that al-Tarsusi, who wrote a manual of war for Saladin that became a classic among the Mamluks, described Frank, Arab and Turkish mangonels as being of three distinct types and either traction fired or using torsion release.

Baybars's machines could be erected on site, a vital consideration considering the isolation of some Crusader castles and the difficult terrain that had to be covered in order to approach their walls. The speed at which Baybars moved between his chosen targets required that the Mamluk regiments ride ahead of the slow-moving carts carrying the unassembled mangonels and begin pressing the siege with smaller arms whilst awaiting the arrival of the big guns.

The *arrada*, a small and simple beam-sling machine was easier to deploy than the larger mangonels simply because it was already assembled, could be brought into action by only a small team and could be towed like a wagon. The *arrada* had a range of at least 120 metres but it lacked the power of a counterweighted mangonel. The ballista and the wheel-crossbow of which al-Tarsusi has left us diagrams could be used to deliver *naft* and their manoeuvrability meant that garrisons and civilian populations could be could be subjected to terror as soon as the Mamluk forces arrived. It is interesting to note how many cities fell so rapidly that there was actually no time for the full application of the Mamluks' mangonels. *Naft* fire was a key element of the Mamluk arsenal and its recipe, as described by al-Tarsusi, was:

> Take 10 pounds of tar, 3 pounds of resin, 1½ pounds each of sandarac and lac, 3 pounds of pure, good quality sulphur, free from all soil, 5 pounds of melted dolphin fat, the same quantity of liquefied, clarified fat from goats kidneys. Melt the tar, add the fats, and then throw in the resin after having melted it separately. Then grind the other ingredients, each one separately, add them to the mixture, put fire under it, and let it cook until all is thoroughly mixed. If you wish to use it in time of war, take one part, add about a tenth part of the mineral sulphur called naphtha, which is greenish and looks like old oil, place the whole lot in a skillet and boil until it is about to burn. Take the pot, which should be earthenware, and a piece of felt. Then throw it with a mangonel against whatever you wish to burn. It will never be extinguished.*

Caesarea had also been subject to sapping under cover of frontal assaults. Sapping could be used more extensively by the Mamluks than by previous counter-Crusaders such as Saladin simply because they were far less interested in the structure of the fortification surviving. If it was a Jordanian castle then they had time to repair it since the Crusaders had such a limited ability to hit back and if it was a maritime fortification then they were going to raze it to the ground anyway. Baybars and his successors also consistently managed to take Crusader positions quickly, in less than six weeks, or the siege was abandoned. The whole strategy of siege warfare was revolutionised under the Mamluks. Long desultory encirclements of cities, attempts to starve out garrisons like the Crusader siege of Antioch from October 1097 to June 1098 do not even seem to have been envisaged. Again the lack of an effective Frank field army meant that the garrison of a besieged city had little chance of

---

* In Hillenbrand, p. 528.

relief, but there was more to it than this. The Mamluks swiftly became experts at delivering distraction and destruction to defenders of bastions and strongholds. The Mamluk army would appear suddenly at the walls of a fortification – it was, after all, a cavalry force – the attack would begin with a hail of arrows being fired at defenders, sometimes with Greek fire, which would also be thrown using hand slings, then the light artillery of *arradas* and wheel-crossbows would be added in and then only a little later the counterweighted mangonels would be constructed and would begin bombardment. All this time other operations at which the Mamluks had become adept such as sapping and filling in of moats under cover of moveable shelters or *dabbaba* –similar to the Romans' *testudo* – would be carried out. So the pressing of the siege was extremely rapid in its escalation and applied in such a way that the defenders would be under bombardment from the sky but also in dread of the walls falling out from under them. Added to this was the constant fear of an assault on the walls by troops who were brave, well armoured and fired with *jihad* and of betrayal by the native troops inside the castle, who could see clearly which way the wind was blowing. All of this took place against a constant and morale sapping background of terrible thunder coming from the beating of huge paired drums carried on the backs of up to three hundred camels. Al-Ansari's manual of war gives clear instructions on how to press a siege:

> And when the armed attack takes place it is necessary that the men of the army fight with the most convenient of arms first then the next most convenient, delaying the use of the largest arms until last of those which they employ in attacking. In this manner it becomes apparent to the people in the fortress that each successive implement is a little more than the proceeding one.
>
> When the investment is under way there should be no pause in the discharging of the mangonels against them and there should be no abating of the amount of mangonel fire in any hour of the day or night. To desist in attack against them is among that which cools their fright and strengthens their heart.*

---

* In G. A. Scanlon, *A Muslim Manual of War*, Cairo: American University at Cairo, 1961.

For this medieval equivalent of shock and awe to be delivered effectively, it required that the number of siege engines that were available for assault be large. Therefore the wood supplied by the Golden Horde was vital to the Mamluks' removal of the Crusaders from their bastions. The number of ballistas and mangonels used by the Mamluks shows a massive jump from the number deployed in siege warfare in the twelfth century. Saladin used no more than ten mangonels at any siege, whilst at the siege of Acre in 1291 the Mamluks deployed over ninety. The Franks were not, however, totally helpless before this onslaught. At Arsuf Baybars's sappers failed when the Crusaders dug a counter-mine to devastating effect. Ibn al-Furat wrote of this event:

> The Franks cunningly drove a tunnel from within the citadel until they got to a point beneath the blockage. They then cut through the earth until they reached the wood that was to be moved under the walls. They had made barrels full of grease and fat and they lit fires, having constructed bellows in the tunnels. The Muslim army knew nothing of this stratagem until the flames had taken hold. This happened at night and the Sultan himself came in the dark; people threw themselves at the fire to extinguish it, and water was poured from waters skins, but it was no use . . .*

Fortunately for Baybars, he had been able to take the citadel by deceit and he applied the principles of dirty tricks and psychological warfare next to the Templar castle of Safad in Galilee as 1265 and 1266 became truly appalling years for the Crusaders and their allies. He had shown his army before the walls of Acre on 1 June 1266 when he had returned to Syria with his army, but the city's French regiment paid for by King Louis IX had just been reinforced and he had moved away, making a feint at the Teutonic Knights of Montfort before suddenly appearing at Safad in early July.

The castle was well garrisoned and had three hundred ballisti operating its mangonels but most of its troops were native Syrian Christians under the command of Templar knights.

---

* In Hillenbrand, p. 532.

Baybars's initial assaults and a bombardment lasting fourteen days failed to bring the castle's defenders to surrender, despite Baybars paying 1,000 dirhams for every stone knocked out by his men. He was almost killed in the trenches by a well-aimed Frankish missile so he turned to more subtle methods. He declared an amnesty for any native Syrians who wished to surrender to him. The Syrians inside Safad had shown no disloyalty whatsoever up to this point but the Sultan's offer put their Templar overlords on guard against their own men. Tensions began to mount within the walls and before long the parties in the castle were at each other's throats. The Syrians deserted wholesale. The Templars' fears were probably not unfounded. In the Ayyubid period the natives of Syria had considered that the Franks were a fact of life and Outremer had by now been in existence for at least two generations. But now it was different, it became evident that the Mamluks were going to extinguish the Crusader kingdom and do it quickly and this realisation hastened the desertion of many of the Franks' native troops. Baybars was able, many times, to use forged letters and amnesties to foster suspicion between natives and Europeans and to cause division among the forces of Latin Syria.

The Templars' forces were now so reduced that they could not hope to cover the city's entire vast ring of walls. One of their native sergeants who had not deserted offered to parley with the Sultan. Whilst he was in Baybars's camp a Frankish spy who had infiltrated the Mamluk base released a carrier pigeon. Baybars grabbed his bow and shot the bird from the sky. After reading the message attached to the bird the Sultan then handed the note to the Crusaders' envoy, saying, 'we will be happy if this tells the Franks all about us'. There was obviously no hope for the Templars and when the sergeant returned to the castle with a forged letter from the Grand Master calling on the knights to surrender under promise of safe passage to Crusader territory they abandoned the castle, only to be decapitated to a man.

The Mamluks garrisoned Safad and moved on. The small city of Toron north of Safad fell at Baybars's first attack and Qara, a small Syrian Christian village between Homs and Damascus, which was not under Crusader occupation but which had been selling Muslims to Acre's slave market, was levelled by a small detachment of his army and all its inhabitants slaughtered. A delegation from Acre asked leave to bury the dead of Qara but Baybars responded that they wouldn't have even to leave their homes to find more than enough martyrs to bury before very long. He then marched down the coast south of Acre and, as if to drive his point home, enacted what can only be described as a pogrom on the Christians of the region. He returned to Egypt in the autumn of 1266.

At this point the Crusaders must have begun to wonder about their decision to lend support to the Mamluks against the Mongols in 1260 and in the early years of the 1260s there was a very understandable volte-face in Crusader policy. Europeans had tried diplomacy with the Mongols before; King Louis IX had sent emissaries to the Mongol Court in Asia before his Crusade of 1248 but the result had been disappointing, the Mongols thought the King's men had been sent to offer tribute and submission not alliance. The Mongol attitude of disparaging the Western Powers continued right up until the effective break up of the Mongol empire in 1260 with the Qubilai–Ariq Boke civil war. At this point the junior Khans seemed suddenly to realise that they needed other allies and were prepared to parley as near equals. Hulegu started a correspondence with Louis IX of France in 1262 and in this he was competing for the attentions of the King with Berke of the Golden Horde. A later letter of 1289 from the Ilkhan Arghun to Philip the Fair of France shows how much the rhetoric of the people with the divine right to conquer the world had been toned down over the years, how far plans for a joint operation had been developed and also shows how much the Mongols were expecting the Christian world to aid them against the Mamluks, a foe that they had become increasingly disheartened about ever defeating:

> We agree to your proposition which you conveyed to Us last year . . . 'If the armies of the Ilkhan go to war against Egypt, We too shall set out from here and go to war and to attack . . . in a common operation.'
>
> And We decided . . . after reporting to heaven, to mount our horses in the last month of winter [1290] . . . and to dismount

outside Damascus on the fifteenth of the first month in spring [1291] . . . if by the authority of heaven, We conquer those people, We shall give you Jerusalem. If . . . you should fail to meet the appropriate day, and thus lead our armies into an abortive action, would that be fitting? Even if you should later regret it, what use would that be to you?*

All this was to come to nothing for the Crusader states. The basic problem was the same one that faced the Mamluk–Golden Horde accord: the distance between the powers was too great to allow for effective coordination. The Crusaders faced a further problem in that they couldn't agree amongst themselves how to operate against the Mamluks and with the Mongols and their other allies. Venice and Genoa fought an undeclared war of attrition against each other around the ports of the Levant and the Hospitallers and Templars were involved in a long political struggle with each other over the spoils of Acre's trade. There was not even any assistance for their ally, Armenia, from the Crusader states other than from the Templars of Baghras when a Mamluk army under the emir Kalavun moved against it in 1266; by the time its king, Hetum, had returned from the Mongol capital of Tabriz his capital had been pillaged.

Kalavun's army had set out from Cairo at the same time as Baybars's summer expedition in 1266 and it made several attacks on the lands around Tripoli – one of Bohemond of Antioch's cities – capturing the forts of Qulaiat and Halba and the town of Arqa before moving on to its primary mission to join up with al-Mansur, the Ayyubid Prince and hero of the Battle of Homs, and then to inflict the maximum degree of damage on King Hetum's lands. The Armenian King had made several attempts from 1262 to 1264 to secure a foothold in northern Syria. He had been repulsed at Aleppo in 1262 and in the same year while he was in the process of sacking Sarmin he was surprised by an expeditionary force of Mamluks that ambushed his army from a prayer house and routed it. It is to be wondered just how many fully armoured Mamluks could get into a prayer house and by extension just how poorly the Armenian army fought, but the

---

* In D. Morgan, *The Mongols*, Oxford: Blackwells, 1990, p. 184.

fact remains that the King only just got away. In 1264 he again assembled an army and enlisted a thousand Bedouin irregulars for another raid, but Baybars's intelligence system allowed him to make a pre-emptive strike against the force from Homs and Hama, and King Hetum was sent back over his border again with a beaten army.

All this defeat finally took its toll and the King became involved in secret negotiations with Baybars to secure some kind of neutrality for his country by a payment of tribute to Egypt but he could not comply with Baybars's demands of the ceding of frontier fortresses for fear of his Mongol allies. In fact Baybars had no intention of even attempting to make peace with Armenia. He often entered into sub rosa negotiations with Mongol allies, as he did with Georgia in 1264, in order to then blackmail them by threatening to expose their subversive activities to the Mongols. The benefits of this intrigue were compliance under duress of the correspondents or a reasonable chance of the Ilkhans punishing their own vassals if the correspondence should, through an unfortunate slip on Baybars's part, end up in their hands. Baybars also used the technique to force the hands of potential defectors from the Mongol government. In 1262 he threatened to expose his secret correspondence with a former Abbasid government officer who continued to hold a high position in the Mongol administration, al-Baghdadi. His mechanism for exposing the incriminating letters was to dispatch two messengers to al-Baghdadi and instruct one messenger to kill the other and to leave the body, complete with the evidence of al-Baghdadi's forged reply and Baybars's offers of asylum, where the Mongols would find it easily. Al-Baghdadi had no choice but to run once the plot had run its course. He escaped to Egypt and was treated well for his defection by the Sultan.

King Hetum was not treated well by the Sultan. His sons waited for Kalavun's attack with the Armenian army in the Syrian gates, a small plain between the coastal city of Alexandretta and the start of the mountains to the city's east, but Kalavun and al-Mansur went straight over the mountains and entered Armenia unopposed and began pillaging. The

Armenian Princes moved quickly to meet the Mamluk army and the forces engaged on the plain to the east of Tarsus. The Armenians were both outnumbered and outclassed and were sent from the field in disorder. The death of one prince and the capture of the other meant the country was now leaderless. Kalavun's forces sacked the cities of Ayas, Adana and Tarsus and al-Mansur took his contingent to sack the capital Sis to the east. King Hetum's palace was ransacked, thousands of the inhabitants were killed and forty thousand captives were taken back to Aleppo. The cathedral was also burnt down and when the King returned from the Mongol court there was very little of the structure of his realm left to govern. Antioch was also now devoid of local allies, excepting the dubious friendship of the Mongols.

This thoroughly miserable period for the Christian East concluded with the defeat of the French regiment of Acre and a contingent of the Knights of the Orders during a counter-raid that they had attempted to launch through what was now Muslim-controlled Galilee. On 28 October 1266 the Crusader army's camp was raided by Bedouin and its lead forces were ambushed by the Mamluk garrison of Safad, which was already proving itself to be a very useful base for the Sultan's forces. The remainder of the Crusader force retired to Acre. The only bright spot was that the normal pre-Baybars rules of warfare in the Levant resurfaced ever so briefly when Bohemond was able to bribe off the emirs sent by Baybars to attack Antioch in the autumn of 1266. It may of course have been an unwise move, though, in that it only made the Sultan angry.

The Sultan's fury was delivered through his army and more specifically through his Royal Mamluks who were, of course, the best-trained soldiers in the army. Indeed, below this level, training was much more perfunctory, because not only did the size of the army increase at such a rapid pace under Baybars that resources must have been strained even as Baybars pushed more and more of the state's revenues into the military, but because it was also politically desirable to limit the training of those outside the Sultan's loyal guard. Overall, Baybars increased the size of the army during his reign to forty thousand horsemen plus infantry and auxiliaries; he had taken over a force of about ten thousand cavalry troopers and auxiliaries at the outset of his Sultanate. Most of the old Ayyubid forces were *halqa*, these were non-Mamluk horsemen, but still a first-class cavalry unit by any other army's standards. They were downgraded under Baybars and the Royal Mamluks became the real spine of the army. The Zahiriyya increased from one thousand to five thousand men through personal purchase and through the Sultan's 'inheritance' of men from dead Mamluk emirs and defeated Ayyubid princes.

A Royal Mamluk's life, in theory, prepared him for little apart from war. After being purchased from the slave dealers, the novice Mamluk would be sent to the *tibaq*, the barrack schools in the Cairo citadel. Each *tibaq* could hold one thousand trainees and by the fourteenth century there were twelve of them in Cairo. No novice could leave the barracks during the training period and transgressions of barrack law were harshly punished. One law that attempted to solve an ongoing problem in the Mamluk military society that worsened during the dynasty's decline gave the death penalty for any novice who was found to have been the object of sodomy by an adult Mamluk. The adolescent boys were under the care of eunuchs in the barracks – perhaps because of the foregoing concern – and came first under the tutelage of religious teachers, they were taught the Koran, how to pray, *sharia* law and the Arabic script. It is notable, however, that reading Arabic began to fade as a discipline as the Mamluk Dynasty became more mature and positively disassociated itself from the local populace almost completely. Their religious education, as it had been in Samarra, was dogmatic and narrow. There was an emphasis during this time too on making the novices fully aware of the splendours of Islamic civilisation for which they were to fight for. One is reminded of the way in which the 'British Way and Purpose' was promulgated to Commonwealth troops during the Second World War.

Upon coming of age, being of eighteen lunar or about fourteen solar years, the Mamluk novices began training according to the precepts of the *Furusiyya*. Al-Maqrizi described a Mamluk who had completed his training thus: 'The glorification of Islam and its people had been merged in his heart, and he became strong in archery, in handling the lance and in riding the horse.' The learning of military skills was formally divided into exercises in horsemanship, use of the lance, archery and swordsmanship. The Arabic word *Furusiyya* is made up of three parts – the *'ulum* (science), *funun* (arts) and *adab* (literature) of cavalry skills – and it is at this point in history that the mounted man as a distinct class in Islamic society appears. In Western society there was an acknowledged division of knights from clergy and labourers from at least the ninth century and such a tripartite division existed in Islam from very early too, but the Mamluks of Egypt systemised it much as chivalric orders did in the West.

The *Furusiyya* was in fact a concept far older than the Mamluk Sultanate. It was certainly already important in the early Abbasid Caliphate. The Caliph al-Mutasim had treatises written for him on the manufacture of steel blades in the early ninth century and the Mamluk polo players of the Mamluk Sultanate of Egypt and Syria continued to use playing techniques and rules, and indeed to continue the copying of *Furusiyya* works on the sport from the early Abbasid period, without introducing any changes or additions to the texts that guided players in Persia in the eigth century.* Indeed, the *Furusiyya*'s history can perhaps be traced back further even than this, certainly the last Umayyad Caliph Marwan II sent his son full instructions on how to conduct war and how to direct the army in a letter of 746 and these instructions bear all the hallmarks of the *Furusiyya*'s scientific approach to warfare. It addressed the management, training and care of the horses, cavalry tactics, riding techniques and the wearing of armour as well as how to wield certain weapons consummately, concerted movement of cavalrymen on the field, techniques for single combat and basic veterinary science. That there was already a wide-ranging body of texts even before the Mamluk Sultanate is evident from the fact that

---

* Cf. S. Al-Sarraf, 'Mamluk Furusiyah Literature', *Mamluk Studies Review*, vol 8, no 1, 2004, p. 197.

many Mamluk authors quote the work of and acknowledge the brilliance of earlier writers.

The Mamluk preoccupation with the *Furusiyya* and with warfare as an end in itself rather than just the vehicle that brought power gave the Mamluk military society its peculiar character. This, added to the ideals of *jihad*, the *khushdashiyya* loyalty code and their separation from mainstream Egyptian society defined the Mamluks and marked out their caste. Although unwritten, the code of this caste embraced virtues such as courage, valour, magnanimity and generosity. A Mamluk manual of war gives the following:

> If it happens that one of the men of the army should retire because of his fear of battle or the suffering of wounds, no other person of the army should obstruct him by standing in his way or should send him back to his position among the warriors; but rather he should be treated gently and be placated until he attains the rear of the battle rankings.*

Such ideals were propagated through Mamluk society; armour commonly carried engravings such as: 'Father of the poor and miserable, killer of the unbelievers and the polytheists, reviver of justice among all.' But, just as with the chivalrous knights of Christendom and the Samurai in Japan, the reality was often very different. Mamluk troopers were as interested in booty as the next man, they were capable of disloyalty and of extreme cruelty to civilians, even cowardice in the face of the enemy was not unheard of, but what was vital to their pattern of life was that there was an ideal and the *Furusiyya* was central to that.

Japanese Samurai spent evenings discussing over and over the *Art of War* and Western knights-to-be, in their childhood, heard tales of derring-do and were told to seek a place in the vanguard for honour's sake when they came of age. In the same way the Mamluk trooper's life's work was based around the *Furusiyya* and we can be certain that whenever he gathered socially with his comrades, dinner arguments were won by

---

* In Scanlon, p. 72.

reference to the *Furusiyya* texts, stories of old victories were rounded out by quotations from it, and defeats and stratagems were qualified by reference to its lessons. Indeed a great deal of what we find in the *Furusiyya* of the Mamluk Sultanate does not fit with contemporary warfare and was often included by authors to show their learning and knowledge of classical Greek and Persian warfare and presumably to allow their readers the opportunity to do likewise. Similarly, it is evident that many texts were just straightforward copies or confabulations of much earlier, and now lost, treaties on warfare from the early Islamic period. For example, the heavy *amud* mace of the early Abbasid period is discussed at length in one Mamluk *Furusiyya* but the weapon had gone out of use long before the Sultanate's birth and the author shows his total ignorance of the weapon's characteristics by giving us its weight as being about half a kilogram, whereas it was in fact commonly some twenty times heavier than this.*

The *Furusiyya* manuscripts of the Mamluks were beautifully illustrated and were obviously treasured. Older texts were sometimes expanded upon and enhanced with new military tactics. This is particularly notable in Mamluk texts on siege warfare, which was revolutionised under Baybars and in the later Mamluk period when the introduction of artillery and firearms to the battlefield challenged the old ways and required a new analysis of strategy. Diagrammatic representations of large-scale cavalry manoeuvres were another addition of the Mamluk Sultanate to the older manuals of war. The formation and make up of armies was also described in these later additions and ruses using fire and smoke screens were illustrated. Even the treatment of wounds was addressed. Fourteenth-century texts show a breakdown of Mongol methods of warfare and an analysis of their tactics. Al-Ansari's text gives this salutary warning, obviously relating to the Mongols:

> If the enemy stimulates flight and raises dust the attack against him should not occur until the dust has settled for fear of an

---

* Cf. Al-Sarraf, p. 177.

ambush. If the enemy turns his back and his rout is certain the entire army should not follow him rather some of the army should pursue while others plunder, and the remainder are employed to cover these operations. For them, as a whole, to pursue the enemy is judged blameworthy.*

The point about treatises being at the heart of military lore is made clearly in the layout of an archery lesson written down by the archery master Taybugha al-Baklamishi al-Yunani (d. 1394). The text equates entering the archery training enclosure with entering a mosque. The trainee was instructed to adopt a reverential disposition through prayer and to use this time also to relax and focus before beginning the preparation of bow and arrows. Instructions in the *Furusiyya* tell the novice archer how and when to tie his sleeves back and how to tie his clothing in preparation for target practice. The parallels between this and *Kyudo*, the art of Japanese archery, are truly telling; when entering the *Kyudojo* novices are told to adopt a contemplative mood, the *dojo* always had a Shinto shrine on a raised platform and novices were instructed on how to tie the *obi* and *hakama* – the waistband and divided skirt.

The Mamluk novice was introduced to archery through using a soft flexible bow. All training was carefully staged, with novices moving through the demands of training from simple tasks and little physical requirement through to highly skilled tasks requiring a great deal of strength and endurance. The Qipchaq boys had all handled bows and ridden ponies on the steppe before being harvested but Mamluk training required that every novice started again with the basics – the 'modern' system so beloved of elite forces of breaking and remaking recruits would have found plaudits among Mamluk instructors. The novice was shown how to make the 'Falcon's Talons' to grip the bow by mimicking the actions of his instructor and he practised without arrows for several days; great emphasis was placed on correct grip and pull. As any archer knows, each and every shot is the same, the height of aim may be adjusted for distance but every arrow is delivered with the same pull,

---

* Al-Ansari, in Scanlon, p. 106.

and consistent shot delivery – especially when shooting as a group – is all. The novice moved on to a featherless arrow that was shot over and over at almost point-blank range at a cotton-filled leather tube called the *buttiya*. Again the correspondence between this and ancient Japanese archery training using *makiwara* targets only a bow's length (two metres) away from the archer are uncanny, in fact the distance in the Mamluk practice was only one *dihra* (66.5 cm). During this practice, which extended over a considerable length of time, the novice progressed through four more bows of increasing pull.* The final one would have had a pull of about thirty kilograms and this was the *qaws* used for combat.

Taybugha wrote a poem of 200 lines that novices were expected to memorise. When recited the poem gave complete instructions for delivering the perfect archery shot right from setting the bow, through the placement of the legs, nocking the arrow, aiming and to execution of the shot. Even Robert Ascham of *Toxophilus* fame would have been shamed by the detail of Mamluk archery manuals, obviously arrow and bow types are covered in detail in these texts, but there is much more, even extending to such minutiae as how to avoid hand and forearm trembling and how to treat and avoid the wounds caused by bowstrings.

The Mamluk trooper was a cavalry soldier and he would almost always be using his bow from the saddle, so first, of course, he had to learn or rather relearn how to ride. The novice began horsemanship on safe mounts made of wood. The horse master taught the trainees how to mount the horse swiftly, and this drill was continued with the addition of a saddle and then progressed to full armour mounting and dismounting. *Furusiyya* manuscripts give descriptions of and instruction on how a horseman should put on his mail hauberk and remove it while his horse was in motion so we can be sure that these drills were practised; being able to remove armour on the move in the Syrian summer was not a luxury, it was a necessity for

---

* Cf. H. Rabie, 'The Training of the Mamluk Faris', in Parry and Yap.

maintaining the fighting ability of troops in a harsh climate. When the novice was ready to move onto live horses he went back to riding without armour and saddle again and progressed through trot, canter and gallop.

Much of the training was like this – two steps forward and one back – with constant reiteration and recapitulation of the basics. Mamluk commanders needed their men to be predictable and consistent in everything they did; if the army and its soldiers are known quantities the field commander can expect manoeuvres to be executed on the battle field as they are on the training ground. The ability to move forward in units even under heavy archery fire had been the key to breaking the cycle of Mongol rearming, remounting and re-entering the battle at Ayn Jalut. The novice practised tight turns, jumping and standing with saddle and stirrups. At this stage he was also expected to study the health and illnesses of horses and to attend to the care of his mount and to his tack. The *Furusiyya* manuscripts relate how a bad soldier can be easily identified from the poor condition of his saddle straps and how any trooper has not completed his education unless he knows how to care for a sick horse and how to nurse it to recovery.

The *Furusiyya* writings are very specific on how the rider should hold the reins and this is extended also to the hold employed for each piece of battle equipment. The idea was that the cavalryman should be balanced perfectly in every move so that weapons could be deployed smoothly without upsetting the horse and rider's movement. It is common for weapons to be paired in the manuscripts, partly to show the particular attributes and applications of different weapons, and also to hint at this required balance and the poise required to become a warrior of the highest stamp. The manuscripts entreated warriors never to be without the *khanjar*, a large dagger, either in war or peace. It could be used in the same way as a sword or dagger and could also be thrown. It was thought to be the perfect accompaniment to the lance because it could be used when the fighting got closer than a spear's length. For the trooper carrying a sword, missile weapons such as a javelin or a sling-shot are recommended. The pairing continued through to the *dabbus* or mace, which accompanied the spear or javelin.

It is notable that whilst the *Furusiyya* manuscripts make extensive use of this device of pairing for almost every weapon the bow is barely mentioned. This is because the bow was so central to Mamluk warfare that its carriage was simply assumed. The highest point of *Furusiyya* training was mounted archery and it would show clearly whether a Mamluk novice had acquired the balance, composure and grace of movement that the *Furusiyya* texts and instructors sought to instil in him. The two main movements that the horse archer had to demonstrate competency in were shooting down at a sand-filled basket – an infantry kill – and a shot up through a ring mounted about seven metres high on a beam and into a circular target behind it – a shot into the ranks of an advancing enemy. Both shots had to be executed at the gallop and the rider stood in the stirrups for both, leaning forward over his horse's ears for the first and hard over to his side for the second. Attainment of one hundred per cent was required if a novice was to achive the status of *faris* or knight.

The high target was called the *qabaq* and shooting it became a popular sport among even high-ranking Mamluks. Ibn Taghribirdi, writing in the fifteenth century, relates a story of the Sultan al-Ashraf Khalil coming to the *maydan* or hippodrome with friends to shoot *qabaq* in 1293, the only difference between the Sultan's tourney and the drills of the *tibaq* being that a perfectly placed shot would release a dove from a silver gourd atop the pole and the first man to free the bird won a robe of honour and the gourd. Baybars, similarly, offered pedigree Arabian horses from Medina to emirs who achieved perfect marks in the *qabaq*. Vegetius may have boasted that the Romans' drills were bloodless battles and that their battles were bloody drills but the Mamluks' leisure activities were equal to drilling. Mounted archery competitions, horseback acrobatics and mounted combat shows were commonplace, taking place as often as twice a week. During the visits of emissaries from the Golden Horde Baybars and his guests watched archery displays that lasted several days.

Polo's popularity has already been discussed and with its need for tight control of the horse in close turns and bursts of speed it mimicked nicely the skills required on the battlefield, Baybars is recorded as regularly playing in two games a week, one in Damascus and the other in Cairo. The novice was introduced to the manoeuvres required by a polo player of Baybars's standard in his *tibaq* through the *bunud*, the lance exercises. He learnt how to tilt the lance during both attack and retreat and how to thrust and parry and disengage from opponents. The manuscripts even give advice on how to extricate oneself from difficulties; the popular notion of a lance as the weapon of reckless all-or-nothing charges is dispelled by the calculated and drilled approach to its use seen among the Mamluks. At the end of his lance training the novice was expected to be able to throw his lance from his galloping mount at a target made up of a tower of seven narrow boxes with a ring on top at about the height of the novice's horse. The novice had to throw cleanly through the ring without dislodging any other part of the target to claim success. He was also tested by several other varieties of target practice. Najm al-Din al-Rammah's *Furusiyya* tells us that cones had to be collected by the galloping Mamluk novice with the tip of his lance as he sped by, twelve rings had to be caught from metal poles and the rider was also expected to strike a ball placed atop a man's, presumably not the instructor's, head. The *bunud* was comprised of a total of 150 exercises that were recorded from the earliest days of the Muslim Empire, these were reduced under the Mamluks to seventy-two exercises emphasising the need to increase the novice's strength in both the thighs and the upper body.

Mastering the lance allowed the novice to move onto training in the *maydan*. These hippodromes were places of entertainment, as discussed above, but they were also the place where novices learnt movement as a unit, how to make concerted coordinated attacks and were drilled in defensive positioning. There was a strong emphasis during these exercises on awareness, at all times, of the trooper's own position in the formation and of that of his comrades. The Mamluk tactics employed against the Mongols drew heavily on these skills and it is not surprising that Baybars built two more hippodromes to supplement the one built in the reign of al-Salih. The novices entered the hippodrome in units based on their *tibaq* and they followed their instructors as they formed columns that diverged left and right to form lines that would then fold in on themselves to make staggered lines from which columns or individual riders peeled off. The *Furusiyya* of the master Lachin al-Husami shows these movements in clear diagrammatic form; despite their simplicity they are quite dazzling.

What was certainly not dazzling was the novice's introduction to sword or *sayf* drills. He started with a sword of about a kilogram in weight. He would progress to a sword of about two and a half kilograms by the end of training. The drills certainly sound tedious. The novice was allowed only to hold the sword between the thumb and forefinger and progressed from a mere twenty-five strikes a day at a soft clay bed placed on a table through to one thousand hits through increments of twenty-five per day. He used the same approach each time, bringing the left leg forward and the right leg back whilst raising the sword to his cheek and then striking down. The exercise was repeated using the left arm. Felt was laid over the clay when the novice had reached a thousand hits, and the novice then had to cut through the felt to reach the clay. The felt was increased from one layer to five over the course of training. Some *Furusiyya* manuals advocate the use of a lead bar instead of the addition of felt but the effect would have been the same – the progressive development of mighty sword arms. Brute force alone was not enough for the instructors, however, and the novice had also to be able to control his stroke for wounding or killing. He had to cut through reams of paper without cutting a soft cotton pillow placed below it with one blow, only then could he move to training with the sword as a cavalryman. The drills here were limited to one sword until the novice showed that he was able to cut a measured piece from reeds of his own height, at a gallop, with his sword. The reeds were placed both to his left and to his right and he was expected to be able to cut all ten at a run. Then he would move onto the use of two swords or a sword with the *khanjar*.

Baybars's ambidextrous army returned to the field in May 1267 and appeared before Acre with Hospitaller and Templar banners that he had acquired during previous campaigns. Using these he was able to get his forces close up to Acre's walls, but the hoax was rumbled before he could inflict any real damage. He compensated himself by ravaging the countryside to such a degree that the Crusaders of Acre sent emissaries to request a truce. The prediction of Shafi ibn Ali, made in 1265, that Baybars would, 'fight until no more Franks remain on the surface of the earth', seemed to be coming true. Also whilst Saladin had made Jerusalem the focus of his *jihad* Baybars's Holy War was much more extensive; he aimed to make Syria a Sunni enclave. The Shiite Ismaili Assassin sect, who had maintained strongholds in northern Syria were the subjects of a long difficult campaign pursued by Baybars's lieutenants between 1265 and 1273, by taming them he also gained the benefit of deploying Assassins for his political killings as required.

Religious zealotry was firing up among the Christian monarchs of Europe just as it was in the Sultan of Egypt. Louis IX of France again took the Cross in March 1267 and there was enthusiasm for a Crusade among the royal houses of England and Aragon. Baybars knew that Louis's enterprise would take considerable time to plan, and he had to prepare for the worst possible scenario, that Louis's and Abagha Khan's correspondence that had begun in earnest in 1266 would lead to a joint attack on Syria and Egypt. Therefore early in 1268 Baybars set off to clear the last remaining Crusader city south of Acre. Jaffa was on the coast and a potential landing point for a Crusader army. On 7 March he appeared before its walls, he was legitimately able to break an agreed peace treaty with the city because the garrison had built mangonels in violation of their agreement. One of these engines launched a missile that killed three men standing close to Baybars, but after only twelve hours of fighting the city fell. Baybars allowed the troops of the citadel to leave for Acre but there was an extensive slaughter of the civilian population and many captives were taken as slave booty. The city walls and the castle were demolished completely, in line with Mamluk coastal policy, and the marble decoration and wood of the structures were sent back to Cairo to become part of the Sultan's new mosque. Baybars then bypassed Acre completely and headed north, set on the destruction of Antioch. Bohemond had continued his policy of close alliance with the Mongols and it was highly likely that he would be an important part of any joint Ilkhanid–European assault. The Sultan stopped at the Templar castle of Beaufort on his way north, where he watched his siege engines destroy the walls over a ten-day period. The foundations of a new fort to the south of the castle that was being built to enhance Beaufort's defences were actually its undoing. Baybars used the level base, the only flat area in the mountainous region, as a base for his artillery. The Templars surrendered and were sent to the slave markets, whilst oddly the women and children were set free to seek refuge in Tyre. The castle was rebuilt and garrisoned as it was inland and straddled a likely Mongol invasion route.

Baybars made a quick move towards Tripoli, one of Bohemond's possessions, arriving there on 1 May, but his reconnaissance held that it was too strong to be taken quickly and he may not have realised that Bohemond was in the city. He continued north, moving past the Templars' strongholds of Tortosa and Safita, both of which sent hurried embassies to the Sultan petitioning for clemency. Baybars accepted the appeals and moved on up the Orontes Valley. The Templars were undoubtedly saved by Baybars's concentration on Bohemond's Antioch. The Mamluk army arrived before Antioch's walls on 14 May, and the city was immediately invested by Baybars with about a third of his forces. Further divisions were sent to Saint Symeon, Antioch's port, to cut it off from supply and reinforcement from the sea, and to the pass in the mountains, the Syrian Gates, to prevent any relief coming from Armenia –unlikely, given the now ruined state of that country – or the more realistic likelihood of Mongol intervention.

Bohemond's constable organised his limited forces along the city's long walls and the defenders were stretched thinly around the city's fortifications. The constable then made the incredibly foolish move of leading a sortie against Baybars's division whilst the Mamluks were in the process of settling in for the siege. He was captured and Baybars immediately put him to work arranging the city's capitulation, but after his imprudent raid the defenders refused to listen to him. Bombardments and assaults began immediately and were then broken off for more negotiations, which also failed.

On 18 May Baybars made a general attack on every sector of the walls; the garrison was stretched so thin that a break-in was inevitable and it came on the Mount Silpius section of walls. The Mamluks charged into the city and there was a whole day of murder and rapine. The city gates were sealed to ensure that no citizen could escape death and only those that escaped to the citadel were able to negotiate for a life in bondage rather than instant death. Baybars called a halt to the slaughter the next day. He ordered an organised and regulated collection of the city's riches and distributed slaves and riches among the 'emirs of one hundred', his senior emirs, with which they could richly endow their one hundred personal Mamluks and perhaps even the leading officers of the 1,000-strong non-Mamluk troopers and infantry that these men also commanded. Baybars wrote to Bohemond of the sack:

> If you had seen your churches destroyed, your crosses sawn asunder, the pages of the lying gospels exposed, if you had seen your enemy the Muslim trampling in the sanctuary, with the monk, the priest, the deacon sacrificed on the altar ... the Churches of Saint Paul and Saint Peter pulled down and destroyed you would have said, 'Would to God that I was transformed to dust or would to God that I had not received the letter that tells me of this sad catastrophe.'*

The collapse of Antioch made the position of practically all Crusader possessions in northern Syria untenable. The Templars abandoned all their castles in the surrounding mountains and other minor fortified towns took on vassalage under the Sultan. Antioch itself was refortified, it was now to be a platform for operations against the Mongol dependencies of Anatolia, but it was never repopulated.

---

* In Hillenbrand, p. 320.

Antioch's first Crusader Prince, the great Bohemond of Taranto, had taken the city in 1098 by cunning and it is to be wondered if these two men, the Norman Adventurer and the Slave Soldier from the steppes would not have held a grudging admiration for each other. Both were superb soldiers, both devious and Machiavellian and both superb organisers of intelligence and vision. Baybars's vision extended to minutiae when it came to the military infrastructure of the Sultanate. Through acquisition and conquest he had solidified the borders against Mongol land attack and Crusader sea assault and through his diplomacy he had helped distract the Mongols from Syrian conquest.

The threat from both foes, though, was still considerable and there was the continued potential for a war on two fronts. Early on, Baybars had turned to the problem of communications and early warning systems in the Sultanate. The military postal service that had existed under the Saljuq Sultanate was long dead by the Mamluk period but it, and the superb Mongol *yam* system that covered the entirety of their lands, provided models for Baybars's new *barid*, or pony express service. The Turcomen whom Baybars had settled in Syria and to whose chiefs he had given robes of honour were charged with supplying horses for the *barid*, just as the nomadic Arabs were charged with maintaining the safety of the roads from Egypt to Iraq and into Africa, each emir of the Arabs was given a fixed territory to guardian and was rewarded accordingly. Stations capable of supplying fresh horses were available all the way from al-Bira in the extreme northeast of the Sultanate down to Alexandria to the west of Cairo. Al-Ansari tells us that the *barid* reduced twenty days' distance to three and that from Qus dromedaries were used to extend the service south to Aswan and Aydhab.

The use of carrier pigeons had been used moderately extensively but unsystematically under Nur al-Din and Saladin but Baybars created a regular network of constantly manned pigeon towers throughout the Sultanate. Al-Ansari's treatise on war includes this assessment of the importance of carrier pigeon communications: 'It is obvious that pigeons are among the fastest means of communication because the pigeon covers the distance of twenty days' walking in less than a day.'* The third line of early warning were new watchtowers on the borders that communicated with each other from the Mongol border at al-Bira and al-Rahba on the Euphrates and down through the communication spine of the Sultanate to Gaza through smoke signals and beacons. From Gaza the ponies and pigeons took over.

The Sultanate's interior lines of communication were made safer and quicker by the addition of roadside guard towers near the Mongol border and the construction of a series of bridges over the Jordan. Baybars's early preoccupation with the destruction of Crusader strongpoints in the Syrian interior gave unimpeded movement within Syria both for the *barid* and of forces sent north to meet any Mongol incursions.

Baybars's ordering of the military state extended to correcting the ad hoc nature of Mamluk government before his accession. Kutuz and his predecessors had led the Mamluks as a *primus inter pares*. This would have been in line with steppe traditions where successful war chieftains were given allegiance but there was no divine right per se as in Western kinghood. Baybars's re-establishment of and investiture by the new Caliph was a key part of his move from being merely a war leader maintaining his position by success and distribution of booty to being a Sultan by right of religion and required loyalty. Of course this was also achieved by reorganising the upper echelons of power in the state. Baybars, as discussed earlier, distributed power among his *khushdash* and senior members of this clique formed his politburo. The army and state therefore became more and more centrally controlled and those outside the clique could not gain advancement. Baybars also took on young Mamluks as a bodyguard, the *khassakiyya*, whilst older officers of the *halqa* found themselves sent to distant border posts away from political power in Cairo. Baybars formed distinct tiers in the Mamluk forces and three divisions emerged among the emirs. An emir of ten was the lowest rank and, as the name implies,

---

* In Hillenbrand, p.547.

this lord was expected to maintain ten Mamluks for service with the Sultan. Next came the emir of forty, who was also titled an 'emir of drums' as he was entitled to have drums beaten during ceremonies. The emirs of one hundred were the most senior emirs, they were entitled to have a military band accompany them; this one hundred was the core around which about one thousand troopers of lower levels of training would be arraigned.

This fixed hierarchy helped ensure that reward in the form of pay was regular and fair and that *iqta* distribution was regulated. After his conquest of Caesarea Baybars had the entire region surrounding the city surveyed and the Frankish villages, or even fractions of villages, were then distributed among emirs of differing ranks. This was reward by booty but in a highly regulated way that allowed Baybars to advance the careers of those men who were one of his own. The wealthier his own men became the more Mamluks they purchased as their personal bodyguard. Therefore the huge pyramid that was the Mamluk state, with the Sultan at the top and the Mamluk troopers at its base was constructed of multiple replicas, each internal structure itself a triangle of loyalty to its *ustadh*. The bond of strength within each unit was the *khushdashiyya*. The structure seems impenetrable but it did have dangerous flaws just as the Western feudal pyramid of fealty did. Both required a strong dynamic and successful leader, without this the higher lords or emirs below would use their personal power base to dispute power. In the absence of a strong Sultan higher Mamluk politics quickly reverted back to the brutal ways of the early years. Bloody purges of higher emirs of the 'old guard' by incoming Sultans and internecine fighting among factions loyal to different candidates for the throne were common, as was the use of impalement and crucifixion by Sultans against those suspected of acts of lese-majesty or intrigue.

Baybars would not have flinched at inflicting crucifixion on even his closest friends in order to retain power. In 1263 he struck first against a conspiracy that included Balaban al-Rashidi, his competitor for the Sultanate in 1260 after Kutuz's murder. Ending the plot also required the death of men close to him personally and in his purge of 1265 he dispassionately dispatched the Kurdish emirs of Damascus, with whom he had ridden and raided in the 1250s; in Baybars's purge of Bahriyya emirs in 1270 the senior emirs Kalavun, Baysari and Baktash were left alone, despite his distrust of them. The disciplined politician in him counselled that they were too powerful to be removed easily. There was even a marriage alliance between Kalavun's daughter and Baybars's oldest son, Baraka. The popular work of fiction, the *Sirat Baybars*, that came into existence after his death romanticises Baybars's exploits but there is also truth in the tales of his disguising himself in order to spy on his own administrators in distant parts of the Sultanate and in his prohibition on the drinking of wine in the army and the finding of husbands for Cairene prostitutes. Camp followers, a medieval euphemism for prostitutes, were anathema to the Sultan. Ibn al-Furat tells us that, 'the army brought no wine in its train nor were there any lewd practices: there were only virtuous women who brought the soldiers water to drink in the middle of the fighting.' There was also legislation against hashish consumption so it was a very sober Baybars who made a secret pilgrimage to Mecca in 1269 whilst everyone thought he was hunting around al-Karak, by doing so he effectively brought the Holy Places of Islam under his suzerainty.

Baybars becoming the protector of Mecca and Medina could only add to the infidel Ilkhans' problems with their rebellious Muslim subjects. Peasant rebellions wracked the Ilkhanate throughout this period. A revolution in Fars in 1265 had been led by a Mahdi and practically all the numerous rebellions that the Ilkhans faced in the south of Iran and Iraq up until the end of the thirteenth century had a religious aspect. In truth, the Ilkhans didn't need outside interference for their subjects to rebel, their own policies were quite sufficient. The Ilkhanate was passing through a period of massive economic decline due partly to the devastation wrought by the initial Mongol invasion and compounded by a policy of taxation that can be conveniently labelled rapine. In brief, the population fell, the land under cultivation fell as the underground irrigation system, the *qanat*, that maintained Iran's agrarian infrastructure was neglected and ceased to flow, and urban life disintegrated whilst state taxes and feudal rent increased and nomadic pastoralists roamed over the wreckage of what had been one of the most fertile countries in Asia. Depopulation was a deliberate policy of the early years of the Ilkhanate: it helped to crush resistance, intimidate the populace and opened up pastureland for the migrational herding that the Mongols practised, but it had certainly gone too far. The writer Saifi collected stories from old men in Khurasan who could remember the 1260s and recorded them in his work of 1321, 'Neither people, nor corn, nor food, nor clothing . . . the people ate only human flesh, dogs and cats for a whole year because the warriors of Genghis Khan had burnt down the granaries.'* Only twelve people were left alive in Herat once the Mongols had passed through, in the fields of Khurasan the ploughs were pulled by men as every ox had been slaughtered and in the fertile valley of the river Kur the grain count fell from 700,000 *khawa* units in 949 AD to 42,000 in 1260. Hamd Allah Mustawfi's verdict was that, 'there can be no doubt that even if for a thousand years to come no evil befalls this country, yet will it not be possible to completely to repair the damage'.† The consequences of this appalling mismanagement of the Ilkhanate's economy would become more and more important as the contest with the Mamluks wore on.

Baybars, meanwhile, had been building the economic base on which his military state relied. Trade relations had been established with Aragon and with the new ruler of Sicily, Charles of Anjou. Baybars had kept up his correspondence with Sicily's previous ruler, Manfred, partly because he was fervently anti-Papal, even sending him a giraffe and Mongol prisoners, but the Sultan had also written in cordial terms to Charles, even before he had usurped the Sicilian throne. Baybars knew that Sicily's naval resources and strategic position in the Mediterranean made it a potential launching pad for any Crusade. He needed to assure its ruler, whoever he was, that

---

* In I. Petrushevsky, 'The Socio-economic Condition of Iran Under the Ilkhans', in J. Boyle (ed), *The Cambridge History of Iran, Volume 5*, London: Cambridge University Press, 1968, p. 484.
† In Petruschevsky, p. 485.

his actions in Syria would not affect the trade revenues that the island gathered from the flow of goods from the Middle East into Europe. Charles's Papal-backed usurpation of the throne had benefited Baybars in that Charles's territorial ambitions in Italy, plans for the conquest of Constantinople, now back in Byzantine hands, and his designs on Outremer had all frightened the maritime republics of Genoa, Venice and Pisa to such an extent that they all looked to solidify their position in the eastern Mediterranean by making trade treaties with the Sultan. He, after all, controlled Alexandria and it had almost the monopoly on the trade of India now that the Crusader ports of Syria were withering away.

These economic relationships became politically important in 1270 in the miring of King Louis IX's last crusading venture. The Crusade had looked, during its initial preparations in 1267, to be a great threat to the Mamluks. Louis's reputation had been enough to bring even the Kings of Aragon and England into the project. Therefore Baybars continued his preparations to meet the expected Crusade with a treaty with Lesser Armenia in 1268. He released Prince Leo, captured by Kalavun in 1266, and the Armenians ceded border fortresses. He also responded to calls for a truce from Acre with an agreement allowing a temporary cessation of operations against the city. Despite the truce he still arranged for the Assassins to eliminate the leading baron of Acre, Philip of Montfort, and he completed the demolition of Ascalon in case it should be used as a disembarkation point by the Crusaders. He had already fortified Alexandria and given it a new watchtower to identify hostile ships. Damietta was also refortified and the Nile was dredged to ensure that the flooding that had destroyed the Crusade of 1218 could be repeated. The Sultan also investigated the possibility of importing Indian war elephants to give the Crusaders a nasty shock, but transportation proved too difficult.

So Baybars was braced for the storm but it never came. Enthusiasm for the Crusade was not universal and the Italians, who were needed to carry the army to the Levant, were dragging their feet and the King's own brother, Charles of Anjou, strangely enough, appeared reluctant to attack Egypt. The Crusade was eventually diverted to Tunisia on the rather odd assumption that its ruler was a likely convert to Christianity; it turned into a disaster. Pestilence did more damage to the Crusaders than the armies of Tunisia could ever have hoped to. King (later Saint) Louis died in Tunis of dysentery. Prince Edward of England arrived only after the King's death and he left shortly after for Acre. Then Charles of Anjou assumed command of the project but soon abandoned it after securing trade and tribute agreements for Sicily from the Tunisians. The Aragonese had suffered shipwrecks before getting any further than Barcelona and only a handful of them made it to Syria under two bastard princes. Nothing was achieved.

The emergency was over and it was back to work for the Sultan. His last campaign against the Crusaders set out in 1271. In February he took the White Castle of the Templars and then moved on to the great prize of Crak des Chevaliers, the immense Hospitaller castle that sat between the Mamluk cities of Hama and Homs. The castle was encircled on 3 March and despite heavy rain slowing down the bringing up of siege engines a brief but very effective barrage began on 15 March. The same mistake had been made at Crak as had been made at Beaufort: earthworks had been constructed by the Franks on a neighbouring hill in order to keep enemy siege artillery at a distance but the Hospitallers' limited manpower meant that it could not be held and it made the perfect platform for Baybars's engines. Crak, on an otherwise impenetrable mountain, also had one accessible spur and the final successful assault was launched along it after sappers brought down one of the massive towers on the outer wall. The Mamluks swarmed into the outer ring of defences and two weeks later they were able to force their way into the inner enclosure. There was a spirited defence of one last tower by the knights but after ten days they capitulated and were given safe conduct to Tripoli. Baybars then moved south to the smaller Hospitaller castle of Gibelcar. The Mamluks had great difficulty pulling the siege engines up the wooded hills that surrounded the castle, but Baybars showed his usual resolve and helped to dig out the platforms for the engines and steered carts through the forests carrying timber for their construction. The castle fell in twelve days once the bombardment began and on 12 June the Teutonic fortress of Montfort also fell after only a week-long siege. There was now not one inland castle left to the Franks.

It was at this point, however, that constant weakness in both Baybars's and the later Mamluk Sultans' military response to the Western threat began really to show itself. The problem was the navy, or the lack of it. The Mamluks had galleys and Baybars built about forty more vessels during his reign but still couldn't keep up with Western maritime power. Baybars sent a fleet to raid Cyprus in June 1271, concerned that with Prince Edward of England's arrival in Acre there might be new Cypriot-backed raids from the Crusader cities into the interior. The ships were painted black like Christian ships and their flags bore the Cross but due to poor seamanship and bad weather they were wrecked off the island's coast and eighteen hundred sailors and troops were imprisoned. Baybars also failed at Maraclea, a small fort built on a rock just off the coast near Tortosa. A joint naval–land operation turned into a debacle and the Mamluks were beaten off.

King Hugh mocked Baybars's naval failures and Baybars replied that he had captured Montfort and that a ship could be built in a day but a fortress couldn't. This was just bluster, though, and as he seemed unable to keep up in the naval arms race the policy of destruction of the cities and harbours of the Syrian coastline continued unabated. This however, didn't address the core reasons why the policy was needed and the Mamluks still had a huge 'navy gap' to make up when action was absolutely forced upon them by the arrival of the Portuguese in the Red Sea in the fifteenth century. More important than this was that the policy showed how the major power of the Islamic world had turned in on itself. The Mamluks rejected expansion and venture just at the time when the Western nations were beginning to fully embrace it. Their simplistic policy of defence by denial of a place to land was certainly unimaginative and restrictive and this inflexibility eventually extended into their intellectual approach to grand strategy. The huge advantage that the European nations were later to gain from their continued investment in naval power and navigation of the oceans, later leading to the eventual dominance of the West and the near impotence of the countries of the Middle East in the modern age had its origins in the golden period of the Mamluk era but the Mamluk Sultans of the thirteenth century could not possibly foresee this. For them, making policy – as it is for the politicians of our time – was in many ways simply a process of reacting to events, and the medieval Middle East was never uneventful.

6

DUBIOUS ALLIES AND UNTRUSTWORTHY FRIENDS

BAYBARS'S LAST CAMPAIGNS

> I am full of fatal arrows
> My merchandise is pain and death
> Learn by what thou have seen of me
> I am the blight of this wide world
> *Inscriptions on Mamluk bows*

PRINCE EDWARD OF ENGLAND'S Crusading forces were small, he only had about one thousand men. Consequently he was only able to manage a few raids into the Plain of Sharon near Mount Carmel in 1271. However, he was able to enter into a correspondence with the Ilkhan Abagha. The Ilkhan had been distracted once again from Syrian affairs by an extensive invasion of Khurasan by the Chaghatay Mongols in 1270, which he had defeated in the Battle of Herat in July of the same year. In 1271, as a reprisal, he sent a large division of his forces into the Chaghatay Horde's lands to sack and burn Bukhara. The Ilkhan himself had been badly gored by a boar whilst hunting, but despite this and his Transoxanian commitments he was still able to send a Mongol force of ten thousand troopers from Anatolia to Syria at Edward's behest. The Mamluk garrison of Aleppo fled under Baybars's orders, trying to draw the Mongols further into Syria and closer to his main force at Damascus. As the Mongols advanced towards Maarat al-Numan Baybars started to move north with his heavy cavalry and a large number of auxiliaries. He also called for another three thousand troopers from Cairo. The Mongols denied him the battle he wanted by quickly evacuating Syria, but one detachment of the Mamluk army was able to reach Harran in Mongol territory and capture part of its small garrison as it came out to challenge them. They were unable, however, to take the city but it was demolished shortly after by the Mongols and deserted. Such was the intensity of the Mamluk raiding around it that holding on to it was untenable. The Mongol incursion had been brief, too brief for Edward's liking, and Abagha's perceived inability or reluctance to commit sufficient forces to assist his Western allies was to have a damaging effect on Crusader–Mongol relations in the future.

The Mongols and Mamluks meanwhile returned to what they had been doing for the last eleven years of their cold war – probing and testing along the border. Mongol activity had been increasing in intensity and, despite his obvious unwillingness to launch a full invasion, Abagha evidently still had his sights set on taking Syria. It had taken him a while to gain full control of the internal politics of the Ilkhanate but even as early as 1269 his letters to Baybars had been becoming more and more truculent and confident:

> When the King Abagha set out from the East, he conquered all the world. Whoever opposed him was killed. If you go up to the sky or down into the ground, you will not be saved from us. The best policy is that you will make peace between us. You are a Mamluk who was bought in Siwas. How do you rebel against the kings of the earth?*

If Baybars did not submit, Abagha warned, 'God would know of it', and of course Abagha considered himself as God's instrument on Earth. Baybars's cool reply was to refuse submission and remind Abagha of the fate of Kit Buqa, but he knew the letter heralded a heating up of the war. Baybars had other concerns too, in Upper Egypt. He therefore decided to grant a truce to Acre in order to reduce the risk of Mongol-

---

* In Amitai-Preiss, *Mongols and Mamluks*, p. 121.

Crusader operations against him. The treaty between Edward and Baybars was mediated by Charles of Anjou, who wanted to preserve a weak Outremer until he was ready to bring it into his dominions. The peace was negotiated to last ten years, ten months, ten days and ten hours, a timeframe in accordance with the Koranic provisions for *hudna* – a truce that can interrupt *jihad* if there is an advantage to be gained by the Muslims from a cessation of hostilities against the infidel – and was signed on 22 May 1272. As a further guarantee of peace from Edward in the future Baybars decided to have him assassinated. Edward was stabbed by a poisoned dagger as he lay sleeping in his chamber, the initial wound was not fatal but the Prince lay near death for several months afterwards and as soon as he was well enough he departed the East, leaving for England in September 1272. It is to be wondered if dealing with Baybars made an impression on the young man, certainly as Edward I of England he gained a reputation as being calculating, ruthless and cold and as having a superb military mind.

Baybars's catalogue of destruction against the Crusaders gives the impression of unceasing enmity but the picture is not complete without an appreciation of the Sultan's use of peace treaties to widen the political fissures that ran through Outremer. In 1267 he made an accord with the Hospitallers, then in 1268 his campaigns were against the Templars and Antioch. His treaty with the Lady Isabel of Beirut in 1269 practically made the city and the person of the lady a protectorate of the Mamluk Sultan and effectively neutralised its strategic value to the Franks. Article twelve states that, 'the lady shall not enable any of the Franks whomsoever to proceed against the Sultan's territory from the direction of Beirut and its territory. She shall restrain from that, and repulse everyone seeking to gain access with evil intent.'*

These treaties were not made between equal parties. Baybars's negotiation method was akin to that of the nineteenth-century British in China, the Sultan's gunboat being his Mamluk army.

---

* In P. Holt, *Early Mamluk Diplomacy 1260–1290: Treaties of Baybars and Kalavun with Christian Rulers*, Leiden: EJ Brill, 1995, pp. 42–7.

Baybars's biographer Ibn Abd al-Zahir tells us of one of his missions to Acre:

> Their king sought to temporize to obtain the best possible conditions, but I was inflexible, in accordance with the instructions of the Sultan. Irritated, the king of the *Franj* said to the interpreter, 'tell him to look behind him'.
>
> I turned around and saw the entire army of the *Franj*, in combat formation. The interpreter added, 'the King reminds you not to forget the existence of this multitude of soldiers'. When I did not answer, the King insisted that the interpreter ask for my response.
>
> I then asked, 'can I be assured that my life will be spared if I say what I think?'
>
> 'Yes'.
>
> 'Well then, tell the King that there are fewer soldiers in his army than there are Frankish captives in the prisons of Cairo'.
>
> The King nearly choked, then he brought the interview to a close; but he received us a short time later and concluded the truce.*

The truce with Edward left Baybars free to pursue a new project, but it was one that would become truly Sisyphean and would frustrate every Mamluk Sultan to the end of their line. Nubia had always been important to Egypt for its mines but it had equally always been an unpleasant if not particularly dangerous neighbour. In August 1272 Nubian tribesmen under King David raided the important Red Sea port of Aydhab. Baybars sent the governor of Qus on a punitive raid into Nubian territory that pushed up the river Nile above Aswan. Baybars followed this up with an expedition in 1276 that took a pretender to the Nubian throne from his court in Cairo right to the Nubian capital of Dongola. King David's army was slaughtered and the new king, Shakanda, was enthroned. Nubia was no longer to be independent, the King was also to be the Sultan's governor and half the annual revenue of Nubia was to be remitted to Cairo. The Christian Nubians were made to pay the *jizya* poll tax and territory was annexed up to Aswan. Baybars set out

---

* In Maalouf, pp. 250–1.

the Nubian policy of the Mamluk Sultanate – vassalage, tribute and punitive measures. Ultimately, well beyond the death of Baybars, the policy failed, as it was impossible to suppress revolt in the hostile area.

For the remaining years of his reign Baybars was concerned almost exclusively with the Mongols. The war had effectively, and very successfully from the Mamluk point of view, become a stalemate. Al-Bira up on the northeast had been the main focus of the war thus far, the Mongols had raided around it and had attempted to take it many times, Baybars had supplied it for over ten years now with food, weapons and siege engines to resist. Likewise the Mamluks had been sending *wafidiyya* over the border and Mamluk patrols had been fighting a dirty war of attrition on the Mongol side of the line since 1260. It was time, however, for a fresh initiative and to take the war to the Mongols; Baybars had long before realised where the Mongols might be vulnerable and it was perhaps time now to make a play in Anatolia.

As discussed earlier, Anatolia had been under a Mongol protectorate since 1243 but Mongol control in the region was not particularly strong and as early as 1262 a dissident Saljuq prince in hiding in Constantinople had attempted to get Baybars to invade the protectorate. Baybars was not sufficiently secure in his own lands to pursue such a conquest and even when the Mongols' choice for regent, Mu'in al-Din Suleiman, whose Mongol title was the Pervane or keeper of the seals, started to correspond with the Sultan in 1272, Baybars still held tight.

There was, however, still the problem of maintaining the status quo on the al-Bira front before any operations could be mounted in Anatolia. As noted above, Abagha had been becoming more active and had also entered into serious negotiations with the Pope. Such was the advanced nature of these negotiations that in 1274 Gregory X preached a Crusade at the Council of Lyons, briefly uniting the Western and Eastern Churches and putting the West on a war footing to back their unbaptised Mongol friends in the East. Fortunately for Baybars the old Pope died soon after and once again the Western nations fell into antagonism against one another. Abagha, it seemed, would have to go it alone. Baybars injected a little pace into his diplomacy with Mongke, the Khan of the Golden Horde, during this period to distract Abagha and also made sure that Abagha knew that joint operations against him, however unlikely this was in reality, were still planned. This from Baybars's letter of September 1272 to Abagha:

> The Sultan greets you and says that the envoys of Mongke Timur have come to him several times so that the Sultan should attack [your lands] from his side, and King Mongke Timur will attack from his side. Wherever the horses of the Sultan reach, that land is his, and wherever the horses of Mongke Timur reach – that is his.*

Abagha was reportedly so disconcerted by this one missive that he left the room and Baybars's emissaries in some degree of distress. His reply to Baybars indicated a desire for peace, or *sulh* in Arabic. However, this was not a weakening on the Ilkhan's part. The word for peace in Mongolian is *il* and it can be read both as peace or as peace granted after subjugation and total submission. Baybars dismissed the offer as standard Mongol 'manifest destiny' world-conquering hyperbole expounded as much for the consumption of Abagha's men as for the Mamluks. Al-Bira stood stubbornly in the way of this world conquest and the Mongols sent out an army once more to take it in November 1272. Baybars had already been preparing his forces in Damascus as he had been receiving vague intelligence that the Mongols were on the move since August. He moved north despatching a small Mamluk force backed by Bedouin ahead of the main army to bolster al-Bira's garrison. Baybars himself went via Hama to pick up small boats that were then transported by camel to the Euphrates. Some three thousand Mongols were reported to have massed on the east bank of the river and Baybars reached its west bank on 11 December.

The Mongols were well advanced in their siege operations by the time the Sultan's army arrived. Mangonels and siege machinery, under the direction of the Chinese engineers who

---

* In Amitai-Preiss, *Mongols and Mamluks*, p. 127.

had been sent by Qubilai to Hulegu along with thirty thousand more Mongols in 1264, were already assaulting the fortress. The Saljuqs of Anatolia had also been compelled to provide three thousand troops and the force guarding the river was in fact closer to five thousand troops rather that the earlier reported figure of three thousand. These five thousand troops took up position at a point in the river that looked easy to ford but was in fact somewhat treacherous, they dismounted and built a palisade. They obviously planned to stop the Mamluks before they could get any further than the riverbank. Baybars sent his river boats loaded with foot archers downstream; the archers were to cross the river, scout for Mongol reinforcements and provide some cover for his main crossing. Then the Mamluks crossed the river at the fording point opposite the palisade, swimming and leading their horses by their reins. The emir Kalavun led the first wave whilst Baybars brought the main contingent of the army across. The army must have crossed in good order because they were almost immediately engaged in heavy hand-to-hand fighting with the Mongols and, despite the Mongol's obvious advantage in numbers and their preparations for this precise attack they were defeated. Their commander, Chinqar, was killed and two hundred troopers were taken captive. The Mongols besieging al-Bira were just out of sight of this action but, when they were faced by the unedifying spectacle of their own flank defence running and riding pell-mell towards them, they too took flight. It seems that they were on the verge of taking the fort and the old cliché of the last-minute arrival of the cavalry seems to have applied here to Baybars's deliverance of the besieged garrison. Baybars was delighted and rewarded the defenders of al-Bira whilst sending detachments to pursue the Mongols further up the river. Abagha was furious and exiled the expedition's general.

With al-Bira secure, Baybars's strategy began to swing back towards Anatolia again. The Armenian fortress of Kaynuk was attacked in July 1273 under the pretence that its men were attacking Muslim merchants. This was certainly true, even though the Armenians wore Mongol headgear in their sorties in an attempt to disguise themselves, but it is also notable that the fortress city is close to one of the mountain passes that link Syria to the Anatolian plain. The city was sacked, the men were massacred and the women and children taken as slaves. The Mamluk army then swung east to attack the city of Trush, south of Mongol-controlled Abulustayn. Later the same year Baybars called a general assembly of all the horsemen in the kingdom; there were rumours of a Mongol invasion but it is more likely that the Sultan used the threat as an opportunity to ensure that even the Turcoman irregulars and the men of the *halqa* were on their toes. Baybars frequently reviewed even the lower orders of the army and always ensured that his surprise inspections were linked to pay parades, thus ensuring a full turnout and thereby reducing the opportunity for the borrowing and sharing of armour and horses between men who were prepared to take pay but not provide themselves with the means to fight. The *Sirat Baybars* tells us that he reviewed a different part of his forces every Monday and Thursday and that the parades were magnificent spectacles that sometimes lasted all day. This imbued a culture of readiness and of pride in their profession among the troopers:

> During this time the Sultan ordered the emirs, the soldiers and their Mamluks to maintain their equipment complete. So all were completely absorbed in preparing the war trappings of horses, making coats of mail, polishing coats of mail, inlaying the helmets, and making frontals for the horses . . . No one took any interest in anything except in the completion of his useful equipment. In every house there was an instructor for training in lance-fighting, and a great number of the Zahri Mamluks learned the fire game on horseback. None had any desire but to busy himself with war equipment, for the people always follow the custom of the King . . . before this, the soldiers spent their money on useless things which would not be pleasing to God.*

One can only wonder what these 'useless things' that the *Sirat Baybars* discusses were. The reviews were not just carried out to catch out unsoldierly soldiers; the *Sirat Baybars*

---

* See earlier note on the *Sirat Baybars*.

continues: 'Not a single man passed under review without the Sultan looking into his case carefully, and whoever among the soldiers complained of his employer, he ordered justice from the latter.' The similarity between Baybars's attitude towards military justice and that of Genghis Khan is striking. Liddel-Hart in his *Great Captains Unveiled* identifies this aspect of Genghis's attitude towards his forces as being one of the keys to his success as a leader. It is mystifying why Liddel-Hart failed to include Baybars in his survey of military greatness.

The mobilisation of 1274 was more extensive even than Baybars's normal meticulous checks on his forces and was part of the Sultan's preparations for fresh assaults on Armenia. Armenia, it was claimed by Baybars, had ceased sending tribute and had not sent 'true information' about the Mongols to Cairo. It is difficult to see how King Leo could have fulfilled either of these vows given the fact that he was subject to the Ilkhan and had Mongol garrisons of at least twenty thousand standing troops on his soil. Still, Baybars needed a justification and his real reason for the attack – that the Pervane had again been in touch, offering the Anatolian throne to the Sultan if he would come and claim it, and that Armenia stood in the way – was certainly not to be publicised.

In late 1274 a preparatory invasion began under the Mamluk forces stationed at Aleppo. It raided up to Marash, devastating the countryside en route and destroying the suburbs of the city. Baybars set out with his main force in February 1275 and once he was in northern Syria he sent a small detachment towards al-Bira to give the impression that his intentions were towards the northeast. This force caused such panic in the Mongol zone above al-Bira that it was able to raid in the Jazira unopposed and proved to be a very useful diversion while the main army was moving through the Syrian Gates. The Sultan moved through the mountain pass on 20 March, having sent small detachments under senior emirs into the mountains either side to protect the army's flanks. The army marched along the coastal plain before heading inland. Kalavun was once again in the van and his troops surprised and massacred the inhabitants of al-Massisa. The capital Sis was razed again, as in 1266, but the citadel

4. In Middle Eastern paintings the bow and quiver are ubiquitous, marking out their importance to the warrior class of the region in this period. In this piece the artist has marked out the quivers in lively colours and has even gone to the trouble of showing the quiver behind the grounded warrior. Note also the strong stable saddles allowing for mounted archery. *The Diwan of Khwaju Kirmani*, 'Combat of Humay and Humayum', Baghdad, 1396, painted by Junayd. © *British Library Board. All Rights Reserved. 18113. f23.*

(*above*) 2. Sultan Baibars's addition of a square tower to Crak de Chevaliers can be seen here at the near end. *Bean Edge.*

(*below*) 3. The Mamluks called for jihad against Acre in 1291 in Damascus's Great Mosque. *Bean Edge.*

(*bottom*) 4. Aleppo's Mamluk Citadel had a moat so wide that boats could sail on it. *Courtesy of the Syrian Government.*

(left, from top)

5. The memory of the Crusaders' nemesis lives on in Italy. This bar sign is in Arezzo; the city still holds jousting contests which require knights to strike a whirling effigy of a Mamluk. *Author photo.*

6. The Mamluks, despite their polytheistic origins, both built and enhanced mosques. This is the mihrab of the al-Azhar mosque in Cairo. *T. Thornton.*

7. Ottoman Janissaries, the Mamluks' nemesis, were also slave soldiers and superb archers. *New York Public Library Archives.*

(below) 8. This portal in Sultan al-Nasir's mausoleum was taken complete as booty from the church of Saint Jean in Acre by the Mamluks in 1291. *Bean Edge.*

(*above*) 9. Four horsemen riding in unison around a pool.
(*below*) 10. High-quality steeds from Medina were offered as prizes by the Mamluk Sultans for troopers who excelled in military games.

(above) 11. A Mamluk showing one of the uses of *naft* or Greek fire, his shield is deliberately ignited.

(below) 12. Horseback acrobatics with two swords demonstrated by a Mamluk trooper.

(right) 13. Bloodless drills to prepare for bloody battles.
(below) 14. A Mamluk with a typical *qilich* shape sword. Even today the British army general officers' sword is modelled on the Mamluk blade which the British encountered in the hands of nomadic Turks during their Central Asian campaigns of the nineteenth century.

(above left) 15. An illustration that accompanies a helpful text on how to tackle bears when hunting.

(above right) 16. Even immense moats like this one at Crak de Chevaliers were no obstacle to the Mamluks' assaults on Outremer's castles. *Bean Edge.*

(below) 17. Goya depicted Napoleon's Mamluk regiment charging at the Spanish revolt of the Madrilene in May 1808. Napoleon also retained a Mamluk bodyguard, a certain Roustan who, perhaps wisely, refused to follow the Emperor into exile on Saint Helena. *The Charge of the Mamluks by Francisco de Goya (1814).*

18. The heavy cavalry that was the core of the Mamluk army had a longer heritage in the Middle East than has been commonly acknowledged. As early as the First Crusade the writer of the *Gesta Francorum* describes *Agulari*, heavily armoured Persian horses. Alexander Battling the Zangis, from a Khamsa by Nizami. Safavid Period, Iran. *Freer Gallery of Art, Smithsonian Institution f1908. 279a-b.*

(top) 19. Aleppo was a key point of the Mamluks' defence of Syria against both the Mongols and the Ottomans.

(above) 20. The walls of Acre were assaulted by the Mamluks with the largest mangonel barrage ever seen in the Middle East.

(left) 21. The minarets of Circassian Mamluk mosques reflect their patrons' origins garrisoning Cairo's towers. *Bean Edge.*

(*above left*) 22. Mamluk emirs of forty were entitled to be accompanied by drums and would have started their career in the Sultan's bodyguard, the Khassakiyya. *Illustration J. Reilly.*

(*above right*) 23. The Royal Mamluks were the greatest soldiers of the medieval age and carried Egyptian bows, Damascene swords and Aleppan shields. The light leather armour illustrated here was copied by Crusader knights and came to Europe as the hauberk jaseran. *Illustration J. Reilly.*

(*below*) 24. The Cairo citadel was largely a construction of Saladin's but it became so central to Mamluk power and politics that after his conquest of Egypt the Ottoman Sultan Selim I had all its armaments removed. In the background can be seen the Ottoman mosque of Muhammad Ali.

(*above*) 25. The Castle of Athlit was destroyed by the Mamluks to deny European Crusaders a bridgehead on the Syrian coast.
(*below*) 26. Caesarea was conquered after Mamluks made rope-ladders from their horses' bridles to pull themselves up and over its walls.

(*above*) 27. A Damascene sword maker, an artisan producing the most desirabl
blades in the Middle East.
(*below left*) 28. This nineteenth-century portrait sketch shows a Mamluk warrio
with his *khanjar* and Circassian-style helmet.
(*below right*) 29. These Ottoman swords are very much in the Mamluk style.

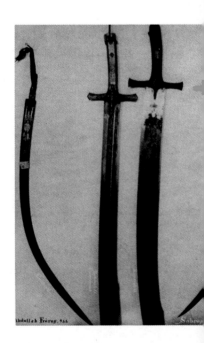

(left) 30. The Bedouin often performed as auxiliary camel and horse cavalry for the Mamluk army but equally they were often in revolt against the Sultanate and the Mamluks exhausted a lot of resources in bloody reprisals against the tribes of both Egypt and Syria. Note this tribesman's long spear, the Arab spear was lengthened during the Crusades period in response to Western lance charges.

(below left) 31. Mamluk mausoleums were the central landmarks of medieval Cairo. *Bean Edge.*

(below right) 32. The heads of Mongol emissaries were hung from Cario's gates in 1260 as a frank declaration of war. *Bean Edge.*

33. The Hospitallers of Margat Castle allied themselves to the Mongols and paid for it with the destruction of their stronghold by the Mamluks.

34. It was the destruction of the tombs of the Kings of Jerusalem and the slaying of monks in the Church of the Holy Sepulchre by the Khwarazmians in 1244 that prompted Saint Louis to attack Egypt in 1250. His Crusade was the catalyst for the Mamluks seizing power.

35. 'Mamlukdom' was not just a territorial fact, it was also a mindset. This classic Syrian style black and white portal is in an Egyptian Mamluk building. *Bean Edge.*

(above) 36. Even today Circassians are to be found in the Middle East making up the Royal Guard of the King of Jordan. This trooper is from the Ottoman period.

(below) 37. In this picture of the 1880s taken by a British military mission to Syria entertainment in the form of horseback acrobatics are being provided by Circassians. Such exercises were common even as early as 1265 when emissaries of the Golden Horde witnessed such spectacles at Sultan Baibars's court.

stubbornly resisted. Baybars rode out into the environs of the city and captured Mongol women and children who had been deserted by their men. The Armenian army was also curiously absent; perhaps after the disasters of 1266 a confrontation with the Mamluks was beyond comprehension for King Leo. Later there was a successful battle to be fought with a small detachment of some fifteen hundred Armenian troops and five hundred Franks near the coast, but this was only after Baybars had enjoyed a comfortable rest in Sis during a Muslim religious holiday whilst despatching emirs to raid Tarsus and the sea coast. The city of Ayas, the Ilkhanate's main port and an important source of revenue, was also burnt and its inhabitants massacred, many of those who escaped in boats drowned. The army then moved back towards the Syrian Gates and attacked Tall Hamdun on its way. By 1 June 1275 the Sultan was back in Damascus.

The Pervane was coming more and more under suspicion from his Mongol overlords; he was called to Abagha's court in September 1275 along with the Ilkhan's brother, who had been sent to Anatolia several years before and who was equally under suspicion of planning the assassination of the Pervane and making himself an independent ruler under the protection of Baybars. The Pervane's calls on Baybars to invade therefore became even more intense in 1275 but Baybars was still – despite his successful campaign – unable to guarantee success in Anatolia, and Abagha was active once more. Al-Bira was besieged by the Mongols again in November 1275 with a force of thirty thousand men, but only half of it was Mongol. The Pervane was once again compelled to send Saljuq troops, and Kurdish and Iraqi troops were also used. Baybars set out from Damascus on 8 December and the Mongols started a precipitate withdrawal on the same day. It is tempting to suggest that the Sultan's name alone was enough to send the Mongols into retreat, but more direct causes were the death of horses in appalling weather conditions, a lack of supplies, disease among the besiegers and a number of successful sorties by the defenders that had destroyed several of the Mongols' mangonels. Added to this the Mongols had become fearful and suspicious of their Anatolian levies; there was a very real risk of desertion to the Mamluks once Baybars's standards were in sight.

In 1276 Baybars was ready to mount an expedition to Anatolia. Whilst the Pervane had only secured the absolute loyalty of a handful of these emirs there was a consensus amongst the rest that the Mongols should not be apprised of the plot and that they would wait to see which way the wind was going to blow. Baybars too decided to undertake a little procrastination to see how firm this pledge of loyalty was. When he received the letters vowing allegiance he sent back a reply stating that the rivers were too low at present – this from a man who campaigned in every month of the year – and that he would come after the spring rains. The Pervane's subterfuge was by this point almost running out of control. He sent a detachment of Saljuq troopers to the Mongols at Abulustayn under the pretence that he had heard that the Sultan was marching that way, but with secret instructions to its leaders to desert to the Mamluks at the first possible opportunity. He also made contact with a Kurdish lord in the borderlands who was preparing to flee to Syria after murdering several Mongol officers in order that Baybars might be informed of the preparations now taking place. Added to all this the poor man had to organise the wedding of a Saljuq princess to Abagha Khan and had been called upon, once again, to explain to the Khan exactly what was going on in Anatolia. At this point Baybars sent two Mamluk raids into Ilkhanate lands. These were not just sent to disturb the Khan's honeymoon but to gather intelligence. One was sent to the lands around Mardin, well to the east of al-Bira as a distraction for the more important mission to the Anatolian frontier that returned with several defecting Saljuq emirs and their troops, promising news that the province was in disorder and more letters of support.

Unfortunately the Anatolian princes were not politicians of the first rank like Baybars or even of the second like Abagha. There were disputes among the conspirators leading to murder and reprisal and they attempted to set off the rebellion before Baybars's forces were ready, thereby alerting the Mongols to such a degree that thirty thousand Mongol troopers were dispatched to Anatolia under the Pervane and General Tudawan, who was effectively a Mongol watchdog. Several princes escaped to Syria where Baybars, despite their political ineptitude, greeted them warmly since their propaganda value alone was enormous. Those who could not get out in time were put on trial by the Mongols. The worst of the punishments was to be beaten, executed and then have one's organs circulated around the province as a warning to others. The warnings seem not to have been heeded; the Pervane went back, once again, to his secret letters to the Sultan, there were more grass roots disturbances and Abagha had to send another of his brothers to Anatolia just to bolster the Mongol presence in the province's politics. Meanwhile in August 1276 Baybars returned to Cairo and began serious preparations for his invasion. Anatolia was still the obvious place to set up a new front against the Mongols. A successful occupation would close off one of the Mongols' routes of entry into northern Syria and deny them its Saljuq troops; Armenia could be isolated from its Mongol protectors and the propaganda coup of reclaiming an Islamic state could not be discounted either. This said, we still cannot be sure that Baybars didn't envisage his Anatolian campaign as little more than a diversionary assault to keep the Mongols distracted from their designs on Syria.

The army of Egypt set out in February 1277 and was joined by most of the forces available to Baybars in Syria as he headed north. However, the army of Aleppo along with a Bedouin force was sent to the al-Bira border in case the Mongols should respond by crossing the border into Syria. Baybars's force dropped its baggage train near Aleppo and moved on into the mountains. He crossed the river Gok Su and by April he was in the passes of the Taurus Mountains; the passage across the river and though the mountains was extremely difficult, and a small force was sent ahead of the main army to reconnoitre. Methods of locating the enemy in mountainous terrain are discussed in *Furusiyya* treatises: the scout would take an empty quiver, place it on the ground and then to place his ear to its side to listen through this amplifier for the sound of hooves or of marching feet. Perhaps this was how they detected the three-thousand-strong Mongol cavalry force that they subsequently engaged in the mountains to the east of the main army. The Mongols fled and some prisoners were taken. From interrogation of these men Baybars learnt that the Mongol army was nearby in the plain beside the garrison town of Abulustayn. The decision was made to engage these forces and the Mamluk army entered the plain at its southeast corner. The Mongols under Tudawan along with their certainly unwilling ally the Pervane and his troops were at the plain's southwest corner watering their horses in the River Jayhan.

Rashid al-Din, a Persian and absolutely pro-Mongol writer tells us that there were three Mongol *tumen* present at the battle but that gives a number of thirty thousand men and Baybars's force could not have had more than fourteen thousand, including irregulars, so it seems unlikely that these *tumen*, as was common, were actually comprised of ten thousand men. Whilst we can certainly discount the deprecatory evidence of Kalavun's biographer, Shafi Ibn Ali, who claims that Baybars only faced five thousand Mongols, we can be sure that Baybars would not have engaged a force much larger than his own so far from home. Therefore Al-Umari's figure of eleven squadrons of one thousand Mongol troopers each seems closest to the truth with the addition of three thousand Georgians riding in their own unit. The Pervane's contingent was separated from this main force by a considerable distance and consequently never had the chance to join battle – perhaps they were simply not trusted.

The Mongols opened the battle with their left wing crashing into the Mamluks and actually reaching Baybars's *sanjaqiyya* or standard bearers. It is difficult to determine from the sources whether this means that they rode at the Mamluk centre, where the standards would normally be, swinging across the battlefield to hit the middle of the Mamluk army at an oblique angle or that the Mamluks were initially disorganised and unready for battle when the Mongols attacked. Either way, Baybars had certainly been caught unprepared for once and, realising that if he lost his standards so far from home and safety there would be certain panic among even his most battle-hardened troops, he rode with his bodyguard, the *khassakiyya*, into the fray. The physical shock of the Sultan's guards' charge was enough to push the Mongols back and to relieve the centre, but by this time the Mamluk left was also in trouble. Their Bedouin auxiliaries had deserted them and the remaining troops were on the point of caving in under a furious Mongol assault. Baybars sent directions to the army of Hama to bolster the left wing and this was enough to put the battle back in the balance. Baybars was then able to organise a general advance and counter-attack. The Mongols were pushed back and as at Ayn Jalut it seems the cyclical nature of Mongol warfare had been broken by the Mamluks' ability to match them in the initial engagement and then go over to the attack. This time, however, one thing was different: the Mongols did not flee the field. They dismounted and many, many of them fought to the death. The Mamluks almost had to wade through the slaughter on their armoured horses but eventually they had slain enough of the brave Mongols to break their opponents' will to hold the field. Even then, though, one detachment tried to make a stand in the surrounding hills and when they were surrounded they also dismounted and refusing surrender, died where they stood. The Pervane also fled the field but his son and several other Saljuq emirs were captured. Some Mongol emirs were executed and the Mongol commander, Tudawan, was either killed in the battle or executed; either way, he did not survive the debacle. Many of the Mongol troopers were freed, perhaps transporting them home was logistically too difficult, and several took service with the Mamluks. Kalavun took two of these new men, Qipchaq and Salar, into his entourage.

In both this engagement and the battle at the Euphrates around al-Bira we see the Mamluks in action against dismounted Mongol troopers. The Mamluk military theses of the time are quite detailed on the engagement of infantry so we can be certain that drills for dealing with foot soldiers and the stubborn resistance they were capable of were practised by the Mamluks. The texts discuss what weapons are most suitable for dealing with infantry. The horseman was advised to use a spear, javelin or arrows when meeting infantry, the use of the sword or mace were not suggested as their use brought the rider too close to his enemy. Getting in among the infantry is given as the most foolhardy thing a cavalryman could do and the texts tell us that separation from supporting riders whilst engaging infantry is almost certainly fatal. The texts' discourse on infantry would certainly have been influenced by the Mongols' use of the lasso and of large hooks that could pull cavalrymen from the saddle. These could be used both by mounted Mongols and by troopers fighting on foot.

The *Furusiyya* texts also make a judgement on the merits of both arms of the army. They tell us that, whilst each is superior to the other in different ways, cavalry is the real master of the battlefield because it enjoys a greater variety and power in the weapons it uses; it has greater speed of deployment and strikes harder at the enemy and can more effectively pursue the enemy and feign a retreat. This leads us to a very intriguing question. The Mongols were, excepting the Mamluks, the best cavalrymen of the medieval age, so why did they dismount at Abulustayn? One explanation is that they had simply decided to fight to the last man and dismounting would have improved the accuracy of their archery and they could use their horses as defence. But for the decision, 'last man, last arrow', to be made men have to be driven to desperation. Looking a little deeper we are once again drawn to the conclusion that the Mongols were simply outclassed by the Mamluks on the battlefield. The Mongols dismounted because what they were doing on horseback just wasn't working. Returning to what we know of Mongol warfare provides many of the reasons for the Mongol failure at Abulustayn. The following is from John of Plano Carpini:

> It should be known that when the Mongols come in sight of the enemy they attack at once, each one shooting three or four arrows at their adversaries; if they see that they are not going to be able to defeat them, they retire, going back to their own line. They do this as a blind to make the enemy follow them as far as the places where they have prepared ambushes. If the enemy pursues them to these ambushes they surround, wound and kill them ... if they can avoid it, the Mongols do not like to fight hand to hand but they wound and kill men and horses with their

arrows; they only come to close quarters when men and horses have been weakened by arrows.*

The problem was that it was the Mongols who were weakened in the archery exchanges, not the Mamluks. Mamluk high-volume shooting or 'shower shooting' put down a much higher rate of fire than that of any other force in the medieval world. The Mamluk archer held several arrows, up to five, by the nock end between his palm and the last three fingers of his bow-drawing hand during firing so he did not reach to his quiver between each shot. Al-Yunani, the archery master, set a standard of delivering three arrows in one and a half seconds for graduation from the archery school and Mamluk texts tell us that their perception of accurate fire was striking a one-metre target from seventy-five metres. Mongol tactics required them to close to fifty metres in order to ensure armour-piercing shots before firing and retiring. In the last twenty-five metres before being able to deliver their own arrow barrage they would therefore have been assaulted by three arrows per Mamluk. Furthermore, battle plans from *Furusiyya* documents indicate that the Mamluks took up staggered defensive lines so that each rank could reload their quivers behind the ranks of another moving forward to fire, the fire was therefore continuous and the texts tell us of the enormous camel-loads of arrows taken on campaigns.

It wasn't however only the rate of fire and range of their fire that failed the Mongols. It was also their mounts. Small steppe ponies cannot carry even lightly armoured troopers at full gallop for a protracted period of time, indeed times as short as ten minutes have been suggested before a replacement mount would be required.† The larger Arab horses, on the other hand,

---

*   In J. Smith, 'Mongol Society and Military in the Middle East: Antecedents and Adaptations', in Parry and Yapp, p. 257.
†   Cf. Smith, pp. 256–8. The hypothesis is that a small horse of 300kg cannot carry more than 17 per cent of its own weight effectively and a Mongol trooper tilts the balance well over this point. An Egyptian horse weighs in at 500kg and its endurance is certainly more impressive than its steppe cousin's. A steppe pony could only maintain battle for eight

were able to carry a fully armoured man right through the course of a battle. The chronicles never mention the Mamluks bringing more than one fresh mount to the battlefield with them. The Mamluks inflicted enormous slaughter on the Mongols at Abulustayn and while it is likely that much of this was done during the later stages of the battle when the Mongols were dismounting, their forces must have been severely degraded in the early confrontations, otherwise there was no reason for them to be driven to the extreme measure of leaving the saddle. Such was the pressure of the Mamluk riposte and counter-attack that there would have been no time for changing mounts. The reason for the Mongols dismounting from their horses was born of the total exhaustion of their horses, being outclassed in the very kind of warfare in which they excelled and the desperation that this realisation engendered in the weary troopers. Put in its most basic terms, the Mongols were exemplars of the cavalry soldier but the Mamluks of Baybars were its quintessence.

Baybars set off for the Saljuq capital Qaysariyya the day after the battle, his forward guard surprising a group of Mongols who knew nothing of the previous day's battle, capturing a few of them and watching the others scatter into the night. Baybars arrived at Qaysariyya on 20 April where there was a warm reception. Markets were set up and festivities took place but Baybars, upon learning that the Pervane had already passed through the city and taken the puppet Sultan Ghiyath al-Din away with him to his fortress at Dokat could not enjoy such frivolities. Coins were being struck with his image as the new Sultan of Anatolia but he was far from confident that his rule could be solidified whilst the Pervane was still at liberty and held the Sultanate's legitimate ruler. Baybars received a letter full of congratulations but no commitment from the Pervane during the celebrations. Quickly he wrote back inviting the Pervane to return to the capital to be rewarded and confirmed in his old position. The Pervane's reply to this was that he would

---

to ten minutes maximum before needing to be changed. In modern Mongolian steppe races children are used as jockeys and even then the mortality and morbidity among the ponies is frighteningly large.

present himself at the new Sultan's feet in fifteen days. The tone was just too obsequious and fifteen days was too long. It was obvious that Baybars was to be delayed until Abagha could be alerted and could intervene for the Pervane with a new Mongol army. Baybars took stock and, taking into account his depleted supplies – his baggage train was in Syria – and his distance from support should Abagha appear at the head of a fresh force, he decided the risk of trying to hold Anatolia was too great. The Mamluk army set out for home on 20 April but Baybars found one more use for the Pervane. In his reply to the Pervane's letter the Sultan wrote that he would lead his army to Siwas. Knowing that this information would immediately be sent to Abagha by the untrustworthy minister, he set the army's course in the opposite direction moving southwest back past the battlefield of Abulustayn. Here Baybars ordered a count of the Mongol dead: it totalled 6,770 and was out of all proportion to the light casualties that the Mamluks had suffered. The army re-entered the mountains while the Sultan watched with a rearguard. His action was recorded as a lesson for later commanders by al-Ansari:

> If the commander of the army should come across a narrow place or mountain pass or river or similar things along the line of march he must pause until the army, to the very last man of it has passed safely. If he doesn't do this perhaps each one of them would demand precedence for himself over his fellows and confusion will occur and disagreement among the army will be occasioned, leading to the stirring up of sedition. It was related of al-Malik al-Zahir Baybars that when he entered the land of Anatolia and conquered Qaysariyya and was returning it was he who supervised this matter himself and paused at the narrow places and at the river fording until the army had passed one by one.*

The journey through the mountains was difficult again but by 16 May the army was back in Harran where it received fresh supplies and Baybars received emissaries from another group of rebellious Anatolian Turcomen who had gone into revolt

---

* Al-Ansari in Scanlon, p. 84.

against the Mongols around the city of Konya. The Sultan had only warm words for them; the Anatolian diversion was over for Baybars and he returned to Damascus in early June.

For the Pervane the affair was fatal. Abagha, having surveyed the field of Abulustayn, flew into a rage and was set on following Baybars into Syria. He was dissuaded by a deserter from the Mamluk army, a certain Aybeg al-Shayki who had been beaten and humiliated by Baybars and who now reported to Abagha, after giving him the full details of how his men were vanquished, that the Sultan's army was enormous in size and that the Syrian summer was sure to defeat the Mongols before they could even make contact with the Mamluks. He also catalogued the Pervane's crimes in extreme detail, giving dates and details of the governor's correspondence with Baybars. Abagha, finally, decided enough was enough. The Pervane was executed and Abagha and other senior Mongols were served his flesh at a presumably not very merry dinner. Aybeg's desertion and Baybars's reportedly appalling treatment of him seems strange given that they were old *khushdash*; He was also extremely well briefed on the Pervane's activities by a Sultan renowned for secrecy. It is also odd that shortly after Abagha made him governor of Malatya he rather ungratefully emptied the treasury and fled back to Syria. Was he the sting in the tail left behind by the Sultan to ensure the Pervane's doom and complete Abagha's misery? With Baybars any trick was possible.

Death, however, as the classic Middle Eastern tale *Death in Samarra* relates, cannot be tricked,* and Baybars died on

---

* Somerset Maugham related the tale thus in the final act of his play, *Sheppey*, London: Heinemann, 1997:

Death Speaks:
  There was a merchant in Baghdad who sent his servant to market to buy provisions and in a little while the servant came back, white and trembling, and said, 'Master, just now when I was in the marketplace I was jostled by a woman in the crowd and when I turned I saw it was Death that jostled me. She looked at me and made a threatening gesture; now, lend me your horse, and I will ride away from this city

1 July 1277 whilst in Damascus, at the age of about fifty. His achievement had been immense. He had ripped the Mamluk Sultanate from the hands of a man he had fought alongside and then murdered, but the state that he had acquired by his treacherous deed was an exhausted, distracted and frightened one. The state that he left behind was one that boasted a powerful well-organised army, secure borders, regular relations with foreign states, an efficient bureaucracy and judiciary and a firm economic base. But he left his successors much more than that, he left them a model for them to follow. He campaigned both during the heat of Syrian summers and through winters that even the Mongols retreated from. He was ever alert and active and expected perfection and dedication from his men but also from himself. He was without doubt one of the greatest men of his time, but as a man, he was a mass of contradictions. He created a bastion for the survival of Islamic culture and artisans and scholars fled to Mamluk Egypt from every part of the old Islamic world to escape from the Mongol yoke, and yet he himself was a stranger from the steppes, a barbarian from outside the *Dar al-Islam* whose chief entertainment was daily training in the military arts from noon until evening. He was enthroned by a Caliph who hailed from a family that had been titular heads of the Islamic world for five hundred years whilst he himself had no parents beyond his slave merchant and first master. He fought, even as Sultan, under the yellow banners of the family of Saladin but he had killed, with his own hands, the last Ayyubid Sultan of Egypt. One story of his death has it

---

and avoid my fate. I will go to Samarra and there Death will not find me'.

The merchant lent him his horse, and the servant mounted it, and he dug his spurs in its flanks and as fast as the horse could gallop he went. Then the merchant went down to the marketplace and he saw me standing in the crowd and he came to me and said. 'Why did you make a threatening gesture to my servant when you saw him this morning?'

'That was not a threatening gesture, I said, it was only a start of surprise. I was astonished to see him in Baghdad, for I had an appointment with him tonight in Samarra'.

that he died after drinking *kumiz* that had gone bad. This was the fermented mare's milk that was the Mongols' and Turks' favourite firewater and which was always drunk to excess, and yet he banned wine from his army and his capacity for 'office work' and for organising, administering and for planning does not betray the weaknesses of an inebriate. He was confident and brave in his dealings with his adversaries and in public but it is reported that he slept poorly and suffered from dyspepsia and nightmares. He kept loyalty with his *khushdash* but he was cruel in the extreme to enemies. He was not, however, rage driven like Abagha or Hulegu, for him terror was a political instrument. He was king of the Egyptians but he married a daughter of the Khwarazmians and rarely spoke Arabic and was as much a Turkish warrior chief as an Islamic Sultan. He rose by virtue of merit through a system that gave nothing by inheritance or by blood line but he tried, unsuccessfully, to secure the Sultanate for his family's line. He was the champion of orthodox Sunni Islam but he kept his own Sufi, a religious mystic who predicted the fall of Crusader cities and who practised a form of Islam more akin to the steppes than to the cities of Egypt. He ruled from his war charger but his mausoleum in Damascus is now Syria's national library; he was a patron of a renaissance in the arts, and there are magnificent Korans from his time and fine pieces of glasswork carrying his emblem, the red lion.

He was adept in international diplomacy but as likely to use assassination as negotiation. A second version of his death has the Sultan drinking from the wrong glass after flavouring its contents with poison meant for a minor Ayyubid emir. His biographer, al-Zahir, has it that, 'fortune made him king', but the Sultan al-Malik al-Zahir Rukh al-Din Abul-Fath Baybars al-Salihi al-Najm, also the war chief Baybars al-Bunduqdari, was in fact the avatar of the self-made man.

7

THE PATTERN OF POWER

THE KALAVUNIDS

What must be done if the army is weak and the enemy is strong:

Confronting him at the very outset while he is in this condition is not permissible. To do so is comparable to one stirring up a serpent from its lair while one is unarmed, in order to oppose and defeat it, thus presenting oneself to peril and courting death by one's own hand. By delaying battle you do that which benefits you.

Al-Ansari's manual of war, c.1399

BAYBARS HAD ATTEMPTED TO secure the Sultanate for his son Baraka by making him joint ruler in 1264 and by marrying him to the daughter of Kalavun, the most important emir in the Sultanate, and for a little while the dead Sultan's settlement worked. News of Baybars's death was kept from the Cairo elite by his chief minister and the succession was not disputed. A few weeks later Baraka repaid the minister for his loyalty to Baybars's house by poisoning him. A new appointment to the office was made from Baybars's household, but he too was to die soon enough, this time in prison. Baraka's problem was that Baybars's Zahiriyya Mamluks still retained many of the higher positions of government and were never likely to step down from power voluntarily. They therefore restricted the ambitions of the new Sultan's *khassakiyya*. A career in the *khassakiyya* was structured roughly thus: emancipation following training, service as a bodyguard, companion and confidant for the Sultan, followed, it was hoped, by promotion to the status of emir, granting of an *iqta* and a high administrative post in the government. Baraka needed to satisfy the ambitions of his own men according to this pattern in order to ensure a loyal power base but couldn't afford, early in his reign, to antagonise the senior emirs too much. What was needed was a deft political touch to outmanoeuvre and slyly and slowly replace the old guard but unfortunately for Baraka he had none of the skills required for intrigue that his father had enjoyed in abundance and his blundering soon antagonised the senior emirs into forming factions against him. He countered with a clumsy pattern of arrests, even imprisoning his maternal uncle for a short time. Despite a display of outward strength, Baraka's powerbase was weak, his alienation of the Zahiriyya was perhaps inevitable but he had also managed to achieve, through his persecutions, his estrangement from the Mamluks of the Bahriyya. Things still looked calm, however, in March 1279 when Baraka took the army to Damascus. From there he dispatched his father-in-law Kalavun and another leading Bahriyya emir Baysari to Armenia. The two emirs carried out their assigned duty well, Kalavun raided up to Tarsus and Baysari pillaged the lands around the fortress of Qalat al-Rum but even while looting and burning both had their thoughts fixed on the Sultan. Neither had been fooled by his ruse of sending them away while he dealt with their less powerful friends in Cairo and Damascus; they held back from full engagement in Armenia.

Baraka had appointed Kunduk, a Mongol who had come into Baybars's hands as a young man, as his chief minister. Kunduk had shared his education with Baraka but after giving him the job Baraka found that his new minister and childhood friend was not as pliable as he had hoped for. Kunduk particularly upset Baraka's *khassakiyya* and they even tried to assassinate the minister before he was finally deposed by Baraka. Kunduk hastily made contact with Kalavun and Baysari in Armenia whilst gathering support for a coup among the Bahriyya in Cairo. A suspicious Baraka headed out for Damascus, but Kalavun took his forces past Damascus and was in Cairo before the Sultan had word of his desertion of the northern campaign.

Baraka hurried back to Cairo, only to find it under the control of a Bahriyya faction led by his father-in-law. He managed to secure the citadel but he had no support in the city and he was surrounded. His mother negotiated on his behalf and his family ties to Kalavun and the memory of his father were enough to secure an honourable abdication and a gilded cage – the semi-independent fortress of al-Karak – to retire to. As in 1250, the senior emirs put up a puppet Sultan, Baraka's seven-year-old brother Salamish, while they decided how power was to be divided. After three months Salamish was deposed and also sent along with another brother, Khadir, to al-Karak, which was now proving to be a very convenient rest-home for prematurely retired Sultans. From the horse trading that then took place Kalavun emerged as the emirs' choice for Sultan. He was arguably an unusual choice in that he was about sixty years old when he came to the throne but perhaps some of his supporters viewed him as a stopgap allowing them time to prepare their own later power bids. He was also very generous, perhaps too much so, in his promises to supporters.

Kalavun was a Qipchaq Turk and, like Baybars, had served in the Bahriyya as a young man, but he had been taken from his homeland as a man of about twenty rather than as a boy as Baybars had. Because of his extreme good looks he had, acquired the nickname of al-Alfi, 'of one thousand', as this was the high price that had been paid for him in the slave market, whereas Baybars had been sold at a clearance price after being returned by his first master because of a cast or squint in his eye. He was also an impressive soldier and despite Baybars's intense mistrust of anyone who was not of his *khushdash* or of the Zahiriyya, Kalavun had shared in the decision-making processes during the Mongol war and had been in control of the river citadel in Cairo that was the political hub of the Bahriyya. As the new Sultan Kalavun did nothing to antagonise the Bahriyya emirs, using them to neutralise the power of the men of Baybars, the senior Zahiriyya, whom he purged from the upper echelons of the army. Baraka's *khassakiyya* were bribed off with political patronage, and Mamluks of the Zahiriyya who had achieved no rank under Baybars were promoted by the new Sultan to the positions lost by more senior Zahri men; thereby effectively becoming Kalavun's men. Knowing that the Bahriyya were elderly men Kalavun simply waited for them to die off. The office of Sultan apart, there was no hope of inherited office for the sons of Mamluks in the early days of the Sultanate, it was a one generation elite and a Mamluk's progeny had to find employment in the civilian world. Kalavun used the core of Mamluks that he had already acquired as a senior emir to form a power base that he would eventually use to replace the Bahriyya. He took the enthronement title of al-Mansur and his personal regiment was called the Mansuriyya.

Despite his caution there was immediate resistance to the new Sultan. The senior emir Sunqur al-Ashqar declared himself independent ruler of Damascus upon Kalavun's accession, echoing al-Halabi's revolt against Baybars in 1260, but Sunqur's support was more extensive than al-Halabi had enjoyed. There were rumours that he had been promised Damascus by Kalavun for his support in Kalavun's election to the Sultanate and this gave him legitimacy in the eyes of many. He had the backing of Hama, Aleppo and Safad and elements of the Bedouin. Kalavun immediately sent a force to meet this challenge under the joint command of Aybeg al-Afram and, ironically again, Sanjar al-Halabi, who could at least be expected to know how these revolts worked. Sunqur was defeated at Gaza in May 1280 and again at Damascus on 21 June. His allies deserted him and he fled to the north where he retained a number of strongholds. He was still strong enough to maintain effective control of northern Syria and this was continued through an agreement with Kalavun in June 1281 by which he forwent his claims on Damascus and lent his support to the Sultan against the Mongols. He was only removed from his lordship of Antioch and Latakia by Kalavun's Syrian governor in 1287.

At al-Karak the sons of Baybars were looking a little too independent for the Sultan's peace of mind. Their wealth and core of household Mamluks was enough to attract some adventurers to their cause and they might have become more of a challenge had not Baraka died of a wound in 1280 after falling from a polo pony, suspicion of having a hand in the death fell on the Sultan but nothing was proved. His two brothers were eventually banished to Constantinople but the family returned to Cairo in the thirteenth century and as late as 1488 we can still trace a descendant of Baybars in Cairo.

Kalavun was settling his internal affairs just in time. Abagha had been receiving intelligence on the difficulties of the Sultanate since the death of Baybars but had been held back from taking advantage by his own problems. During 1278 and 1279 he had to deal with an invasion of eastern Iran by Mongols of the Afghan Khanate and in 1279–80 he faced invasions from the Golden Horde. Furthermore, there was also a plague spreading over eastern Iran during these years, decimating cattle herds. Even with all this the Khan started to organise a Syrian expedition as early as the summer of 1280. Sunqur had been in touch with Abagha at this time, encouraging him to invade in support of his Damascus rebellion. Sunqur had married a Mongol girl during what sounds like a very comfortable captivity under Hulegu and Abagha in his youth and was allied to pro-Mongol Bedouin. His loyalties were, to say the least, conflicted. His new pact with the Sultan caused him, however, to turn his back on his former jailer and friend, and once Kalavun had had Kunduk – the emir who had brought Baraka down – drowned in Lake Tiberias for attempting to start a coup among Mamluks of Mongol origin, renewed Baybars's peace treaty with Bohemond VII of Tripoli, made a fresh agreement with the Franks of Acre and brought most of the Bedouin who had joined Sunqur's rebellion back into the fold, he was ready, politically at least, to meet the threat.

But was he ready militarily? Baybars's war machine had been badly weakened by both Baraka's and Kalavun's purges of the Zahiriyya. The new Mamluks of the Mansuriyya were inexperienced and dedication to training and maintenance of the army's effectiveness had not been anywhere near as impressive under Baraka as it had been under his father. Also Abagha was coming to Syria with a huge force; it seemed that the Mongols had learned the lesson of Ayn Jalut and were aiming for overwhelming superiority in numbers. Abagha's preparations were slow, however, and whilst Aleppo was plundered in September 1280 by a small force, the Mongols evacuated after realising that Sunqur was no longer going to aid them and the main expedition didn't reach Syria until the autumn of 1281. By this time Kalavun had scratched together an army, even recruiting auxiliary forces from the sons of the Bahriyya, which might just be capable of facing the Mongols.

The intelligence service sent estimates of the Mongols' forces of between eighty to a hundred and twenty thousand men. The army was being led by Abagha's brother Mengu Timur but only under the tutelage of two experienced generals Tukna and Doladai. Abagha himself waited on the banks of the Euphrates with a small escort for news of success. There were also reports from spies in Tripoli that Mongols had been seen in boats arriving at the city and it was feared that Abagha was putting a second force ashore behind the Mamluk position. More concrete intelligence soon showed, though, that these were just Franks wearing Mongol headgear attempting to confuse the Mamluk strategy. More accurate details of the Mongol army's disposition came to the Sultan via a Mongol deserter. Mengu Timur was in the centre with forty-four thousand Mongols, whilst his right wing was made up of five thousand Georgians, three thousand regular troopers of the Anatolian army under the Mongol overlord who had been imposed on the Anatolian Turks since the rebellions of 1277, two thousand Turcoman tribesmen and a large number of Armenians under King Leo. There were also an unspecified number of Franks, probably Hospitaller Knights from Margat, along for the ride. The left wing was comprised of further Mongol divisions and the Mongol line extended some twenty-four kilometres from Hama to Salamiyya. They left Hama in the evening of 28 October and rode south overnight. Moving in column was not practical as the army needed pasture and water and advancing on a wide front was the best way to find it.

The battle took place, or rather two battles took place, in the early morning of 29 October. Kalavun had been able to put together an army totalling about thirty thousand men from every part of the Sultanate. On his extreme right he had placed the Bedouin forces of Syria and on his extreme left he had positioned Syrian Turcomen and the garrison army of Hisn al-Akrad, as Crak de Chevalier had been renamed after its conquest. The Mamluk army's line extended beyond that of the Mongols, despite having fewer men; the wings were also stronger at the expense of a weaker centre. Kalavun's fear was that the Mongols' superior numbers would allow them to roll up the Mamluk flanks and envelop his army. On the centre left Sunqur's forces and al-Halabi lined up backed by some *halqa* squadrons and on the centre right the armies of Damascus and of Hama were joined by the forces of al-Mansur, the hero of the first Battle of Homs in 1260, and were supported by more *halqa* troopers. In the centre Kalavun placed his young Mansuriyya Mamluks along with the *wafidiyya* and experienced Mamluks of the Bahriyya. The Sultan himself sat just to the rear of the centre on a low rise with the standards and drums and a corps of eight hundred Royal Mamluks, his *khassakiyya* and a reserve of *halqa* troopers. Kalavun's dispositions at the centre were in depth and al-Ansari's war treatise suggests that, 'if the numerical strength of the enemy be great put the army into five lines'. His manual of war continues in its advice for situations where the army is outnumbered, as the Mamluks were at Homs, 'delegate for each of the wings a squadron of supporting cavalry as compensation for the [line] bending towards the centre'. This is evidently what Kalavun intended and he hoped to be able to plug gaps as they appeared by rapid deployment of his Royal Mamluks and *halqa* reserve.

The Mongols advanced to the attack and their right wing had immediate success against the forces of Sunqur and al-Halabi on the Mamluk left, which broke and scattered. So panic stricken was the flight of some of the Mamluk emirs that they were to reach Damascus and even Egypt before they really felt safe. The Mongols and their allies rolled on to the shore of Lake Homs, well south of the main battlefield, after chasing and massacring the local infantry of Homs and looting the baggage train of Sunqur and al-Halabi's men. So convinced of total Mongol victory and so far away from the rest of the action were the men of this army that they sat down to rest on the pleasant lakeside to await news of the left and centre. This was a mistake because things were going rather better for the Mamluks in the other battle.

The Mamluk right had withstood an initial series of Mongol charges and had then moved over into a counter-attack. This assault pushed the Mongols of the left wing back, folding their line onto the Mongol troops in the centre. The Bedouin of the far right then added their weight to the attack and may also have got around the back of both the Mongol left and the centre in order to raid the Mongol baggage train. The Mongol historians tell us that Mengu Timur's indecision at this point gave the Mamluks victory on the main battlefield, but he was only nominally in charge and had two experienced generals with him. What actually happened is that the push of the Mamluk right and arrival of the Bedouins was matched by an advance of the Royal Mamluks and the Mansuriyya in the centre led by the senior emir Turantay. It is also possible that the Mamluks had employed a technique they trained for almost endlessly; they would search out standard bearers in the Mongol lines and select them for their first arrow strikes during a charge. Such an assault on their communications would inevitably have caused chaos in the Mongol army. Also, at some point during the Royal Mamluks' thrust, Mengu Timur was injured and fell from his horse. Mongols surrounding the Prince then dismounted to secure his safety and this, perhaps with memories of Abulustayn still fresh in their minds, stirred the Mamluks to increase their efforts and charge again. The Mongols of the centre and left became one confused mass that struggled to clear the field under the hacking of Mamluk sabres and showers of arrows. The Persian historian Wassaf has it thus:

> Mengu Timur's troops succumbed to the grief of utter destruction and the Prince . . . out of terror and dread took to the highway of flight. Suddenly Mengu Timur was struck by an arrow, the tongue of whose notch read out to him the letter of the doom predestined for the souls of all men. The valiant warriors of Syria and the men of Egypt put the whole of the Mongol army to their whetted swords . . .

Such was the excitement of the pursuit among the Mamluk forces that Kalavun found himself virtually deserted when the entire Mongol right wing reappeared on the battlefield after having realised during their lakeside sojourn that something was amiss. The Sultan ordered the banners to be furled and the drums to stop and he undoubtedly held his breath, hoping not to be seen with his small force. Eventually the disaster that had occurred dawned on the returning men and they set off to join the Mongol retreat. This retreat cost the Mongols even more in casualties than the battle, as bloody as it had been. They were chased by Mamluk troopers and by Turcomen and at one point a mini-battle broke out between Mongols and their Georgian allies over the allocation of horses for what was fast becoming a rout rather than a retreat. Many died simply of thirst or exhaustion and others were killed by vigilante villagers. The Euphrates made a formidable barrier to escape and many Mongols drowned or were incinerated when the Mamluks set fire to the reed beds in which they were hiding. The garrison of al-Bira annihilated a force of Mongols and the Armenians suffered similarly as they passed by the Mamluk fortress of Baghras.

For the Mamluks' part, they had once again defeated the Mongols but they had undoubtedly been lucky this time. The battle was won by the army that Baybars had bequeathed to his successors and Kalavun's command had been solid but uninspired. Indeed, he had been arm-twisted into fighting at Homs by his senior emirs; he had wanted to fight closer to Damascus to allow for retreat into Egypt should the battle be lost. He had failed to understand that one of the reasons for the Mamluks' continued success against the Mongols was their veterans' fervour for battle with their foe and their stubborn desire to defend all of Syria from the Mongols. Mamluk society put primacy upon the military vocation, and their basic security as a dynasty was in military success and whilst this success was predicated on superior patterns of logistics, armament and tactics, their military expertise was as nothing without *amour propre*. By facing down and defeating the Mongols consistently they were building up a lore of invincibility; half-hearted battle plans do not sustain such traditions. Confusion in the Mongol command and the failure of their right wing to return to the field in time certainly played a part in the Mamluk victory and Kalavun should be commended for maintaining communications, at least with his right and centre, especially considering the inexperience of many of his centre troops and his employment of the ever-ephemeral Bedouin on the extreme right. Doubtless the Mongols were also tired after their all-night advance and their tactical error was made to look all the more glaring by the Mamluks being able to enjoy three days of rest prior to the battle.

Perhaps in the last months of his life as he drank himself to death with *kumiz* Abagha might have wrestled with the question of continued Mongol failure against the Mamluks. Certainly he had made a gross error in 1271 by not working harder at launching a joint operation with Edward and by virtue of this failure to act in concert he had set the Crusaders against a joint operation in 1281. He had tried to repair the damage with envoys to Italy in 1276 and to England in 1277, but his previous inaction spoke louder than mere words could. It was a pity for both him and the Franks, Kalavun's victory had been a damn close run thing and the presence of a Frankish enemy force in his rear, however small, could have swung the battle and thereby the war. Apart from a few renegade Hospitallers the leaders of Outremer had tied their forces into pacts of neutrality with the Mamluks and this was to continue. The wording of the accord between Kalavun and Acre in 1283 makes it clear that the men of Outremer had given up hope of rescue either from the West or from the East and hoped to survive through the Sultan's clemency alone. They were not even supposed to make efforts to make it harder for the Mamluks to end Acre's existence:

> The Franks shall not restore any wall, castle or tower or fortress, whether old or recent, outside the walls of Acre, Athlit and Sidon.
>
> If one of the Frankish maritime kings or others should move by sea with the intention of bringing harm to our lord the Sultan and his son in their territory to which this truce applies, the Lords

of the kingdom and Masters in Acre are required to inform our Lord the Sultan and his son of their movement two months before their arrival in the Islamic territory covered by this truce . . .

If an enemy comes from among the Mongols, or elsewhere, whichever of the two parties first learns of it must alert the other. If – may God forbid it! – such an enemy marches against Syria and the troops of the Sultan withdraw before him, then the leaders of Acre and the masters there may protect themselves, their subjects and territories as best they can.*

The Crusader kingdoms were safe for now as the Mamluk army was in no condition to launch any offensives against them. Kalavun was not even able to prevent Sunqur from taking up his old appanages in Northern Syria. The Mamluk historians' accounts of the Battle of Homs give ridiculously low figures of two hundred killed, but in fact the army was shaken to its foundations by the effort of repelling the Mongols. The Sultan's prime preoccupation, therefore, was to rebuild it. The way that Kalavun went about restoring his Mamluk core was to be highly significant later. He widened the net for captives, buying mostly Circassians† from the eastern Caucasus, but also Mongols, Georgians, Greeks and other Europeans; Lachin, who would later become Sultan, was a Prussian. Kalavun would end his reign with more than twice the number of Mamluks that Baybars had been able to acquire. His elite were the Mamluks of the Cairo citadel, a unit of about three thousand strong, which garrisoned the *burj* – the towers of the citadel – and from this they took their name, the Burjiyya. Kalavun was as thorough in his training programme as Baybars had been, therefore bringing the army up to full strength was a slow process but the investment was worth it.

Kalavun was at least strong enough in the early years of rebuilding to launch two campaigns into Armenia, in 1283 and 1284. Iron and wood were both needed to repair the Mamluk war machine and Egypt was poor in both these resources whilst

---

* In Holt, *Early Mamluk Diplomacy*, p. 81.

† Today Circassians make up the ceremonial guard of the King of Jordan.

Armenia had them in abundance and was weak enough to be brought to a humiliating peace treaty in 1285, yielding an annual tribute of 250,000 *dirhams* and its equivalent again in wood and iron as well as livestock. The Armenians were therefore heavily punished for their presence at Homs.

Fortune smiled on Kalavun in the internal difficulties that afflicted the Ilkhanate after Abagha's death. The Mongol *quriltai* called after his funeral elected his older brother Teguder to succeed him and passed over the claims of his son Arghun. Teguder, however, proved to be an ineffective leader and may also have guaranteed his eventual assassination by converting to Islam and taking the name Ahmad. His first foreign policy move was to offer peace negotiations with the Mamluks. Kalavun's intelligence service made sure that the Sultan was apprised of the unreadiness of the Ilkhanate for war, the divisions that had opened up among the senior Mongols under Teguder Ahmad and the continuing war of attrition that the Mongols were being forced to fight in Anatolia against rebellious Turks. The offers, made in 1282 and 1283, were treated coldly by Kalavun and these shameful rebuffs weakened Teguder's position even further with the Mongol elite. In short, Teguder was arrested by his own officers while he fought a civil war against Arghun in 1284 and executed by having his back broken – royal blood was, of course, not to be shed.

Arghun was little better than Ahmad. He delegated everyday government to professional Jewish and Persian bureaucrats and only personally headed the army twice. Both of these outings were forced upon him by incursions of the Golden Horde, in 1288 and 1291. Perhaps his obsession with longevity – the mercury and sulphur-based potions he took to ensure long life were to kill him in 1291 – restrained him from endangering himself in battle. From 1289 to 1294 the entire region of Khurasan was in rebellion under its Mongol military governor, Nauruz. Such was the appallingly bloodthirsty nature of Nauruz's forces' devastation of Khurasan that the herders of the region claimed that they could not make their cattle drink where Nauruz had been as the water held his evil reflection. The political disintegration of the Ilkhanate and ineptitude of Arghun required that his diplomacy with the West be sanctioned by the Great Khan and was even carried by Qubilai's emissaries to Europe. In his letters the Ilkhan offers what he was obviously incapable of delivering, this is from his letter to Pope Honorious IV in 1285:

> We send you the said messengers and ask you to send an expedition and army to the land of Egypt, and it shall be now that we from this side and you from your side shall crush it between us with good men; and that you send us by a good man where you wish the aforesaid done. The Saracens from the midst of us we shall lift and the lord Pope and the Great Khan Qubilai will be lords.*

He received no answer and by 1291 he was willing to offer more concrete enticements than the simple crushing of the Saracens. In his letter to Phillip of France Arghun wrote: 'Now if, fulfilling thy sincere word, thou sendest thy troops at the time agreed upon, and if, blessed with good fortune by heaven, we conquer these people, we shall give you Jerusalem.' The Pope and the King were treated as equal to the Great Khan in these missives; things were obviously bad in the Mongol self-image department and they were about to get worse. Arghun's brother and successor, Geikhatu, added debauchery to ineptitude. The continuer of Bar Hebraeus's chronicle tells us that, 'he had no thought for anything except . . . how he could get possession of the sons and daughters of the nobles, and have carnal intercourse with them.' By 1294, due to pestilence and the financial chaos that ensued after an abortive attempt to introduce paper money into the Ilkhanate there was not even a single sheep to be found for the Ilkhan's table. Geikhatu's cousin, Baidu successfully rebelled against him in 1294, more as a response to a beating he had received by Geikhatu's retinue after he had insulted the Khan at an all-night drinking session than for any political ends. Geikhatu was strangled with a bowstring but Baidu was not long to survive him. He was put to death by his own supporters in a

---

* The Latin translation is in the Vatican Library. Quoted in A. Moule, *Christians in China before 1550*, London, 1930.

pleasant garden in Tabriz in October 1295 after meeting Arghun's son, Ghazan in an inconclusive battle. Ghazan was to stop the rot and would even enjoy brief success against the Mamluks, but in the period between 1281 and 1295 this catalogue of inept Ilkhans left the Mamluks virtually free from any fear of interference. If anyone ever finds Genghis Khan's grave they might find him still spinning in it at the thought of such progeny.

Kalavun was happy to keep peace with the Mongols. Al-Ansari records how he

> used to treat them kindly, maintaining relations with them and bestowing gifts upon them ... one day he heard some of his *khassakiyya* conversing together. Some were saying that the Sultan gave gifts to the Mongols out of fear of them. He upbraided them and said, 'that which I bestow upon the Mongols, all of it, does not equal the cost of the shoes of your horses when going out to do battle with them.'*

Peace with the major threat in the region gave him freedom to operate against his lesser enemies and he used this freedom well. In 1285 he brought his army up to the walls of Margat. The Hospitallers, as the Armenians had, were to pay for their presence at Homs but the castle was positioned atop a mountain and its mangonels fired down upon the Mamluks as they tried to bring their machines within range. Many of the Mamluk siege engines were smashed and the siege went badly for a month before Kalavun's 1,500 engineers fired the mine they had dug beneath one of the main towers and deep into the inner defences of the castle. After the collapse of these walls, resistance was obviously useless and the Hospitallers took an honourable retirement to Tripoli. Kalavun rebuilt and garrisoned the castle and moved on.

Once again the lack of an effective Mamluk fleet meant that the reduction of Kalavun's next target, Maraclea, the little fort that had defied Baybars, would be both time consuming and difficult but when Kalavun threatened Tripoli and gave as his

---

* In Amitai-Preiss, 'Mamluk Espionage Among the Mongols and Franks'.

price for withdrawal the evacuation of Maraclea Bohemond VII hurriedly arranged it.

Acre was horrified by the loss of Margat but, as discussed above, it could expect no aid from the Mongols or from Europe, especially as Charles of Anjou, now Outremer's absentee titular king, had fallen in the revolt known as the Sicilian Vespers in March 1282 and the rest of Europe, including his son, was too busy taking sides and finding allies for the Angevin–Aragonese confrontation over the fate of Southern Italy to be bothered with the fate of the Crusader states. The Pope's message of 1288 in response to entreaties for assistance from the leaders of Acre was that they should remain vigilant, which was probably good advice but availed them little. News of Charles's death reached the Levant in 1285 but Kalavun was inactive until 1287, when an earthquake levelled a good portion of the walls of Latakia and the Mamluks simply walked in to take its surrender. Perhaps the shock of even nature being against him was enough to kill off its overlord, Bohemond VII, in October 1287 and it may have been due to his age that Kalavun acted more slowly than Baybars ever had; he didn't move against Tripoli until 1289. Perhaps he was just more subtle, Al-Yunini claims that Kalavun had been colluding with the family of the mayor of Tripoli, the Embracio, against Bohemond VII since 1279 and had even sent Muslim hill tribesmen to the Embracio to use against the possessions of their political enemy. The Sultan also let the factions that erupted in Tripoli after the death of the childless Bohemond mature fully before he attacked. The political manoeuvrings inside the city set the nobles against the military orders and the merchants of the commune against, at different times, just about everyone else. Indeed, the antipathy between the Venetians and the Genoese in the city, which ended with the Genoese backing Bohemond's sister's claim on the city and the Venetians appealing to the Sultan for assistance in their struggle with Genoa, gave him his pretence to revoke the treaty of 1283.

Kalavun had been prepared to march for Tripoli in 1288 but the death of his favourite son stopped him in his tracks. In March 1289, however, the Egyptian army began the siege of Tripoli. Unity suddenly ensued among the Christians within the city's walls. Six galleys under Venetian and Genoese colours were assembled in the harbour and Pisa donated a number of smaller vessels to supply the city. The French regiment bequeathed to Outremer by King Louis IX had already marched down from Acre to bolster the garrison and knights and galleys came over from Cyprus. The sixteen-year-old Ayyubid emir Ismail Abu'l Fida who was present at the battle said this of the difficulties of reducing Tripoli. 'The city of Tripoli is surrounded by the sea and can be attacked by land only along the eastern side, through a narrow passage. After laying the siege, the Sultan lined up a great number of catapults of all sizes opposite the city and imposed a strict blockade.' It was certainly hard going for Kalavun's men, the thin peninsula reduced the options for attack and it was hard to make their superior numbers tell on such a narrow front. The defenders meanwhile could employ all of their admittedly small forces on one small section of wall. The city fell, in the end, under pressure of bombardment. Fire was concentrated on the southeast corner of the land walls and after nearly a month of continuous battering the Tower of the Hospitallers and Tower of the Bishop, both key defence points, simply crumbled away. At this point the Venetians packed up their possessions and began to pull their vessels out of the harbour, with the Genoese following suit. There was just time for a quick and bloody argument between the two over ownership of various boats before their joint desertion. There was panic and disorder inside the city following this betrayal and, choosing his moment, Kalavun ordered a general attack on 26 April. In the carnage that followed, every man caught was killed and every woman or child found was reserved for the slave markets. Most of the higher-ranking Franks made it out of the city and reached Cyprus but the commander of the Temple was slain, as was the mayor and former friend of Kalavun, Embracio. Abu'l Fida conveys both the extent of the massacre and even more so the zeal for murder among the Mamluks:

A short distance from Tripoli, in the Mediterranean Sea, there was a small island, with a church. When the city was taken, many *Franj* took refuge there with their families. But the Muslim troops took to the sea, swam across to the island, massacred all the men who had taken refuge there, and carried off the women and children with the booty. I myself rode out to the island after the carnage, but I was unable to stay, so strong was the stench of the corpses.

Other sources say that the Mamluks rode their horses as far as they could into the sea and then swam whilst pulling their mounts along by the reins to the island. It would seem that even in urban warfare they would not be separated from their chargers. Bohemond VII's bones were exhumed and strewn around the city by its Muslim populace. The campaign against Tripoli, was about much more than *jihad*, though, it was aimed at preventing the Genoese from replacing the dying power of the old Crusader kingdoms in the Levant. Yes, the Italian merchants were the commercial allies of the Sultanate but attempts to build empires on the Syrian coast could not be tolerated. The fortresses of Botron and Nephin fell easily after Tripoli's capture and as Kalavun was supervising the levelling of Tripoli's walls another Embracio, Peter, offered the submission of Jebail.

After this success and the large amount of booty it gained for the emirs there were calls for extinguishing Acre. Kalavun was, however, his normal cautious self and whilst he sent an envoy to Acre to show his anger at the presence of men from Acre's Teutonic, Hospitaller and Templar garrisons at Tripoli's defence, he easily accepted the excuse that Acre's truce had been made with King Henry and not with the military orders and the truce was renewed under the usual ten years, months and days formula. The Sultan knew that the reduction of Acre would require another massive investment in siege machines and he used the false peace of the new *hudna* to have built, among other things, the largest mangonel ever seen in the Middle East, *al-Mansura*, the Victorious.

Acre, knowing that the peace was phoney, went into a flurry of diplomatic activity while the Genoese of the Levant attempted to take revenge on Egypt by a campaign of piracy. The campaign was brought to an abrupt end when Kalavun closed Alexandria to the pirates' mother republic and when the Genoese ambassador came to the Sultan's court to repair relations he found he had to wait behind a Byzantine ambassador and representatives of the Holy Roman Emperor. The embassy from Yemen brought a rhinoceros with them to impress the Sultan and the Genoese, despite bringing a dog that was recorded as being as big as a lion, must have felt that they had slipped down the pecking order somewhere along the line. Now that Acre was obviously doomed, everyone wanted a piece of the Egyptian port action. At this time Kalavun's government was issuing travel and trade permits to Indians and Chinese, accruing duty on the import of goods from the East and duty on their subsequent export to Europe. They were also making money on the export of copper from Europe to the Orient.

So the Sultan's war chest was full and Acre's calls for aid fell largely on deaf ears; of those who might have listened, Edward I was embroiled in Scottish affairs and everyone else was dealing with the fallout from Charles of Anjou's fall. The only response to calls for Crusade was from the Aragonese, who – surprisingly, considering their antipathy towards the Papacy and Venice over the ownership of Southern Italy – sent five galleys, and from Tuscany and Lombardy where gangs of unemployed city folk and excited peasants took the Cross. They were placed in the care of the refugee Bishop of Tripoli and transported to their new home by the Venetians who, in their ongoing battle with Genoa for commercial hegemony in the Mediterranean, did care enough about Acre to commit twenty galleys to its defence. The Italian rabble it carried to Acre would soon enough require that defence to be made.

On the surface, 1290 was a peaceful year. Muslim caravans brought their loads to Acre for transport to Europe as normal, but unfortunately the newly arrived Italian mob didn't understand the social compact that kept Acre in business and, full of religious passion and possibly other spirits of the alcoholic variety, they began to harass and then openly attack Muslim merchants. Then in August a riot ensued over what the writer Shafi Ibn Ali claimed was the seduction of a Christian wife by a, presumably, smooth-talking eastern merchant. The

Italian rabble rushed through the streets killing every bearded man they could find, which was unfortunate if you were a bewhiskered Christian or Jew. The city authorities were able to restore order but it was too late: Kalavun had his justification and his army was ready for the great siege. He set the wheels of *jihad* in motion and also put out the message, for foreign consumption, that he was sending an army into Nubia. Then the Sultan who had been so very lucky in the way that events had favoured him during his rule was finally deserted by fortune. Al-Malik al-Mansur Sayf al-Din Kalavun al-Maliki al-Salihi led his army out of Cairo on 4 November 1290 but he was to die only five miles into the march. Added to the despair he must have felt at dying before the work of finally removing the *Franj* from Syria was complete was the pain of not seeing his dead favourite son take the throne but instead a younger wholly untrusted scion, al-Ashraf Khalil, about whom Kalavun once said. 'I will not set Khalil over the Muslims'.

8

TRIUMPH AND DISCORD

THE END OF OUTREMER

Because of you no town is left in which unbelief can repair, no
   hope for the Christian religion!
Through al-Ashraf the Lord Sultan we are delivered from the
   Trinity and Unity rejoices in the struggle!
Praise be to God, the nation of the Cross has fallen, through the
   Turks the religion of the chosen Arab has triumphed!
Panegyric to the Sultan after Acre's fall by Ibn al-Furat,
d. 1405

DESPITE HIS FATHER'S RESERVATIONS, Khalil's succession
was relatively smooth and only required a few
judicial murders. Perhaps Kalavun's crushing out of
all resistance in the Sultanate during his reign made it so, the
body count among suspected political enemies was at least as
high in his reign as in Baybars's, or perhaps it was because
the *jihad* against Acre required a Sultan to lead it and, despite
Kalavun's death, enthusiasm for the venture was still high.
Khalil rejected pleas from Acre for clemency in January 1291
and marched for Syria in March after using his father's funeral
to further inflame the Egyptians' fervour for Holy War; the
call to the Syrians for *jihad* was made in the Great Mosque of
Damascus. Such was the effectiveness of the preaching that
the number of *ghazi* recruited outnumbered the men of the
regular army employed for the reduction of the city and Men
of the Pen – jurists and religious teachers – also helped push
the new mangonels to Damascus' outskirts. These men were

normally a thorn in the side of any military dictatorship in the medieval Middle East, much as they often are today, but *jihad* allowed the medieval military elite to harness their energies, so some things are unchanging. Heavy snowfall delayed the army of Hama in its march from the north and the moving of al-Mansura, the vast mangonel, from Hisn al-Akrad to Acre, a journey that normally took only eight days, took a month as oxen pulling the one hundred carts its disassembled parts required died of exposure. The problems didn't cease once the army had reached Acre. The Franks had prepared their defence well and desperation had given them courage. Al-Yunini tells of the arrival of the Sultan at the city:

> The *Franj* had sought aid from the people of Cyprus and other islands, sending messages to their great kings, with the result that a large number of Hospitallers and Templars had gathered in the city. In their letters to the Frankish kings, monks and priests the Akkans mentioned that there remained no Frankish port on the whole coast in which they could take refuge save the fortress of Akka and if it were captured there would be no place left for the Franks to remain. Accordingly the kings sent many men and the city was refortified . . .*

Again Mamluk weakness at sea counted against them. Ismail Abu'l Fida describes Frankish defence from the sea and land:

> [My] contingent from Hama was stationed at the head of the right wing, as was their custom, so we were beside the sea, with the sea on our right as we faced Akka. Ships with timber vaulting covered with ox hides came to us firing arrows and quarrels . . . they brought up a ship carrying a mangonel which fired on us and on our tents from the direction of the sea. This caused us distress until one night there was a violent storm of wind, so that the vessel was tossed on the waves and the mangonel it was carrying broke . . . During the siege, the Franks came out by night, surprised the troops and put the sentries to flight. They

---

* In D. Little, 'The Fall of Akka in 690/1291: The Muslim Version', in M. Sharon (ed), *Studies in Islamic History in Honour of Professor D. Ayalon*, Leiden: EJ Brill, 1986, pp 159–81.

got through to the tents and became entangled in the ropes. One of the knights fell into an emir's latrine and was killed there.*

Zabdat al-Fikra tells us that, 'the Franks did not close most of their gates and did not even draw a curtain across them', leaving them open in order to fight the Muslims at the foot of the walls. The Muslim sources state that Christian knights rode out daily to offer battle and single combat. Of course, they recorded a 100 per cent success rate for the Mamluk champions in these duels. The Mamluks applied their siege hardware to Acre's defences. The bombardment lasted six weeks and involved ninety mangonels, the largest number ever assembled against the walls of any Middle Eastern city. Abu'l Fida tells us that there were four types: *Franj*, *Shaqtani*, *Qarabugha* and *al-Lasib*: the Frankish, a lightweight counterbeam engine, the Devilish, which was a simple traction engine but which was extremely mobile and capable of being moved by only a few men, the Black Bullish, adapted to shoot large arrows, and the sardonically named Playful. The Franks padded the walls with cloth and straw to dampen the impact of the mangonels' missiles but the Mamluks' incendiary arrows cleared these obstacles to the walls' destruction. The action around the city, as recorded by the attackers, has a curious similarity to urban fighting in the twentieth century, with holes being punched through obstructions with artillery and then a handful of infantry occupying key areas from which, by probing and leapfrogging over each other, they moved towards the heart of the city. This account is from the Mamluk Baybars al-Mansuri, Kalavun's biographer and veteran of the battle of Homs:

> Amidst all this I was searching for a place at which opportunity might knock, a corner which might permit a stratagem, but found none. While I was exercising my thoughts and letting my sight and perceptions roam, I suddenly noticed that one of the towers damaged by mangonels could now be reached. Between this tower and the walls a wide open space had been uncovered, but,

---

* In P. Holt, *The Memoirs of a Syrian Prince*, Wiesbaden: Steiner, 1983, pp. 16–17. A quarrel is a short, heavy square-headed ballista arrow.

being surrounded by arbalests, could not be traversed unless a screen was erected over the entire area to protect anyone who entered. So I availed myself of some felt, stitching all of it together in the shape of a large cloud, long and wide. Between two posts opposite the dilapidated tower, I placed a pulley rigged with ropes, similar to a ship's. There I hoisted the felt cloud into place as a dam. This was done at night unbeknownst to the Akkans who, when they arose in the morning and saw the screen, fired mangonels and arrows against it. When a stone fell into the screen, the felt would slacken beneath it and break its thrust, and the arbalesters could not penetrate it with their arrows.*

His men moved backwards and forwards across the dangerous open ground under this improvised cover, filling in the ditches between the broken walls with dirt and rubble whilst under fire from the towers above. This was the route the Mamluks would eventually take to storm the city.

The bravery of the knights of the military orders in pressing counter-attacks is attested to by al-Yusufi, who relates how the Franks displayed bucklers and cuirasses they had snatched during attacks on the Mamluk camps on Acre's walls. Such assaults infuriated the Sultan and on 9 May he had a number of his emirs arrested on suspicion of collusion with the enemy and berated all the others for their poor performance. On the Crusader side the King of Cyprus arrived and the spirits of the besieged were lifted. The elation did not last, however, and the King, who was ill, left the city three days later, realising that the position was untenable. The Mamluks redoubled their bombardment and applied engineers to every one of the towers, which started to come down one by one. The Crusaders abandoned and burnt the Tower of King Hugh on 8 May as it was crumbling away from the mines placed beneath it. The Tower of the English was next to fall followed by its neighbour, Countess Blois's Tower, a section of the walls above Saint Anthony's Gate and the Tower of Saint Nicholas. With the fall of the Tower of Henry II the Mamluks were able to charge through the outer walls, clearing them of their last defenders and investing the

---

* In Little, pp. 159–81.

inner walls. There was vicious fighting around Saint Anthony's Gate, where only the Templars' and Hospitallers' bravery denied the Mamluks entry into the city proper. The leaders of Acre came out to plead for a truce with tribute on 17 May. The plea was refused out of hand as was Khalil's counter-offer of Crusader abandonment of Acre and safe passage from the city. The meeting was then broken up by the Crusaders attempting to kill the Sultan with a well-aimed rock from a mangonel. The furious Mamluk artillery barrage recommenced.

Then on 18 May Khalil ordered a general offensive. The attack began at dawn with the continuous beating of three hundred drums and volley after volley of arrows pouring onto the walls' defenders. Every part of the walls was assaulted but the focus was the Accursed Tower. The Mamluks forced the tower and despite a desperate counter-attack by Templars and Hospitallers the Mamluks were able to fight their way along the walls and secure the inner gateway of Saint Anthony's Gate; after this the Muslims simply poured in. Within three hours the Mamluk and *ghazi* banners were on the battlements. The sack of the city by the irregulars began in earnest. Even Muslim inhabitants of the city were killed as a mob of soldiers slaughtered men indiscriminately and seized women and children. Richer inhabitants were tortured until they revealed where their gold and silver was hidden.

The regular Mamluk troopers were unable to join in the pillage as they were still trying to reduce four tall towers that the Templars, Teutons, Hospitallers and Armenian knights had holed up in. The Templars asked for safe passage in return for their surrender and this was granted, but as Mamluks entered the tower they began to grab at women and children in order to secure the best of the batch. The Templars roared with rage and closing the tower's gate they killed every Mamluk inside the tower and threw down the banner that the Sultan had sent them to secure their safety. Despite this the other besieged groups gave up their positions under renewed pledges of safety given by the emir Kitbogha. The Templars held out for another three days before accepting another offer of honourable surrender that, as they were departing the tower, was broken by Mamluks exacting revenge for the murder of the emir Aqbugha who had been killed by the Templars whilst negotiating for the Sultan. A massacre quickly ensued and the remnant of the Templars in the tower responded by throwing five Muslim captives from its windows. The surrender then turned into a messy and bloody mêlée with Mamluks and Muslim civilians also trapped in the tower and the Templars making furious assaults from its gate and walls. An anonymous Mamluk writer left us this account:

> I was among the group who went to the tower and when the gates were closed we stayed there with many others. The Franks killed many people and then came to the place where a small number, including my companion and I, had taken refuge. We fought them for an hour, and most of our number, including my comrade, were killed, but I escaped in a band of ten persons who fled in their path. Being outnumbered, we hurled ourselves toward the sea. Some died, some were crippled, and some were spared for a time.*

The Sultan, by now exasperated, ordered the tower mined. Bar Hebraeus claims that he also ordered two thousand Muslim troops into the tower and that the tower then collapsed, killing everyone inside, but Muslim sources describe an evacuation and demolition. Khalil ordered the complete destruction of Acre's walls before moving on to accept the surrender of the last few cities held by the Franks. Abu'l Fida describes this simple task: 'After the conquest of Acre, God struck fear into the hearts of those *Franj* still remaining on the Syrian coast. Thus did they precipitately evacuate Saida, Beirut, Tyre and all the other towns. The Sultan therefore had the good fortune, shared by none other, of easily conquering all those strongholds, which he immediately had dismantled.'†

Tacitus' famous statement on Roman peacemaking, *Solitudinem faciunt, et pacem appellant*, they make desolation and call it peace, applies *mutatis mutandis* to the Mamluks' Syrian policy, only the wounds of this destruction were inflicted upon

---

* In Little, pp. 159–81.
† In Maalouf, p. 261.

themselves not others. They tore up, for fear of a return of warring Crusaders, entire portions of habitable coastline, and in doing so they devastated their own harbours and coastal cities and made desolate the economy of Syria for centuries to come. Such actions in the later campaigns against the Crusaders are hard to comprehend as surely the threat was extinguished, but the existence of a Muslim legend of the fourteenth century that new Kings of Cyprus would sail in the dead of night to the ruins of Acre to undergo secret coronations suggests that the ghosts of the *Franj* lingered on in Muslim minds even after this period. Abu'l Fida's final thoughts on Khalil's campaign close with what amounts to a prayer: 'With these conquests all the lands of the coast were fully returned to the Muslims, a result undreamed of. Thus were the *Franj*, who had once nearly conquered Damascus, Egypt and many other lands expelled from all Syria and the coastal zones. God grant that they never set foot there again!'*

The Muslim–Crusader conflict has two discernable trends. There was initial fierce Christian unity in the early twelfth century that degraded over time to such a degree that, even though Western naval superiority could have very probably brought the Mamluk Sultanate to its knees through a blockade of Egypt's ports, this weapon was never applied as feuding and defence of profits between Emperor and Pope, Venice, Pisa and Genoa and the Angevins and just about everybody else precluded it. Running parallel to this was an early Muslim response to the Kingdom of Jerusalem that was hobbled by both a shortage of well-trained regular troops in the Syrian arena and a lack of a unified and consistent response to the Crusader threat. At the close of the period the Mamluks were campaigning almost annually, single-mindedly and in both winter and summer against the Franks and they had constructed the best army of the medieval world for which Outremer could have no match.

As Khalil looked around him after the fall of Acre, he might have been worried. There was no clearly discernable enemy left

---

* In Maalouf, p. 261.

to fight. The Mongols were in disarray and the Franks were gone. He was secure now but he knew that inactivity for the army could soon lead to demands for increased pay and reward and, of course, the Mamluks were an urban aristocracy; the great emirs resided in Cairo with their personal Mamluk households, effectively small armies, which had become increasingly large as more and more revenue was derived from the trade of the Orient and from the booty accrued from conquests in Latin Syria and Armenia. The Praetorian dilemma that the Caliphs of the ninth century had faced in Baghdad could very well rematerialise in Egypt. The Sultan decided that new tasks were the key to managing this problem. The Franks were gone but the Caliph, who really only saw the light of day when the Sultans needed him, was wheeled out to proclaim a new *jihad* against the schismatics and heretics of Syria and against Armenia.

Armenia's main fortress on the Euphrates, Qalat al-Rum was reduced in short order by the mangonels left over from Acre's destruction in May 1292 and it was forced to hand over three more fortresses in the spring of 1293 just on the threat of action by the Mamluks. In the mountains north of Beirut, however, whilst trying to bring the Nusayri Shiites, Druze and Maronite Christians to heel, the Sultan's chief Syrian emir, Baydara, was ambushed and such was the difficulty of his position after the surprise attack that he had to negotiate with the tribesmen he had been sent to annihilate just in order to bring his army, or what was left of it, safely out of the mountains. Baydara was excused by Khalil but the Sultan revenged himself on several of Baydara's companions on the expedition and at this point it became obvious that the Sultan was actually arresting and executing emirs simply to acquire their estates and revenues. The great emirs began to plot as it also became clear that the Sultan's desire for land in Cairo for a new *maydan* and a congregational mosque that would have as its centrepiece the entire doorway of the Church of Saint Anthony that had been taken as a trophy from Acre would require many more appropriations from deposed emirs.

Then there were his grandiose schemes for conquest. He sent letters to Geikhatu threatening to make Baghdad his new capital.

In fact his idea, given the appalling condition of the Ilkhanate under the Ilkhans between Abagha and Ghazan, may not have been so ridiculous, but – as discussed earlier – Mamluk grand strategy and indeed the Mamluk mindset had been shaped by their Syrian coastal policy and expansionism did not fit into their perception of what was needed to protect their state. Khalil had also wisely corrected Baybars's error by building up the fleet to a degree that it was at least now able to protect the coast from Frankish pirates, but then he claimed he wanted to invade Cyprus and needed even more ships. Such dreams of conquest of course required vast amounts of money and Khalil therefore planned a redistribution of the *iqta* of Egypt, redrawing the income from land and trade to benefit the Sultan's treasury to everyone else's cost and this also of course, set many of the emirs against him. Khalil had made the mistake of allowing the emir Lachin, who was related to him through marriage with one of Kalavun's daughters, to escape the purge that followed the debacle in the Syrian mountains on Baydara's pleading. The Sultan attempted to disgrace Lachin by making him a Mamluk of Baydara but in fact he only succeeded in cementing a union between the two men. Late in 1293 Khalil quarrelled with Baydara over cuts to the emirs' share of trade revenue but he dismissed Baydara's antipathy and went hunting west of Cairo in December 1293. He was unescorted when he was set upon by Lachin, Baydara and a gang. Lachin shouted out as he slew the Sultan, 'Let he who would rule Egypt and Syria strike a blow like this!' But there would be a lot more bloodletting before Lachin would rule.

Things returned to form with a child Sultan being placed under the tutelage of a group of protectors, all jockeying for real power. Baydara had claimed the throne for himself but he was dead within a few days. His liver was cut from his body and eaten raw by one of the emirs that killed him; his supporters had their hands cut off before being crucified on the backs of donkeys that were led through the streets of Cairo. Lachin escaped the clutches of the junta that raised the eight-year-old son of Kalavun, al-Nasir Muhammad, to the throne. Kitbogha, the Mongol who had been recruited by Kalavun after

Abulustayn, became effective leader after securing the position of *na'ib al-saltana* or vice-regent of Egypt. His main opponent over the next year was Sanjar al-Shuja'i, who took the second of the two most important posts in the Sultanate, that of *vizier* or senior minister. In brief, Shuja'i attempted to kill Kitbogha and was killed in street fighting by Mongol Mamluks and Mongol *wafidiyya*, as a new racial angle to Mamluk politics now began to cut across the older *khushdash* loyalty.

At the end of 1294 Kitbogha declared himself Sultan, but found his power base of new Mongol Mamluks and men from outside the old Kalavunid government was too weak and he solicited the support of Lachin, who had resurfaced again to lead the Circassians of the Burjiyya. In 1296 Lachin, by now the *na'ib al-saltana*, attempted to kill Kitbogha, which was enough to persuade the Sultan that retirement was preferable to assassination. Sultan Lachin was murdered in January 1299 whilst praying in the citadel's mosque by two Mamluks of Sultan Khalil's old household, the Ashrafiyya. Lachin had been attempting to overhaul the *iqta* system and it had cost him just as it had Khalil.

In fact both these Sultans' attempts to reorder the system were not purely related to greed. Despite Baybars's reforms, division of revenue in the Sultanate was still essentially based on Saladin's arrangements made over a century before. The *halqa* had, for example, been in decline as a force ever since the first mass buying of Mamluks under Baybars and the revenue required to maintain it was therefore far less than that needed by the Sultan and the senior emirs to maintain and increase their household Mamluk forces. The Sultan, having the most Mamluks, bore the brunt of this expense and it was logical that the division of revenue should favour him. Unfortunately for Khalil and Lachin this was not how the emirs saw it, and the emirs were becoming more and more powerful in the 1290s. An emir's power was, of course, based on the number of Mamluks he possessed and in this period slaves from the Caucasus had become cheap as civil war had erupted in the Golden Horde between Toqta Khan and his leading general Noghai. Captives were sold by each side to the Genoese at rock-bottom prices.

Toqta's eventual victory in 1299 didn't stop the discounts flowing as drought and a cattle epidemic affected the steppes from 1300 to 1303 and many nomads were compelled to sell their children to slave dealers. The instability in the Mamluk Sultanate and the weakness of its Sultans in this period was directly related to the increasing size of the magnates' personal armies.

Al-Nasir, the boy Sultan who had been packed off to al-Karak by Lachin, was returned to power. This time he was the front for a struggle between Baybars al-Jashnakir and Sayf al-Din Salar. Baybars represented the new men, the Circassians, whilst Salar was a Qipchaq. The year 1299 was shaping up to be just as dangerous, politically, as preceding years had been and now there was also an added threat as the Mongol monster was coming back to life. Ghazan, the Ilkhanate's ruler from 1295 to 1304, was without doubt the most gifted of all the Ilkhans and he was unfortunate to be following a line of incompetents. His agrarian reforms were based on the sensible logic of his minister Rashid al-Din. 'It is fitting that rulers have three exchequers, firstly of money, secondly of weapons, thirdly of food and clothing – The exchequers of expenditure. But the exchequer of income is the peasants themselves, since the treasury is filled by their good efforts.'* This doesn't seem particularly startling but apparently, for the Mongols, it was. They do not, until this point, seem to have made the link between paying for an effective army and not killing the goose laying the golden eggs and Ghazan had to sell his plan well. 'I am not protecting the Persian peasantry. If it is expedient, then let me pillage and rob them all. But you must consider, if you commit extortion against the peasants, take their oxen and seed, and cause their crops to be consumed – what will you do in the future?'†

Ghazan, despite opposition, got his way and the economy improved. He needed it to for he had decided to take a different approach to the war with the Mamluks and to take a different kind of army into Syria. At Homs in 1281 the Mongols had

---

* In Petrushevsky.
† In Morgan, *The Mongols*, pp. 167–71.

invaded with numerically superior forces and it had not been enough to secure victory. Ghazan was going to ensure numerical superiority again and he was going to add 'weight' to his army by developing a core of heavy cavalry. He was, in effect, going to try to make Mamluk cavalrymen out of Mongol troopers. His first problem was the inferiority of Mongol arms. The migratory Mongols that invaded the Middle East had no industrial base and were on the whole reliant on home-made weapons. This situation should be compared to the fact that a full year in the hands of a skilled artisan was required to produce a Mamluk compound bow and that Mamluk metalwork, a spin-off of fine armour production, was export quality. Wealthier Mongols imported armour and weapons from Europe and China but the numbers of heavy cavalrymen this yielded was tactically insignificant. The Mongols could have used the resources and artisans of Iran, before their invasion one of the richest states in the world, to supply their military but of course Mongol Iran was an economic basket case until Ghazan's reforms, and an effective war economy had never fully developed.

Ghazan copied the Mamluk-style quiver and ensured that there were lances, maces and swords for all troopers and not just for those who could afford them. He attempted to increase armour production from two thousand sets per year to ten thousand. Iran was ultimately unable to achieve this and the shortfall was made up by Italian imports. The new Mongol armour was a knee-length coat, divided at the waist to fall over both thighs, with horizontal overlapping strips of leather bolstered with narrow vertical metal plates; it was far heavier than its predecessors as were the horses of this new model army. There were to be fewer horses per man but they would be stronger by virtue of being stall fed and not simply pastured. It was hoped that by reducing the number of horses per man from five to three more men could be kept in Syria for longer.

The last part of Ghazan's reform of his army was in its training: whilst the Mongols were disciplined in terms of their loyalty to their leader – a central tenet of the Great *yasa* or law code of Genghis Khan – and they operated well as units with their *battue* or great hunts engraining this in the novices, they were still inferior to the Mamluks, who spent their life in training. Taybugha, the Mamluk archery master, chides those who might dismiss formal training and a constant review of skills. 'The purpose of manuals is to instruct the ignorant and to remind the conversant of what they may have forgotten or overlooked,' whilst the later archery *Furusiyya* of 1419 by al-Sughayyir denies the title of *ustadh* or master to this same Taybugha because he was not considered truly learned in the art of the bow. The perfection achieved through this unending training is evident in contemporary descriptions of the firing of untipped arrows at the blade of a sword. A successful hit meant that the arrow would be split down its length. First this was practised on foot, then 'you may also try the same thing on the back of a horse, shooting several arrows and galloping in succession against the blades of the swords.' All I can say to any readers wanting to replicate their accomplishments is the best of luck and that such feats could not possibility be attained without rigorous daily training and slavish application. Ultimately that was Ghazan's main problem – the Mongols were free. Migratory nomads, used to the freedom of the steppe, could not be disciplined in the same way that a man whose life had been purchased could be. It is notable that the force that finally destroyed the Mamluks, the Janissaries of the Ottomans, were also manumitted slaves and Ottoman training manuals required such extremes as bending the bow 500 times in each daily session. Edward I's banning of football and cockfighting in England so that men would concentrate on archery looks feeble by comparison.

Despite these problems, Ghazan still hoped for success against the Mamluks in 1299 as they continued to squabble. The decade-long bloodletting between higher lords for the throne had, however, not physically damaged the Sultanate that much. There had been no civil war to affect either the state's revenues or stability as a whole but rather just street fighting between factions, and whilst there had been a drought in 1294–5 and a famine in 1294–6, it was business as usual in Egypt for the state and the military in the 1290s. The army was still ready and able to meet Ghazan's invasion, but what was affected was the Mamluks' political cohesion. Indeed it was the defection to the Mongols of the Mamluk governor of Damascus, Qipchaq, in fear of his life from the Sultan Lachin in 1298 that encouraged Ghazan to invade. Ghazan had needed to do something against the Mamluks simply because they were causing him so much trouble in Anatolia. Lachin had invaded Armenian Cilicia again in 1297 and Mardin in northern Iraq had also been captured by the Sultan, Mamluk agents were again inciting Anatolian rebellions and had even convinced the Mongol governor of the province, Sulemish, to revolt against Ghazan in 1298.

So in December 1299 poor Qipchaq found himself serving in an army of Mongols, Armenians and Georgians that was invading Syria whilst the Sultan he had fled from, Lachin, was already dead. Ghazan's army swept down past Aleppo and Hama and headed for Homs. For once the Mamluk early-warning systems failed; perhaps they just didn't expect the Mongols to come in winter. The Egyptian army mobilised late but quickly and made a forced march to meet the Mongols. Its progress was, however, slowed by a revolt among Oirat Mongol *wafidiyya* who planned to murder the boy Sultan, al-Nasir, and replace him with the retired Kitbogha. The Oirat Mongols had entered Syria in 1295 as political refugees from Ghazan. In order to maintain legitimacy in Persia after the disastrous reigns of their predecessors, the Ilkhans, from Ghazan onwards, made a political conversion to Islam. Ghazan's conversion was followed by widespread persecution of Christians, Shamanists and Buddhists and the Oirat had fled, ironically, to the kindly embrace of the Mongol Mamluk Sultan, and head of the Islamic world, Kitbogha. Now hundreds of them were executed as their revolt was put down by the Mamluks before the army pushed on.

The Mamluks' march was impressively fast and on 23 December 1299 they cut off the Mongol advance at Wadi al-Khazindar just north of Homs. Ghazan held back from battle to prepare his dispositions. He sent the entire left wing of his army off on a wide detour around the Mamluks in order to strike at their rear and, remembering the battle of 1281, he detached a further body of troopers and positioned them behind his main force ready to counter any flying assaults by the Mamluks'

Bedouin auxiliaries. He decided to give battle the next day and therefore ordered his men to dismount and rest and water their horses in the wadi. The Mamluks, though, misread Ghazan's troop movements, thinking either that the Mongols were abandoning the field or that the battle proper was beginning, and the army commanders, Baybars and Salar, ordered a charge on the Mongol centre which was, at this point, dismounted with their horses at pasture. The Mamluk charge probably wasn't as foolhardy as it would seem later as they certainly surprised the Mongols but the problem was they couldn't get past the Mongols' loose horses. The *Gestes de Chiprois* tells us how close to victory the Mamluks came:

> The Saracens, who were coming in their armour on horses covered in chain mail and wearing helmets [chamfrons] threw themselves, with their lances levelled, against the Tatars so that these retired close to four bowshots back, and they brought down many with blows from their lances. When the king of the Tatars saw his people retreating from the field and the Turks so vigorously delivering blows among them, and better mounted and armed than his people he doubted less his people should lose the heart to do battle and set themselves in flight. Thus he bethought to himself of a great thing, which people mounted on horseback are not wont to do in battle, for he put his feet on the ground and ordered his people to make such piles out of their beasts that the Turks would not be able to fight in their midst . . .*

The charge lost its impetus against the wall of horses and the Mongols stood bravely and shot or pulled Mamluks from their horses as the attack disintegrated into chaos. A degree of order was returned to the Mamluk ranks when they heard the war drums of the Mongol commander in the right wing of the Mongol army and, thinking that they could cut their way through to Ghazan and kill him, they reformed and made a second charge towards the sound of the drumming. They killed a large number of Ghazan's personal bodyguard but in fact the

---

* J. Boyle, 'Dynastic and Political History of the Ilkhans', in J. Boyle (ed.), *The Cambridge History of Iran. Volume Five*, . Cambridge: Cambridge University Press, 1968, ch. 4, pp 303 –421.

drums had been a ruse, Ghazan was fighting in the centre. The Mamluks were then overwhelmed by the Mongols' detached left wing that returned to the main field and struck them in the rear. The Bedouin cavalry did attempt to assist the trapped Mamluk army but Ghazan's reserve dispersed them and they fled the field; by this time everyone in the Mamluk army was trying to flee. The carnage was terrible. The Armenian chronicler Hetum wrote of it in 1306, 'The Tatars smote the enemy so much that out of all the great quantity of people that the Sultan had brought in his entourage, few escaped who were not dead or fatally wounded.'

The Sultan, Baybars and Salar made it clear of the field and nightfall saved the Mamluks from a worse disaster. A retreat was organised and the Mongols followed cautiously but did not move in for the kill, Ghazan may have feared that such a precipitate withdrawal was a ploy that would lead to an ambush, he did, however, send smaller flying detachments to raid down to Gaza. In the mountains of Lebanon the Mamluk army was set upon by the same Nusayri Shiites, Druze and Maronite Christians that it had failed against in 1292. The cumulative effect of these military disasters was that the whole of Syria, with the exception of the fortified towns and castles, fell to the Mongols. They walked into Damascus having already acquired the Sultan's treasury, which was found discarded on the battlefield, and they helped themselves to a great deal of the Mamluk army's equipment that had been abandoned in the city. They were unable, though, to take the citadel, which was stoutly defended by its Mamluk commander, Sanjar, who even made raids into the main city to burn the mangonels brought up against him by Ghazan. His resistance tied down the Mongol occupying force but more importantly it made it obvious to the people of Syria, who might be thinking of switching allegiance to the now Muslim Mongols, that the Mamluks had not gone away. Sanjar's response to calls for his surrender from Damascenes was, 'Your Sultan is still in power!'

The Mongols began finding it more and more difficult to maintain control in Syria as the populace rebelled against their plundering and they had insufficient siege machinery with them to reduce the Mamluk strongholds. Furthermore, the loyalty of the Mamluks who had come across to them in 1299 was becoming suspect. For example, Qipchaq bribed the Mongol governor of Damascus to withdraw his forces and by late spring 1300 every Mongol was back over the Euphrates and Syria was back in Mamluk control. Ghazan could see that though he had won a battle he hadn't destroyed the Mamluks' military capability and the Egyptian army was readying itself to reclaim Syria. Perhaps if he had chased the Mamluks harder after the battle he could have completed the annihilation of their army, an obvious prerequisite to the occupation of Syria, and it was this thought and the fact that the Mongols had at last bested the Mamluks in the field that made Ghazan attempt another invasion the very next year.

Wassaf tells us that in preparation for the 1300 expedition fifty thousand camels were loaded with fodder for the horses and the troopers were given six weeks' worth of provisions. Ghazan did not intend to live off the land and also meant to stay in Syria with all his forces for long enough to finish the job. Right from Ayn Jalut onwards the Mongols had faced the problem that they needed a vast superiority in numbers to defeat the Mamluks but could not maintain such a large army in the field on the pasturelands of Syria alone; they could manage a short campaign but not a prolonged occupation. Hulegu's letter of 1262 to Louis IX of France states explicitly that, 'the better part of our supplies and the pasture had been consumed; it pleased us to return for a little while to the mountains of Armenia'. This had also been another reason for the deployment of smaller raiding parties in 1299 and not pursuing the Mamluks with the entire army – an army not only marches but also gallops on its stomach. The simple act of looking for pastureland for the vast armies the Mongols employed often distracted them from strategic goals, al-Qalqashandi wrote of them. 'It was the custom of the Mongols not to bother with fodder. If the earth was fertile, they would go that way, if it was barren, they would keep away from it.' Of course, the burning of crops and grasslands was an extensive feature of the Mamluk defence plan and 1299 had also proved that even if they were defeated in the field it would take a long time to dislodge the Mamluks from the citadels and castles of Syria.

Ghazan launched his invasion across the Euphrates in September 1300, marching first on Antioch. His progress was slowed by atrocious weather, as was the Mamluk army's progress along the coastal route as it pushed north to intercept him. In the end the weather won. The armies never got close to engaging and Ghazan had to turn back on 2 February; torrential rains and subsequent floods had trapped the army in a sea of mud. The cold that followed the deluge killed both men and animals. The Mamluk army was also a bedraggled mess by this time, their rations convoy had been swept away and the most they could do was to send a small detachment of light cavalry to northern Syria to reassure the garrisons there that the Mongols were withdrawing and that the Mamluks still had a presence in the country.

Ghazan changed tack in 1301, sending letters that offered peace whilst listing the Mamluks' crimes against the Ruler of the World, demanding payment of tribute and for Ghazan's image to be put on Mamluk coinage as well as having his name placed in the *khutba* in every Mamluk mosque. Basically, the Mamluks were to give Ghazan everything he would get if he ever actually conquered Egypt and Syria. Other letters were sent to the Pope, Boniface VIII, giving detailed plans of how the Mongols and Europeans could work in concert to defeat the Mamluks. 'As for now, we are making our preparations exactly in the manner laid down before. You too should prepare your troops, send word to the rulers of the various nations and not fail to keep the rendezvous. Heaven willing we shall make the great work our sole aim ...' The letters give only a glimpse of what had already been, at least in theory, decided upon between embassies. It is evident in this period that the Ilkhan was keeping his politically embarrassing conversion to Islam from the Pope and the intrigue between the Pope and Ghazan came about as a result of rumours that circulated around Europe of the deliverance of Jerusalem after the Mamluk retreat from Syria in 1300. The correspondence ultimately, however, came to nothing as Ghazan was never able to gain enough success against the Mamluks to entice European cooperation. Without absolute cast-iron guarantees of Mamluk defeat in Syria no Western prince was going to commit to an amphibious operation against Egypt.

Ghazan saw an opportunity in 1302 when a group of Syrian Mamluk emirs who felt directly threatened by either one or both of the factions struggling for power in Cairo defected to him. Encouraged by the descriptions of ongoing political strife in Egypt, Ghazan began to organise the army that would cross the Euphrates in the spring of 1303 under the command of his general Qulugh Shah. The Mongols met no resistance at all as they descended into Syria and they reached the environs of Damascus without having made contact with any Mamluk forces. Then on 20 April they found the Mamluk army drawn up and waiting for them at Marj al-Suffar just south of Damascus. The Mamluk position, stretched into lines across the rocky ridges and a small stream that ran east to west across the plain, was an excellent one for defence and a defensive battle was what they had decided to fight. All the victories of the past had been won by defence and counter-attack; the Mongols had to attack, they, after all, had come to conquer and occupy and Wadi al-Khazindar had been a bitter lesson on the consequences of changing strategy. The Mamluks were also outnumbered by their foe, with about twenty thousand Mamluks facing thirty thousand Mongols.

The Sultan was in the centre along with Baybars and Salar. Morale in the army had taken a beating after Wadi al-Khazindar. The chronicler al-Maqrizi wrote that troopers had been taunted in the streets when new taxes were ordered for the army's rebuilding. People called out, 'yesterday you ran away from the enemy, now you want to rob us. You are brave enough against civilians, but your courage fails you against the Mongols!' so the new Caliph had also been brought along. Al-Maqrizi gives him a short speech to the troops before the battle commenced. 'Defenders of the Faith! See your Sultan is with you. Fight for your women and for the defence of your Prophet!' The chronicler tells us that tears flowed from the eyes of the troopers as they listened to the Caliph, but the soldiers wept not so much for his fine words than for the fact that they had to repair the honour lost in 1299. They wept for the slur that Wadi al-Khazindar had put on Mamlukdom and they would fight to clear the disgrace. They would fight to be able to identify themselves with the great warriors Kutuz, Baybars and Kalavun as much as for Egypt. They would fight for *khushdashiyya*, an ideal that had been tarnished in the political frays of Cairo but which was still honoured on the field of battle and they would fight simply to beat the Mongols because winning is ultimately every professional soldier's *raison d'être*. In short, they would fight for honour and when the hour came they fought just as the heroes of Ayn Jalut, Abulustayn and Homs had.

Qulugh Shah's army came on at about midday and his left wing was the first part of his army to make contact with the Mamluk line. The line began to fold quickly and Qulugh Shah pressed his advantage, taking men from the centre with him to push on the Mamluk right wing. Initially the strategy worked as the Mamluk right wing disintegrated under the weight of the Mongol charge but the Mamluk centre and left then met and stopped dead the Mongol centre and right. The Burjiyya fought particularly bravely. The centre and left of the Mamluk army then advanced with the left wing extending to outflank and then fold in on the Mongols. The Mongols retreated and their left wing, which had been pursuing the broken-up units of the Mamluk right, was recalled but it was too late to prevent the envelopment that was taking place in front of Qulugh Shah's eyes. He managed to retreat to a small hill but he was now entirely surrounded. The Mamluks closed up to the base of the hill and reinforced their position as daylight was fading. The war drums were sounded all night in order to recall Mamluk stragglers and to terrify the Mongols trapped on the hill.

At dawn the Mamluks opened their lines just enough to allow the Mongols a chance of escape; they knew that the Mongols were almost crazed with thirst and that they would at some point have to make a dash for it. As al-Ansari's war manual has it: 'No soldier should get in front of a routed army, nor seek to shunt it from its path of flight, nor deny the defeated access to water if they seek it. Standing in the direct path of routed warriors is not sagacious.' The stratagem worked and groups of Mongols started to make their bids for escape from the hill and headed straight for the stream that had been the Mamluk defence line. There was a murderous scene as Mongols threw themselves and their horses into the stream only to have the Mamluks set upon them. It was almost too easy, al-Maqrizi says, 'they harvested their heads as men harvest barley with a sickle'. The Mongols that escaped the carnage attempted to reform for a retreat in the fields to the north of Marj al-Suffar but the local inhabitants broke irrigation channels to flood the fields. Another five thousand Mongols lost their horses in the mud of these fields and had to walk home – a two-month journey. But perhaps they were the lucky ones, as the Mamluks then advanced to assault those Mongols who were still mounted and routed them again. The Mamluk revenge was complete and Ghazan's reported response to the news, a huge nosebleed, added to their delight.

Ghazan certainly wanted to revenge himself on the Mamluks but he died on 11 May 1304. He had been grievously ill for about a year before but he had still been making war preparations. Syria and Egypt must have breathed a sigh of relief at his passing; he had been the most dangerous foe the Mamluks had ever had to face.

Ghazan's brother took the throne after him and chose the coronation name Oljeitu or Fortunate and at the outset of his reign it seemed almost possible that he would live up to his name, as one of his first letters to Phillip of France indicates:

> We, the descendants of Genghis Khan, after recriminating against each other for forty-five years down to these recent times, have now, all of us, elder and younger brothers, reached a mutual agreement, and from the land of the Chinese where the sun rises to the sea of Talu [probably the Mediterranean] our states are joining one another. Now, as for those who shall not agree, either with us or with you, let heaven decide on the manner in which, by the strength of heaven, leaguing against them all of us together, we shall take our stand.*

---

* In Boyd.

It seems almost superfluous to say who 'those who shall not agree' were, as by this time the Mamluks were certainly the Auld Enemy and there was no way they were going to be able to stand up to the might of the entire Mongol Empire, but actually they didn't have to. Such ideas of unity were basically a fiction. In 1313 the Ilkhanate attacked the Mongols of Afghanistan and the Chaghatay Mongols invaded the Ilkhanate in response; even before this, each of the Khanates had enough problems of their own without getting involved in each other's. There is also no evidence of any reply from the French court to this letter, although Edward I of England did reply to an embassy and wished the Ilkhan luck with his extirpation of, 'the abominable sect of Mahomet'.

The extirpation was put on hold, however, by a disastrous campaign against enemies inside Iran. The Ilkhanate army entered the jungles south of the Caspian Sea in an attempt to bring the recalcitrant Gilakis, who had remained unsubjugated despite over fifty years of Mongol rule to heel. If there was a victory it was a highly Pyrrhic one as one Mongol army was slaughtered and a subsequent punitive campaign couldn't make effective contact with an enemy who just kept melting away into the forest. The last Mongol campaign of the long war against the Mamluks therefore didn't set out until December 1312 and once again the Ilkhan was encouraged to invade by dissident Mamluk emirs.

9

VICTORY AND NEW ENEMIES

THE END OF THE ILKHANATE

> If you have met them, stand fast. One should not become disgusted
> at the procrastination of one's enemy, for in the interval of waiting
> is the grasping of possible advantage and acquiring knowledge
> of the enemy's circumstances and that which has been concealed
> of their affairs; and one does not seek victory by engaging him so
> long as victory can be obtained through stratagems.
>
> *Al-Ansari's manual of war, c.1399*

THE MAMLUKS SPENT THE early years of the fourteenth
century re-solidifying their Syrian defences and on its
internal security. Once again there was a campaign
against the 'heretics' of the Lebanese mountains. There had
already been a strike against the area in 1300 as retribution for
the hill tribes' attacks on the retreating Mamluk army of 1299
but in 1305 a concerted campaign was launched as the area
was now in open revolt. The hill tribes were well beaten in a
campaign conducted under a convenient *fatwa* called by the
Sunni jurists of Egypt. The area was divided into *iqta* and settled
with Turcomen. The campaign was important for the way it
reasserted Mamluk control in the whole of Syria, it was bloody
enough to make every other group with thoughts of leaving the
Mamluk fold think twice – as the Chinese say, kill the chicken
to frighten the monkey. The same applies to the brutal quelling
of an Egyptian Bedouin revolt that followed the defeat of 1299.

The espionage system that failed so spectacularly in 1299
also underwent a mini renaissance in this period. It is obvious

that things had been neglected because in 1309 a royal agent, Daw ibn-Sabbah complained about wages to the governor of Damascus. The governor's note to the central administration stated, 'you have cut the wages of the agents who are the eyes of Islam'. The matter was swiftly rectified by Sultanic decree and normal business was resumed.* In 1313 a whole cell of Mamluk spies was arrested in Baghdad but by this time they had already given Cairo vital information about the Mongols' campaign of 1312.

Mamluk politics were smoother after 1310 too. Al-Nasir had attempted to revolt against his overseers, Salar and Baybars, in 1307 but the plot he had been forming with his young Mamluks was discovered. In 1309 he let it known that he was to make the *hajj* but in fact he retired to al-Karak with his retinue and effectively deposed himself. Baybars and his Circassian backers thought they saw an opportunity and Baybars was enthroned quickly in April. He was perhaps the most unlucky of the Sultans so far. In his one-year reign the Nile failed to rise, there was famine and pestilence and he was pelted with filth by the mob every time he showed his face outside the citadel of Cairo; the support for his reign evaporated rapidly whilst al-Nasir had gained the support of virtually all the emirs of Syria. When he marched on Cairo Baybars's support simply fell away and the one-year Sultan fled to Gaza. He was quickly captured and strangled in al-Nasir's presence. Salar was allowed to remain at court for a little while until al-Nasir had consolidated his hold on power and then he was starved to death whilst being questioned about the whereabouts of his treasure. He died in August 1310 after apparently choking whilst attempting to eat his own faeces.

Al-Nasir was only twenty-four years old when he took the throne but he was old beyond his years in his experience of intrigue, his appreciation of the uses of brutality and his weakness for rich living. In 1312 he created forty-six emirs from his personal Mamluks. Then he began to eliminate the veteran

---

* Cf. Amitai-Preiss, 'Mamluk Espionage among the Mongols and Franks', pp. 173–81.

Syrian emirs, the very men who had brought him to power. This was done in the time-honoured manner of raising them higher than they had ever been and then dashing them down. Only two Syrian governors escaped the purge: Qaransunqur and al-Afram, the governors of Damascus and Tripoli, who crossed into Mongol territory with six hundred of their Mamluks. It was these men who would tempt Oljeitu into the last Mongol assault on Syria.

The Mongols set out in October 1312 but of course the Baghdad spy ring had given the Sultan plenty of notice of its march. In fact the Mongols moved so slowly, only managing nine miles a day, that early warning was hardly required but the Mamluks obviously used the time gained well, as when Oljeitu commenced the siege of Rahbat al-Sham on 23 December he found it so well provisioned, garrisoned and ready to resist that the Mongols suffered heavy casualties in their initial attacks and soon found themselves pursuing a lost cause. They had also brought insufficient fodder and provisions with them. The odd claim that the Mongol chroniclers make for Oljeitu's failure is that the weather was too hot for the siege to be pressed; the Mongols packed up and left Syria – never to return – on 26 January 1313, presumably they feared a truly scorching February.

The debacle of Rahbat al-Sham was a microcosm of the ramshackle condition of the Ilkhanate by this point. The currency was debased and the Khanate was split into two administrative spheres in an attempt to placate divisions in the government. Oljeitu's reaction was to turn to drink, or at least more drinking than a Mongol prince would normally have been inclined to anyway, and he died in December 1316. His twelve-year-old son, Abu Said, inherited a throne but no power as the puppet of the Commander-in-Chief of the Armies, Choban. In 1318 the man who had rescued the Ilkhanate's economy during Ghazan's reign, Rashid al-Din, was executed on trumped up charges and in 1319 there was a simultaneous invasion by the Chaghatay and Golden Hordes. Choban's son, the governor of Anatolia, revolted in 1322 at his father's instigation but it was Abu Said's passion for a married woman, Baghdad Khatun, and the failure of Choban to secure the Ilkhan's *droit de seigneur** that finally set Abu Said's mind on ridding himself of his overseer in 1326.

The two went to war in 1327 and Choban was quickly deserted by his forces, captured and then strangled with a bowstring by former supporters, who sent one of his fingers to the Ilkhan as proof of their loyalty. Choban's son in Anatolia fled to the Mamluks but al-Nasir quietly put him to death; he was a political embarrassment as peace had been formally declared in 1322. The Ilkhanate under the full control of Abu Said rolled on for a bit longer and prepared to meet yet another invasion from the Chaghatay Horde, but the game was up. Abu Said died on 30 November 1335, probably poisoned by Baghdad Khatun, now his wife, in a fit of jealousy over a younger woman. He left no children and, surprisingly enough, after years of political mismanagement and policies that would send any people into rebellion, in 1336 this was enough to break up the Ilkhanate. It shattered into petty states and Iran became from this point largely a political irrelevance until the rise of Tamerlane at the end of the century.

The formal peace of 1322 was a tacit acceptance by the Mongols that they couldn't take Syria and Egypt from the Mamluks, but why had they kept trying? The Ilkhanate had faced far greater foes than the Mamluks. The Golden Horde had been a consistent enemy, as had the Chaghatay Horde, yet the Ilkhans continued to return to the Syrian arena. The key reason for this obsession with Syria lies within the Mongol belief that the whole world was the rightful possession of the people of Genghis Khan. Mongol missives to the Mamluks indicate such a worldview and the continual defeats at the hands of the Mamluks were not just an affront to this ideal but also simply infuriating in their own right. The proactive policy of al-Zahir Baybars, especially his assaults on Lesser Armenia and the risk of a concerted and simultaneous Mamluk and Golden Horde attack on the Ilkhanate required that the Mongols at least hem in the Mamluks and if possible bring, as a minimum, northern

---

* The *yasa* of Genghis Khan gave this right of sexual access to *any* woman to Khans.

Syria into their sphere of influence if not their dominion. The spreading of the Muslim faith amongst the Golden Horde and the presence of an, admittedly puppet, Abbasid Caliphate in Egypt would also have alarmed the Ilkhans at least until their conversion in the early fourteenth century. The Mamluks had effectively become the leaders of the Muslim world and the Ilkhans' subject population was overwhelmingly Muslim. These were compelling enough reasons for the Mongols to annex Syria but it is also possible that they simply wanted to reach the Syrian coast in order to complete a dominion of trade routes that stretched from China's eastern coast through to Iraq. This seems unlikely, though – the routes out of the Persian Gulf were lucrative enough and they had access to the Mediterranean through Ayas in Armenia.

Neighbouring Mongol clans, the Chaghatay Mongols, the Golden Horde and the Mongols of Afghanistan blocked other routes for expansion. India appears not to have been considered, the climate and geography may have made it unattractive to steppe people. The Byzantines had worked with characteristic diplomacy to reach agreements with the Ilkhanate and there was always the risk that Constantinople might engage with the Golden Horde or the Mamluks if the Ilkhanate attacked Greek possessions. The Greeks had always leaned towards the Ilkhans in their diplomacy but they managed, generally, to also maintain friendly relations with both the Mamluks and the Golden Horde. It wouldn't have taken much to push them over into the anti-Ilkhanate camp. This effectively left only Syria as an outlet for Mongol aggression and expansion and expansion and aggression were essential policy in Mongol government; continual territorial gain was the *sine qua non* of the Mongol state. Their continual attempts to subdue Vietnam and Japan are examples of this. Indeed, one of the great counterfactuals in history is what would have happened if the Mongols had managed to break out of their beachhead on the shores of Japan in 1281. If the Great Kamikaze Wind had not come, could the Samurai have defended Nippon as well as the Mamluks defended Syria and Egypt?

Then there were the Ilkhans' own men. Mongol tribesmen wanted and needed plunder in the form of ready gold, slaves and new pastureland. There was no profit in peace and no honour either. One of the chief charges against Qubilai made by Ariq Boke in the civil war of 1260 and a cause of later animosity against him from the Chaghatay Horde was that Qubilai was abandoning the way of the steppes for more sedentary ways, and he basically wasn't looting and killing enough. This was tantamount to saying that he'd gone soft. The Ilkhans, now that they ruled a sedentary state and weren't just plundering from the steppe faced the same dilemma as Qubilai. How to keep the dogs of war busy, to keep them from wrecking Persia too badly and to keep up your own Mongol credentials? The answer, for the Ilkhans, was to lead their men into Syria where they could make trouble in someone else's backyard.

And who was to say the feat of taking Syria was beyond them? The Mongols were not so politically and militarily naive as to continue to assault an area that could not be conquered. Certainly the logistics of campaigning in Syria were a challenge, but they must have thought they had at least a reasonable chance of annexing the area permanently, if they didn't think so, what were they trying to achieve by sending armies into battle? As General Fayolle said at the Somme in 1916, 'if a battle is not for breaking through what is its purpose?'

So the Mongols wanted Syria and were sure they could take it but the Mamluks wouldn't give it to them and the Mongols couldn't take it from them because the Mamluks were better soldiers with a belief in their task. Their early Sultans were brave intelligent warriors and Baybars and Kalavun were statesmen of the first order who outmanoeuvred the Mongols diplomatically as well as defeating them on the battlefield and frustrating them on the borders. This is not to suggest that the Mamluks were ever likely to destroy the Ilkhanate. Indeed, Baybars's Anatolian campaign proved that their resources were nowhere near sufficient for enterprises of such magnitude. The Mamluks therefore set themselves the limited task of defending and holding onto Syria and thereby Egypt. The technical and strategic reasons for the Mongols' lack of success against the Mamluks have been laid out above, battle by battle, but ultimately the reasons for the Mongol failure can be seen in the relief of al-Bira in 1272, when Kalavun and Baybars swam the river Euphrates leading their horses. The Mamluks then charged the Mongols, who, despite their superior numbers and the protection of a palisade, could not stop the Knights of Islam with either arrows or the sword. Such feats require leadership, bravery, belief and skill. In short the Mamluks wanted to win more than the Mongols and each victory added to the lore of never submitting to the World Conquerors.

The problem was that once the Mongols went away the Mamluks began a steady decline that was unstoppable. The nobility of the steppe and of war are clichés but they hold a kernel of truth. The Turco-Mongolian tribes are places where men rise by ability to lead, as was the case with Genghis Khan, Tamerlane and Osman, the founder of the Ottoman dynasty. In its early years the Mamluk Sultanate was a meritocracy similar to those of the tribe and steppe but with the overlay of a developed state army structure. Advancement was procured by deed and by experience. Baybars al-Mansuri entered the service of Sultan Baybars in 1261 and it was only twenty-two years later, after years of good service in a time of war that he became an emir of ten. He was awarded the rank because, 'he has the astuteness of a commander and service long enough to make him a candidate for election as an emir'.* Note also that he was only up for election, the Sultan would not promote him without consultation with other high officers. Earned rank was therefore always respected. When Bilik, one of Baybars's favourite personal Mamluks, failed to acknowledge the greetings of a group of emirs he was flogged, on the Sultan's express order. When questioned, Baybars's reply was:

Among my bodyguard there are men who love me and whom I love, and their incomes from the land are small, and there are also men who hate me and whom I hate, but their incomes from

---

* Baybars al-Mansuri, in A. Levanoni, *A Turning Point in History: The Third Reign of al-Nasir Muhammad Ibn Kalavun*, Leiden: EJ Brill, 1995, p. 24.

the land are great. And I cannot bear the consequences if I were to take land from those who hate me and give it to those who love me, for I am Bilik's master.*

Al-Nasir, in the 1320s, on the other hand, with a weakness for attractive young men, bought his Mamluk Qawsun as an adult. Qawsun never went through any Mamluk apprenticeship, never held a field command and yet was given an *iqta* and the rank of emir. Qawsun even boasted. 'I was bought by the Sultan and became one of those closest to him; he made me an emir, awarded me commander of one thousand and gave me the hand of his daughter, while others went from the traders directly to the military schools'.† Baybars al-Mansuri was only made commander of one thousand in 1293 some thirty-two years after his manumission.

Advancement, of course, was linked to salary. One of Baybars's first reforms was to ensure regular pay that was paid according to level of responsibility, length of service and rank. He thereby ensured that his Mamluks looked for advancement through ability, experience in administration as well as in the field and of course through conduct in battle. The wages were low but bonuses were given for valour and ingenuity in the field. Kalavun was given a special reward for leading the riverbank charge at al-Bira in 1272. But al-Nasir's ambition was to be as a king and not as a warrior-chief like Kutuz, Baybars or even his father Kalavun. Consequently he rewarded favourites with gold and flattery and neglected fairness and appropriate recompense. The army quickly became rotten with corruption and emirs spent all their time at court, as they were more likely to gain reward there than at the barracks or training fields. Seeing how easy it was to obtain money from the Sultan, the rank and file commonly rioted for pay and the Sultan himself, ignoring the fact that this went totally against the protocols of rank that Baybars's reform had enforced, often remonstrated with the troopers himself, haranguing them and even once beating at

---

* Ibn Wasil, in Levanoni, p. 23.
† Ibn Hajar al-Asqalani. Levanoni. 35.

them with a staff. Familiarity breeds contempt and in al-Nasir's reign there were even instances of Mamluks going sailing on the Nile instead of turning up for training in the *maydan*, and these were Mamluks of the *muqaddam al-mamalik*, the officer in charge of army discipline. A quick comparison with Kalavun's attitude towards his novices shows how things had changed. Kalavun raised his novice Mamluk, the later Sultan Lachin, in his own house, but we hear from Ibn al-Dawadari that Kalavun, when dealing with his Mamluks, 'put terror in their hearts, and never allowed them to do repulsive deeds.' When a senior emir suggested that the junior Mamluk Salar, who would later be al-Nasir's overseer, should be promoted to the lowest rank of emir of ten Kalavun laughed and said, 'in the name of Allah, a country in which Salar is an emir of ten is not a country!'* Yunini, in later years, described Salar as one of the bravest and wisest men in the state. Both Baybars and Kalavun, despite their political purges show prolonged attachments to men who were loyal; many of Kalavun's higher officials died in office and the head of Baybars's Royal Mamluk School was retained by Kalavun simply because he was outstanding:

> He was one who was awe inspiring, who had a compelling presence, and who commanded great respect from the Mamluks. He was highly respected by the Kings and emirs, and only seldom was there an emir that Tawashi Mukhtass had not at one time struck, cursed or tried. And they had fear in their hearts and great respect for him.†

There was no such classic regimental sergeant major to oversee training in al-Nasir's time but then al-Nasir was dismissive of training too. It took years to graduate from the schools of Baybars and Kalavun whilst al-Nasir permitted two annual graduations. Cadets under the early Sultans were expected to accompany the army on expeditions, Baybars al-Mansuri went with his fellow novices to observe and support the siege of Arsuf in 1264. Nothing of the sort ever occurred under al-Nasir. There

---

* Al-Nuwayri, in Levanoni, p. 22.
† Al-Nuwayri, in Levanoni, p. 18.

were seventeen *tibaq* under Baybars whilst al-Nasir kept only twelve and this was despite the fact that if Baybars had had as many Mamluks as al-Nasir had the Ilkhanate would have been in danger of conquest.

In fairness to al-Nasir, it should be pointed out that it was more expensive to acquire Mamluks in the 1340s. Islam had spread across the steppe and young men were often enticed by payment to present themselves at mustering points rather than having been captured; the price subsequently soared. Kalavun had been exceptionally expensive at 1,000 *dirhams* but in the 1340s buying novices for 6,000 *dirhams* was not uncommon, consequently new recruits were pampered by comparison with the Mamluk novices of the early Mamluk Sultanate.

Of course, right from the origins of the Mamluk system in the eighth century the Sultan had had the first pick of the slave market as he needed the best potential soldiers in order to maintain his superiority over his peers. Under al-Nasir, however, we see the Sultan selecting Mongol novices simply because they bore a resemblance to Abu Said, the last Ilkhan. If the buying process was becoming a beauty contest then it easy to see how novices with true potential like Baybars, the Mamluks' greatest Sultan, would be passed over; as early as 1335 both James of Verona and William of Adam tell us of the importation of specially fattened boys to the Mamluk state for a homosexual love fad.*

Baybars had worked hard to create a uniform administration for the army and to make the army a distinct entity in the state's mechanics. It must be remembered that he had inherited an Ayyubid army that was designed to serve a small ruling elite. Under Baybars the army and its key members became the elite and the state served the army's needs. Under al-Nasir such ideas were eroded and whilst military men were still the elite, joining the ruling clique had more to do with connections, flattery, good looks and having the skills of a courtier than with martial ability and the largesse of the state was spent on horses for the Sultan's stables and table. This is not to suggest that the

---

* Cf. Irwin, *The Middle East in the Middle Ages*, p. 136.

eating of horse flesh was a luxury or even a novelty, it was a steppe custom that the Mamluks had long retained. Al-Nasir's feasts were, however, too sumptuous and far too frequent for his habits not to be called gluttonous.

The pageantry that Baybars had introduced to create a sense of identity for his new state was retained and indeed enhanced by al-Nasir. The *mawkib*, the procession of the Sultan and his emirs through the city – when the Sultan would wear his black turban and robe with its gold tiraz band, accompanied by a selection of swords, two long arrows, and a shield or wearing the red velvet, sable-lined coat of a high emir and the *sharbush*, a triangular crown or the *kalautah*, a yellow cap worn by only by the Sultan – was still a regular event but it was an empty façade. By the end of al-Nasir's reign Egypt was still the greatest power in the Middle East but it was living off past glories and the genius of past leaders, and whilst the Mamluks were still able, largely by virtue of their heavier armament and better organisation, to quell Bedouin revolts and to at least keep a lid on the problems in Nubia and Upper Egypt, they kept their position as the regional superpower only because the region didn't have another. When, in time, they had to face up to determined and credible enemies the damage done by al-Nasir became very obvious. First, though, there were other more pernicious enemies to face but not conquer: plague, famine, dissent and corruption.

There were military successes against second-rate enemies during al-Nasir's reign. Small expeditions were sent to ensure that the lords of Yemen understood their obligations to their masters in Cairo in 1315, 1322 and 1331. The same was attempted in Nubia in 1315 and 1323 but operations up the Nile were difficult and the Bedouin of Upper Egypt hampered supplies and reinforcements; the area could never be brought under full control but the Red Sea port of Aydhab was temporarily secured from incursions of both Nubian and Bedouin tribesmen. Operations against Armenia were more successful. The annual tribute from Armenia was doubled in 1315 to one million *dirhams* and punitive raids in 1320, 1322, 1332, 1335 and 1337 were mounted for tardy payment.

From 1340 it was obvious that the Sultan was dying and he finally expired on 4 June 1341 after nominating his son Abu Bakr as his successor. Al-Nasir's third reign had been long and on the surface successful: the Mongols had finally been defeated, there had been political stability, the Sultan had been able to make the much-needed changes to the *iqta* system and trade revenues were up. But he had sown and cultivated by his actions the seeds of economic and military decline; later *Furusiyya* writers were appalled by the decline into which archery, the keystone of the Mamluk military machine, had fallen under Sultan al-Nasir. He had been a capricious Sultan, fixated on treason, almost certainly as a result of the experiences of his earlier reigns but his purges and persecutions were sometimes just downright vindictive. Poisons were administered by the Sultan's own hand, torture was preferred to interrogation, and starvation, usually to death, was the cheapest and most common choice of punishment. One emir took to his bed and died of fear simply because he had been called before the Sultan, and arrests were made just to sequester men's fortunes. The senior emirs had to hide money to avoid his astronomical taxes on *iqta*s based on sugar production and mining. The Sultan had also preferred to rule through marriage alliance rather than relying on *khushdashiyya* and he had collected more and more power in his hands and those of his favourites. Of everyone else he was suspicious and mistrustful. The reaction this engendered in his subordinates would rebound on his descendants to the end of their line.

The first of al-Nasir's sons, Abu Bakr, was in his twenties on his accession but he was immature and easily led. Qawsun, the Mamluk of al-Nasir, whose meteoric rise was discussed above, ran him and then replaced him with his seven-year-old brother, Kuchuk, whose hand he used to guide for the signing of documents. Abu Bakr and seven of his brothers were sent into exile but Qawsun had overlooked one brother, Ahmad, because the young man was living at al-Karak, having been sent there as a child because al-Nasir had disliked him intensely. An anti-Qawsun faction built up around him and he reigned briefly in 1342 before being returned to al-Karak, deposed, but still in possession of a large part of the treasury and the ceremonial regalia of the Sultan. It was returned only after his murder by a messenger from his brother al-Salih, the new Sultan in 1344. Al-Salih paused only long enough on the throne to order the killing of his other brother, little Kunduk, before dying after a one-month illness attributed by his mother to the sorcery of Kunduk's mother. Al-Salih's step-father, Arghun, a low ranking emir, had run his short reign and replaced him with another brother, Shaban, in August 1345. He was executed in 1346 following a revolt by just about every senior emir in Syria and Egypt, their chief complaint being that he preferred the eunuchs of the palace politically over the Mamluks of the military establishment, but his drinking, cruelty and decision to call himself 'The Snake'* were certainly also factors. Arghun at least stood by him and died soon after in exile.

It was lucky that al-Nasir had been so prodigious in his begetting of sons. Next up was al-Muzzafar Hajji and just for variety he fell from power because of his attachment to a black slave girl and the extravagances he showered upon her during a time of famine and drought. He was deserted by all his supporters as he prepared for a pitched battle outside Cairo with a group of Circassian emirs who had been forced into rebellion by the judicial slaying of one of their ethnic brotherhood, Ghurlu, who had formerly been a favourite of the Sultan. Hajji had panicked at the suggestion of senior Qipchaq Mamluks that he might be deposed if he did not have Ghurlu murdered. Hajji was easily taken by the Circassians who had formerly been his keen supporters and put to death in December 1347. This was the first time the Circassians had acted politically purely on ties of ethnicity. Race was now more important than *khushdashiyya* simply because al-Nasir had done so much to erode the old ideal of brotherhood by his employment of rank favouritism and because the numbers of Circassians within the state was now so large. Their enmity towards the Qipchaqs who had held the lion's share of power through the continued accession of the grandsons of Kalavun until Hajji's reign was recorded by Ibn al-Wardi. 'These Circassians are the opponents of the Tatar

---

* A corruption of his name, the Arabic for snake being *thaban*.

[Qipchaq] race. Al-Muzzafar Hajji turned away from the Tatars towards the Circassians and their like . . .'

As a backdrop to this political turmoil the Black Death entered Alexandria via Black Sea trade ships and spread rapidly across Egypt in 1347. It was also already so well established in the traditional areas for Mamluk harvesting that the Golden Horde had been using the bodies of plague victims as biological weapons by firing them into the Genoese slaving and trading centre of Caffa on the Black Sea before the disease had been heard of in Egypt. The immediate effect of the disease in the Middle East has been estimated as being approximately the same as that experienced in Europe in the same period – about one-third of the population perished. Initially, senior Mamluk officials seem to have been only lightly affected. Only three out of the twenty-four emirs of one hundred in the Sultanate died before the disease's recession in 1349. Being able to leave the city for prolonged hunting trips, not having contact with the local populace and having a rich man's table were enough to see most of them through the epidemic. However, this was not the end of the pandemics as Egypt and Syria were visited next by pneumonic plagues. Between 1347 and 1517 Egypt and Syria were visited by this highly infectious plague over fifty-five times.* It took a heavy toll on the Mamluks, particularly on novices who, freshly imported, had no acquired immunity. Under such conditions a psychological malaise and dark pessimism struck at the heart of the military society and it is not surprising that the fabric of the army often dissolved into indiscipline in these periods of mass death. The *iqta* system was almost destroyed too. Peasants died, so land remained uncultivated and bore no revenue and *iqta* ownerships were disputed as Mamluks drawing their wage from plots of land died in great numbers. The army's revenues were diminished as civilians started to buy themselves low-ranking commissions in the *halqa* in order to then draw funds from an unoccupied *iqta*.

---

* Cf. Irwin, *The Middle East in the Middle Ages*, pp. 134–6.

The political war between the palace eunuchs and the senior Mamluks ended with the death of Hajji. The Mamluks asserted their authority over al-Nasir's boys by banding together to bully any candidate for the throne. They called it a *hilf*, a compact of loyalty to the Sultan, but in reality it meant he became a mere figurehead while real power was dealt out and fought over behind the throne between the most powerful Mamluk emirs. The most successful of these kingmakers in the early period was the Mamluk Manjak, who made himself *vizier* after al-Nasir Hasan had been installed as Sultan. Manjak attempted to balance the books by cutting pay for the Royal Mamluks and getting rid of all the hangers-on at court that had accumulated over the last half-century. He and al-Nasir Hasan managed to last for four years; the regime was popular with the Cairo populace but not with the Mamluk emirs, who had got used to a certain standard of living. Manjak was seized and imprisoned in 1351 and al-Nasir Hasan was replaced by yet another brother, al-Salih Salih in August and imprisoned in the harem, where surprisingly, considering all the distractions there, he devoted himself to study.

Al-Salih Salih's puppet-masters released Manjak and his former partner in power, Baybugha, from prison in order to garner support for the new regime from their followers. This was a mistake, compounded by sending Baybugha to Aleppo as governor. There he was able to organise a revolt in 1354 using the troops of Aleppo and Tripoli, Turcoman tribesmen and local Bedouin. During the advance down through Syria the Turcomen pillaged and burnt in a manner reminiscent of the Mongols. An army was sent up from Egypt but Baybugha's confederate force disintegrated before any engagement was made. Both he and the Turcomen's chief were captured easily and executed.

The year 1354 also saw al-Salih Salih trading places with al-Nasir Hasan and going to the harem whilst his brother retook the throne. Behind the throne an unholy alliance had been formed by the emirs Sarghimish and Shaykhun. Despite mutual hatred of each other an understanding had come about between them to exclude all others from control of the palace and state. Shaykhun, however, only lasted until 1357 when he was struck down in front of the Sultan, allegedly as the result of a private feud with another Royal Mamluk. The later arrest and execution of Sarghimish by the Sultan's *khassakiyya* might make one think that al-Nasir Hasan had been studying something slightly more Machiavellian than religious texts whilst he had been in the harem, if it wasn't for the fact that the next eight years of his reign were to be run by the truly devious emir Yalbugha al-Khassaki.

Whilst any history of the Mamluk Sultanate appears all too easily as a catalogue of cruelty, the men who ran the state should be compared to their contemporaries in the other great societies of the time. The leading families of Florence wouldn't baulk at unleashing their *bravi* on rivals and the Byzantines had a penchant for blinding their political foes, but both civilisations' leading men could be cultured and learned, and so could Mamluk emirs. From their patronage we have mausoleum complexes that are dazzling, a renaissance in Islamic metalwork, outstanding *Furusiyya* texts and insightful histories. And like the Byzantine and Florentine leaders they were also pious men. Shaykhun tended the dying during the plague period and Lachin was renowned for his asceticism. Yalbugha, however, was a different kind of man from all the great emirs who had preceded him because he was a simple brute. Mamluk discipline under the great Sultans was harsh but fair whereas Yalbugha's discipline was severe and totally arbitrary in its application. He finally fell from power in 1366 after failing to mount an effective response to the Crusade of Peter of Cyprus and as a result of the near paranoia that he aroused in even his own household Mamluks who killed him in 1366 rather than accept any more of his random killings and punishments. Before he was killed, however, he did the Sultanate two favours. He started work on a fleet to both protect Mamluk possessions and to revenge himself on the Cypriots and under his guidance there was a small renaissance of *Furusiyya* training that survived his demise.

Tension had grown between al-Nasir Hasan and Yalbugha from 1360 onwards chiefly because Hasan had been raiding the officers' pension funds to build a congregational mosque. He was therefore already deeply unpopular with the military and a collapse of one of the mosque's minarets that killed hundreds of civilians finished his reputation with the populace too. There was a military confrontation outside Cairo in 1361 but it wasn't much of a fight as al-Nasir's Mamluks went over to Yalbugha before the fight really commenced. The Sultan fled but was captured and secretly killed. The Mamluk emirs had finally used up all al-Nasir's sons and it was time now to start on the grandsons. Al-Mansur Muhammad was enthroned, but Yalbugha deposed him in 1363 after learning of an unhealthy interest in sadomasochism. Next was al-Ashraf Shaban who, as the son of al-Nasir Hasan, probably smiled at Yalbugha's murder in 1366 but it didn't gain the Sultan any more freedom as Yalbugha's Mamluks carried on his mode of government. The only difference was that there was an even stronger Circassian element to the junta now.

Al-Ashraf Shaban was popular despite a damaging drought and famine in 1374–5 and everything seemed peaceful in his capital when he set out for the *hajj* in 1377. Perhaps he was too popular; he never reached Mecca, but was ambushed en route and after fleeing back to Cairo he was murdered. In the citadel the second part of the *coup d'état* was acted out. Barkuk, the most senior Circassian emir, placed al-Mansur Ali, al-Ashraf's seven-year-old son, on the throne and when he died four years later he was replaced with his brother al-Salih Hajji. Chronic Syrian revolts finally made the senior emirs decide that the child Sultan should be replaced by an adult and Barkuk was enthroned in 1382. He was the first Circassian Sultan and had also risen from a position outside the Royal Mamluks, very much the new man. He took the throne name of al-Zahir after that of the great Sultan Baybars and although he was not the man that Baybars had been he was pretty good at political survival. When he was deposed in 1389 and al-Salih Hajji was put back on the throne by a duumvirate of powerful emirs he managed to avoid execution and took retirement to al-Karak. Within a year the duumvirate had dissolved itself through mutual hatred and Barkuk was able to return from exile and claim the throne.

Al-Salih and Barkuk organised drinking parties together, but there was no doubt who was the king now, when al-Salih got drunk and overly familiar, Barkuk would tell his Mamluks to, 'take the emir Hajji home'. Barkuk placed Circassian Mamluks of his household in every key position of government and then turned his attentions to founding a dynasty. He died in 1399 having arranged for the succession of his son al-Nasir Faraj.

10

ENEMIES WITHOUT AND WITHIN

THE RISE OF THE OTTOMANS AND TAMERLANE

I that am term'd the Scourge and Wrath of God,
The only fear and terror of the world,
Will first subdue the Turk . . .

Tamburlaine the Great, Part I

THE CRUSADE OF PETER I of Cyprus, launched in October
1365 against Alexandria, came as a complete surprise
to the Mamluks but it had been portended. Knight
Hospitallers had been installed on Byzantine Rhodes by the
Genoese and Cypriot navy in 1308 thus bringing the militant
forces of the West back into the eastern Mediterranean and
Peter had been touring Europe from 1362 looking for assistance
for a Crusade against Egypt. He had secured promises from
the Hospitallers, Venetians and the Papacy. English victories
at Crecy and Calais in the Hundred Years War meant that the
vast numbers of soldiers that the French King had guaranteed
never materialised but there were still 165 ships, ten thousand
men and fourteen hundred horses assembled at Rhodes for the
Crusade. The fleet's destination was put out as being Tripoli
and this simple ruse allowed the Crusaders to be mistaken for a
merchant fleet when they arrived off Alexandria. Peter intended
to attack Alexandria, occupy it and then offer an exchange to the
Sultan of Jerusalem for Alexandria. The occupation of Egypt's
main port would financially cripple the Mamluks and require
them to negotiate.

Alexandria had two harbours, lying east and west of its great lighthouse, and the Crusaders entered the western one, which was reserved for Muslim craft only. At this point the Alexandrians realised that something was wrong but the governor was away on the *hajj* and his deputy only had Arab levies at his disposal. He put his men behind the walls surrounding the harbour and hoped to stop the Crusaders from entering the city proper. Peter first assaulted the western wall but the forces that were ashore proved insufficient to take it. He landed more men and then swung the attack around to the eastern wall. The Muslims were at this point let down by the port's customs officer who barricaded the Customs House that effectively divided the area behind the harbour walls into two halves; he thought he was aiding the city's defence by his action but in fact he prevented the Muslim troops from moving over to the eastern wall to halt the new attack. The Crusaders soon breached the eastern wall and knowing that he was now effectively outflanked, the deputy governor, who was being forced to learn strategy quickly during this baptism of fire, retired with his men to the southern gate. There was still street fighting to be undertaken by the knights and they had to repel a counter-attack by the Muslim troops but within two days the city was theirs and a brutal sack ensued. Perhaps Baybars's executions of Hospitallers and the enslavement of women and children during the fall of Crusader cities in the thirteenth century spurred the Crusaders on or perhaps it was just the simple wealth of Alexandria, at this time one of the richest cities in the world. Certainly the slaughter was indiscriminate, with Jews, Muslims and Christians all being murdered for their gold.

For Peter the sack was a huge problem. It ran out of control, as these things are wont to, and before long all the city's gates had been burnt by the Crusaders as they rampaged through the city and his troops were so satiated by the loot they had acquired that all they wanted to do now was to return to Europe and, presumably, live it up on their new wealth. Peter destroyed the bridge that carried the road to Cairo to slow down the Mamluk relief army that he knew was now coming to effect an all-too-late rescue of the city and he tried to rally his troops, but it was hopeless. The English and French deserted quickly and as the Mamluks reached the outskirts of Alexandria Peter and his Cypriot knights retired before them. The Crusader fleet set sail after only six days in the city, practically thumbing its nose at the Mamluks on the shore.

The Mamluks, as we have seen, were distracted by infighting before and after the Crusade and also by a series of Bedouin revolts in Upper Egypt from the 1340s onwards that disrupted Cairo's grain supply. Mamluk armies carried out punitive massacres in nomad Arab areas, but farmers, the backbone of the agrarian economy, were slaughtered along with rebels, and the Mamluks' actions just drove more and more settled Arabs from the land to join the nomads in revolt. By the 1350s the whole of Upper Egypt was practically beyond control and its revenue was lost. There were problems with Syrian nomads too. In the 1360s and 1370s repeated expeditions were mounted against the Turcomen of northern Syria but they simply melted away into Anatolia whenever a Mamluk army was dispatched and reappeared as soon as the Mamluks retired.

The Mamluks weren't the only ones having trouble with Turks. After the Ilkhanate's collapse, the Anatolian Turks had used their new freedom to make land grabs in Byzantine Anatolia. The Turkish war bands formed around leaders of personality who brought them booty and success in war. The whole area was made up of *beyliks* or mini-states formed around one clan. In the 1300s the most successful *beyliks* in the peninsula were the Ottomans in the northeast and the Karaman in the southwest, the tribes formed around these Turkish families also incorporated Greeks, Kurds and Armenians. Anatolian piracy first engaged the attentions of the Venetians and Genoese, and the Turkish port of Smyrna was taken by a force comprised of Venetians, Cypriots and Papal troops in 1344 to prevent its use by the pirate emirs.

It was not piracy, though, but involvement in the affairs of the Byzantine Empire that would bring the Ottomans, by the end of the century, to a par with the Mamluk Sultanate. A brief summary of the Ottomans' growth from a *beylik* to an empire goes like this. In the Byzantine civil war of 1345 John Kantakouzenos called on Orhan, the successor of Osman, for assistance. The Ottomans were carried across the Dardanelles by the Byzantine navy, but even after winning the war Kantakouzenos found he could not do without Orhan. He married his daughter to Orhan to secure his aid in 1346 and in 1348 he again needed Orhan's help against the Serbians. By now it was obvious to the Ottomans that Greece and the Balkans were ripe for conquest and by 1369 Orhan's successor, Murad I, had conquered eastern Thrace despite a Venetian-backed Crusade being sent against him in 1366. Byzantine embassies begging for assistance were sent home by the Pope with nothing, prompting the Emperor's chief adviser to state, 'Constantinople will be taken, once this city is taken the Franks will be obliged to fight the barbarians in Italy and on the Rhine.'* All this diverted Western attention from the Mamluks. They signed a formal peace with Cyprus in 1370 and in 1375 the Cypriots stood blithely by as the Mamluks finally dismembered Armenia and incorporated it into the Sultanate. Meanwhile the Ottomans were subduing Greece and Serbia and, though Murad I was killed in the Battle of Kosovo in 1389, the damage inflicted on Serbia up to this point was enough to bring about its collapse.† Before his death Murad I had also inaugurated the 'new Mamluks'.

> Of these prisoners that the warriors in the Holy War bring back, one-fifth according to God's law belongs to the Sultan . . .
> They harvested the young men. They took one in every five prisoners captured in the raids and delivered him to the *Porte*.

---

* Demetrios Kydones, in C. Imber, *The Ottoman Empire 1300–1481*, Istanbul: Isis Press, 1990, p. 29. The Papacy's reluctance to aid Byzantium was linked to a desire to weaken the Orthodox Church. Phillipe de Mezieres's Crusade treatise of the fourteenth century argues the need to 'spread Catholicism to the eastern countries'.

† Serbia's collapse was due to Serbian lords rebelling after the battle. The battle itself was not 'martyrdom' for Serbian nobility but rather a very bloody draw. Slobodan Milosevic's 'Serbian sacrifice for Europe' that he used to justify his civil war was predicated on a medieval fantasy.

They then gave these young men to the Turks in the provinces so that they should learn Turkish, and then they sent them to Anatolia. After a few years they brought them to the *Porte* and made them Janissaries, giving them the name *Yeni Ceri*. Their origin goes back to this time.*

The next Sultan, Bayezid *Yildiran*, or Thunderbolt, brought the Ottomans up to the Mamluk borders by a series of lightning campaigns worthy of his name. By 1400 he had brought Anatolia's western and central lands under him. A distant outpost of the Mamluk Sultanate in the far north of Syria, Malatya, was demanded by Bayezid from Sultan Barkuk in 1399. To Bayezid's mind this had more to do with consolidating his position against the Ak-Koyunlu, a Turcoman tribal confederacy that had taken hold of lands in northern Iraq and northwestern Iran following the collapse of the Ilkhanate than a direct attack on the Mamluks. Barkuk was both surprised and angered by the demand but died before he could take action, and the city fell to the Ottomans after a two-month siege during the period of political stasis that always attended the succession in the Sultanate. In Europe Bayezid and his Serbian allies had destroyed both the Wallachians in 1395 and the Crusade of Nicopolis in 1396. By 1402 he had brought Constantinople, by a process of encirclement on land and blockade on the seas, to such a condition that its surrender to him seemed unavoidable. Byzantium was saved and the clash between the Ottomans and the Mamluks was delayed by a violent storm from the East. Tamerlane, the Scourge of God, had arrived in the Middle East.

Tamerlane was from the eastern half of what had been the Chagatay Khanate, but his army was Turco-Mongolian and he spoke Turkish. He was Muslim and claimed the heritage of the Khans through marriage to a princess of the Genghisid line. In the power vacuum that was central Asia after the collapse of the Yuan Dynasty, Ilkhanate and Chagatay Khanate, he quickly gathered a large confederate army around him. He started out

---

* Anonymous Ottoman chronicle, in Lewis, pp. 226–7. The *Porte* was the Sultan's mobile headquarters.

as a mercenary but before long his extraordinary generalship allowed him to begin conquest in his own name. It was fortunate for the Mamluks and the Ottomans that, whilst Tamerlane saw himself as a new Genghis Khan, he and his descendants did not have the administrative ability of either Genghis or Qubilai Khan; the empire he carved out was therefore somewhat ramshackle and he spent a lot of time re-conquering lands that had already been subdued once.

Tamerlane's first contact with the Mamluks had been in 1393 when he had campaigned in west Asia against the successor states to the Ilkhanate and against the Golden Horde. Sultan Barkuk had given refuge to Sultan Ahmed of Baghdad and even sent him back with an army to retake his city once Tamerlane had withdrawn the majority of his forces. Barkuk had also reconfirmed the historical Golden Horde–Mamluk pact as a mutual defence plan against Tamerlane and executed Tamerlane's emissaries. Unfortunately for the Sultan, the Horde was decisively beaten by Tamerlane in a three-day battle near the modern city of Grozny just north of the Caucasus Mountains in April 1395. Tamerlane therefore had his *casus belli*, but Egypt's wealth, the need to deal with the quickly expanding Ottomans and the fact that the Mamluks once again had a child on the throne and their emirs wrestling for power behind it were additional inducements for a campaign in the Middle East in 1399, despite the fact that he had only just completed a bloody one-year campaign in India.

Bayezid sent to the Mamluks seeking an alliance against Tamerlane but the senior emirs responded, 'now he's become our friend. When our master Barkuk died he invaded our country and took Malatya. He's no friend of ours. Let him fight for his country, and we'll fight for ours.'* Tamerlane moved first against the Ottomans. He besieged Sivas, the gateway to Anatolia, in August 1400. The three-thousand-strong garrison surrendered after three weeks under terms that their blood would not be spilt and Tamerlane was true to his word – they

---

* In P. Holt, *The Age of the Crusades: The Near East from the Eleventh Century to 1517*, London: Longman, 1986, p. 179.

were buried alive. There was no Ottoman response to Sivas's fall and the Mamluks were paralysed by internal wrangling, but the slaughter visited upon Sivas should have been a forewarning to both of what Tamerlane was to commit in their lands. His letter to al-Nasir Faraj, the boy Sultan, confirmed his intent:

> The Sultan your father committed many odious crimes against us, among them the murder of our ambassadors without cause ... Since your father has surrendered his life to God, the punishment of his crimes must be brought before the divine tribunal. As for you, you have got to consider your own survival and that of your subjects ... lest our furious soldiers fall upon the people of Egypt and Syria in a cruel slaughter, burning and pillaging their properties. If you are so stubborn as to reject this advice, you will be responsible both for spilling Muslim blood and for the total loss of your kingdom.*

The emirs chose to dismiss the letter and the governor of Damascus cut Tamerlane's emissary in half. Their response was, in hindsight, reckless but at this time, despite its decay, the Mamluk army was still considered to be the best in the Middle East, Syria's fortified cities had withstood Eastern armies in the past and Tamerlane's troops had undertaken almost continuous marches and battles in India, Georgia and Anatolia in the last year; exhaustion of morale and logistics was to be expected. They came to the conclusion that Tamerlane would not be able to campaign in Syria long enough to bring down the fortified cities and could be made to withdraw by threat of the Egyptian army. Still, their decision not to mobilise the Egyptian army at once would be inexplicable if it was not for their obvious fear of plots evolving in Cairo once they had left. Tamerlane swept into Syria and halted before Aleppo in October 1400. The Syrian Mamluk armies of Damascus, Antioch, Homs and Hama had mustered inside Aleppo's walls under the command of the Aleppan emir Timurtash. There was division among the leaders of the army, with one group calling for negotiation with Tamerlane. This was opposed but there were also disputes among the hawks: some

---

* In J. Marozzi, *Tamerlane, Sword of Islam, Conqueror of the World,* London: HarperCollins, 2004, pp. 291–2.

called for immediate all out attack, they are given this speech by Tamerlane's biographer: 'If you are afraid of their warriors and are perturbed at the multitude of their arms and armour then praise be to God, there is a difference between them and us. Our bows are Damascene, our swords Egyptian, our spears Arabian, our shields Aleppan . . .'*

A more cautious approach of simply outlasting the siege was proposed by some of the Mongol Mamluks. 'We are better informed about these people, and we know them well, and we know where this will end. Do not hasten to battle. Do not regard this as a small matter.'† Their advice was ignored in the end because they were seen as suspect by the Circassians and because Tamerlane drew the Mamluk army out to fight by doing everything he could to make it appear that his army was not going to press the siege. His men dug trenches around his camp and erected ox-hide shields and screens as if they were the besieged and not the besiegers. Seeing this, the Mamluks also made camp outside the city and prepared to drive the invader off.

Tamerlane then started sending sizeable reconnoitring parties to harass the Mamluks and to draw them into a full confrontation. At the end of October the Mamluks assembled for battle. Damascene Mamluks under the emir Sudun made up the right wing while Timurtash's Aleppans formed the left. Local infantry were placed in the centre and a folding-in of each wing leading to encirclement of Tamerlane's army was probably planned. Tamerlane's army formed up with his right wing under his son Shah Rukh whilst the left was under the command of two of his grandsons. His armoured elephants, souvenirs of his destruction of Delhi, were under his direct control on the extreme right of his line and he held a reserve of cavalry to his rear atop a small hill.

Tamerlane's right wing moved forward first to engage the Mamluk left. It held but when the elephants were unleashed against them the Mamluks of Aleppo broke and fled. They ran

---

* Nizam al-Din Shami, in Lewis, pp. 104–9.

† Nizam al-Din Shami, in Lewis, pp. 104–9.

for Aleppo's walls and their flight sent the entire army into panic. The army of Damascus disintegrated and fled south. Tamerlane's biographer tells us that, 'The victorious army pursued and attacked at full gallop. They killed so many of their horsemen and footmen that heaps of dead arose, and the gates and streets of Aleppo were so crammed with corpses that the horsemen had to ride over the dead, and the horses and mules could only pass with difficulty.'*

Sudun and Timurtash holed up in the citadel as Sanjar had in 1300 in Damascus. Aleppo's citadel was an impressive fortification and could perhaps have denied Tamerlane as Damascus' citadel had denied Ghazan. Sailboats could be launched onto its moat, such was its size, and its earthworks were so steep that men could not walk up them. But Sanjar had confidently expected the Egyptian army to come to his relief whilst it had become obvious to the Aleppan Mamluks that there was no army marching from Cairo. Furthermore, whilst Ghazan's faith had restrained him from excess violence towards the Muslim Damascenes, the Muslim Tamerlane commenced a slaughter that would only end with the surrender of the citadel. His message to Timurtash read: 'If you wish to save your lives, it will go well with you. Otherwise you will be sacrificing yourselves, your wives, your children.'†

Timurtash and Sudun surrendered but Aleppo's fate was unchanged by their act; the slaughter continued. Women were raped within the Great Mosque and their children were put to the sword. Aleppo's streets were filled with the dead and then Tamerlane's men turned to looting. After four days there were twenty thousand heads in piles outside the city's walls. Aleppo, the city of Nur al-Din, hero of the *jihad* against the Crusaders, was a broken place of death and the road to Damascus was open to Tamerlane's advance. Hama, Homs, Beirut and Sidon all fell quickly and at last on 26 November the Sultan and his army left Cairo. Faraj's army arrived just south of Damascus in time to watch it being surrounded by Tamerlane's forces. The senior

---

* Nizam al-Din Shami, in Lewis, pp. 104–9.
† Nizam al-Din Shami, in Lewis, pp. 104–9.

emirs feared that they too might be encircled, so the Egyptian army left almost as soon as it had arrived. Faraj dispatched assassins to kill Tamerlane but they were caught and returned, *sans* ears and noses, to him. The forces in Damascus, upon seeing the Egyptian army, attacked Tamerlane's rearguard as his main army had moved away to better pastureland. All this pushed Tamerlane's fury even higher than its normal level of simple malevolence and he sent detachments after Faraj's army that managed to kill some of the Sultan's bodyguard.

Tamerlane talked peace with Damascus, however. Protracted negotiations ensued with the historian and philosopher Ibn Khaldun being winched down from the walls of the city to parley with Tamerlane before being given safe passage from Damascus in early 1401. The negotiations left Damascus open and Tamerlane placed guards at each gate to prevent his horde from sacking the city. Initially everything seemed calm but then Mamluks in the citadel revoked their surrender, sallied out of the fortress and slew a thousand of Tamerlane's men. For twenty-nine days Tamerlane set his siege engines and sappers against the walls of the citadel. Only forty Mamluks survived the bombardment and hobbled out to surrender; the Mamluk governor was beheaded, and in final retribution Tamerlane decided to destroy Damascus. To the rape and murder that Aleppo had endured torture was added. Men were cemented into walls, crushed in olive presses, set ablaze or suspended over fires, buried alive only to be dug up again and have the process repeated, and dismembered by the pulling of horses. The Great Mosque was set on fire after it had been filled with civilians. Only a blackened shell filled with orphans remained of what had been the greatest city in Syria as Tamerlane retired. There was panic on the streets of Cairo when the news from Damascus was received but Tamerlane was not coming to Egypt to murder and sack. The army he had dispatched to Baghdad was not meeting with success, but what was more important was that while the Mamluks had been cowed the Ottomans were still there, to his north. He therefore turned north to better pastureland from where he could watch Bayezid and prepare himself for a march on Baghdad.

Baghdad was surrounded by 120 towers of skulls and its river, the Tigris, was red and bloated with corpses when Tamerlane had finished with it in the summer of 1401. He then moved slowly west to challenge Bayezid. The Mamluks, meanwhile, had re-established themselves in the wrecked cities of Syria and were spectators to the greatest battle that Tamerlane had yet fought. He met the Ottomans at Ankara on 28 July 1402. A massive defection from Bayezid's army of his Tatar levies to his opponent sealed the Sultan's fate; he was captured by Tamerlane and his army was destroyed. It looked like the end for the Ottomans but they were saved by Tamerlane's desire to emulate Genghis Khan the World Conqueror. By the spring of 1403 he was already recrossing Anatolia, moving towards Samarqand and from thence to begin his conquest of China. He died on his way to challenge the Ming Emperor in 1405. He had set up a motley assortment of petty principalities in Anatolia before leaving. His control of the area was very loose and all he really expected of his vassals was tribute. Under such a shaky settlement one of the now dead Bayezid's sons Mehmed was able to raise enough men from the remains of the Ottoman army to defeat his brothers in a civil war without interference from Tamerlane's vassals and he was still able to rely on the support of his Serbian vassals against attacks by Byzantium, Wallachia and Venice. By 1417 the phoenix-like Ottomans were at least the par of any power in Anatolia and in the Balkans. By 1421 reconquest had begun and the Empire of Tamerlane was already in decline.

The Mamluk decline was actually worsened by the re-occupation of Syria as it widened the scope for political dissent within the Sultanate, and reconstruction drained the treasury. The new governor of Damascus, Shaykh al-Mahmudi, one of Barkuk's old guard, welcomed political refugees from Cairo who were fleeing the continuing fighting around the throne of Faraj. The most important emir to find refuge with Shaykh was Yashbeg, a tutor to the young Sultan, who for a brief time had been the power behind the throne. The governor of Aleppo, Jakam, joined these two in a revolt in May 1405, but after heavy fighting around the Cairo citadel the two Syrian magnates fled to Safad and Aleppo whilst Yashbeg went into hiding in the capital. He was reconciled with the Sultan but then Faraj abruptly abdicated after indulging in the luxury of one last wild drinking binge and then going into hiding in September 1405. The great magnates were unfazed and they simply replaced him with his half-brother, but by November Faraj had sobered up and shaped up. Yashbeg worked inside the city to garner support for his return, which in the end was unopposed and almost triumphal. The faction of his half-brother, al-Mansur, fled from the city and the little ex-Sultan was sent to Alexandria where he died soon after amid rumours of poison.

Faraj's second reign can be summed up in one word, Syria. He campaigned five times in the province, not against outsiders, but against Mamluk rebels. Jakam declared himself Sultan in Aleppo with Shaykh's support, and in 1407 Yashbeg – of all people – joined Shaykh and together they captured Damascus. Yashbeg was killed in battle at Baalbak in September of the same year but Shaykh escaped from the battlefield. Faraj seemed to be getting some success but it was like fighting a Hydra, the body of which was Barkuk's Mamluks. In January 1411 the previously loyal governor of Damascus rebelled and joined with Shaykh to raid Cairo while Faraj was occupied in Syria with another rebellious emir. Tired with hacking at the heads, Faraj was finally driven to assaulting the beast's body; he purged Barkuk's Mamluks in Egypt, but this just stiffened resistance to him in Syria and eroded what support he had in Cairo. Faraj was trapped with an expeditionary force inside Damascus in March 1412 after being attacked en route to the Syrian capital. Shaykh, again the head of the rebellion, negotiated the Sultan's surrender on 23 May. Faraj was put on trial by the emirs and, to give the trial a gloss of legitimacy, they also put *sharia* jurists on the panel. The plan nearly backfired as the religious judges were unwilling to condemn Faraj but then Shaykh produced his secret weapon. He had captured the Caliph, al-Musta'in, along with the Sultan and had pressured him to accept the throne of Sultan. The Caliph as the – at least theoretical – head of the Sunni world was able to influence the jurists and Faraj was condemned to death. The Caliph's tragedy was not perhaps as acute as that of Faraj, but he aroused the sympathies of Ibn Taghribirdi. 'The Caliph became homesick for his kinsmen in the vast palaces of the Citadel; he was uneasy at the lack of visitors. In vain did he regret the position into which he had entered. To speak of his regret would not bring emirs or anyone else to his aid, so he kept silence about his distress.'*

He didn't have to endure the loneliness for too long, he entered Cairo as its Sultan and Caliph in July 1412 but by November he was only Caliph as Shaykh took the throne. Al-Musta'in died soon after and the Islamic world would have to wait for the Ottomans to conquer Egypt for the Caliph-Sultan to become a standard convention and political convenience for the Ottoman rulers. In March 1414 Shaykh acted against the Syrian emirs who had brought him to power. Their leader, Nawruz, was acting like an independent ruler in Damascus and Shaykh had to bring the entire Egyptian army into Syria in order to defeat him. After four months and a heavy toll of casualties on both sides he finally managed to surround the remnants of Nawruz's forces in Damascus. Shaykh offered an amnesty to Nawruz and a legally binding written oath was produced to this effect. Nawruz had his jurists look over the document but evidently their skills were somewhat lacking as the Arabic text had been written so badly, deliberately so, that it was in effect worthless. Shaykh had Nawruz and his supporters executed the very moment they stepped outside the city walls. It required another expedition the next year to make Syria finally accept its new Sultan and then Shaykh was ready to retake lands lost to the petty states set up by Tamerlane before his retirement from the region. He set out in March 1417; Tarsus was conquered after a brief siege and Abulustayn was also sacked. The Sultan returned to Cairo in the winter, having brought most of southwest Anatolia under control. Karaman, the early rival of the Ottomans, had had its wings clipped and the Dulkadarids to their east had been made a vassal state. Shaykhs's son, al-Sarimi, campaigned successfully in 1419 and reached Qayseri, the Karaman capital, but Shaykh's plans for building a dynasty,

---

*   In Holt, *The Age of the Crusades*, p. 182.

the thwarted dream of every Mamluk Sultan, began to unravel when al-Sarimi died in June 1420 and the Sultan himself became a sick man. He hurried to get the senior emirs to swear the *baya* oath of allegiance to his one-year-old son Ahmad before his death but it wasn't enough to prevent a coup forming among the magnates even before Shaykh's body had been interred. Shaykh died on 14 January 1421 and by August 1421 Ahmad had been removed from power and the emir Tatar took the throne. Tatar's reign was ironically even shorter than that of the boy Ahmad's, and his ten-year-old son and anointed successor, al-Salih, was deposed by a junta just as Ahmad had been on 14 March 1422. Al-Salih's main supporter and *atabeg* had been Janibek. He was thrown into jail by the junta but escaped to cause mischief later.

Barsbay al-Zahiri was the chosen Sultan of the military clique that had ended the Tatar dynasty before it really got started, and in their choice of ruler they did the Mamluk military state an enormous service. Over his reign of sixteen years he reversed the fortunes of the Sultanate to a sizeable degree and achieved what had been denied to every Sultan before him – substantial victories at sea. Frankish pirates sailing out of Cyprus had been raiding Egypt's commercial shipping and in June 1424, after he had finished dealing with a series of small revolts in Syria, Barsbay sent Egyptian and Syrian galleys against Cyprus. The raids were small but successful and the ships returned with both prisoners and bounty from Limassol. Barsbay started constructing more warships, employing the new technology of cannons on each vessel, and planning more raids on Limassol to fund the work. He may have benefited from reading the only known *Furusiyya* text on naval warfare written by Ibn Mangli al-Qahiri in the reign of Shaban, which gave extensive advice on tactics, armament of vessels and useful advice for the individual fighting at sea.

The Genoese governor of Cyprus's eastern port, Famagusta, offered assistance to Barsbay and Mamluk galleys sailed there in the summer of 1425. Detachments of cavalry were disembarked and the fleet then sailed westwards along the south coast while the mounted units raided inland. The fleet of Limassol was engaged twice and there was also heavy fighting on the island itself. The Mamluks withdrew before King Janus and his field army could enter the fray. Barsbay attacked the island again in the summer of 1426, the fleet heading straight for Limassol and taking its citadel on 3 July. The Mamluks then marched on Nicosia, King Janus's capital, but the King surprised them while they were stretched out and marching in a long column. Many of them had taken off their armour because of the heat and none of them was really prepared for battle, furthermore, they were seriously outnumbered, especially in the first battle where only seventy Mamluks faced almost all the Latin troops of Cyprus. Defeat seemed the most likely outcome but then it was as if the Mamluks suddenly remembered that they were Islam's greatest warriors. In the van there was a detachment of Royal Mamluks and they charged the Cypriot army shouting, 'So are the spoils of war!' The Cypriots flew into disorder at the first charge, but such was the size of their army that that King Janus was able to hold his ground and steady his troops. Then more and more detachments of Mamluks arrived on the field and added their assaults to the seventy's initial attack. The Cypriots reeled under the onslaught and started to fold and desert the field. King Janus was captured and the Mamluks pursued his defeated troops into Limassol itself where they looted his palace. It was like the return of the Bahri years of *jihad* in Cairo. King Janus was exhibited to the populace during a victory parade through the city and then humbled before the Sultan. He was only allowed to return to Cyprus after the payment of a heavy ransom and after undertaking that he and all his successors would remain the vassals of the Mamluk Sultans in perpetuity.

In 1427 a delegation came from Rhodes to pay homage to Barsbay; the war unleashed on Cyprus had frightened its leaders into seeking assurances that they would not be next. An ongoing general theme of the period following the Crusades was Western superiority at sea, so at first glance the freedom of action that Barsbay's small navy enjoyed against Cyprus seems surprising, but Venice, the possessor of the most powerful Latin navy, and Byzantium, a reduced but still-potent naval force, were both caught up in their struggle with the Ottomans who were threatening Venetian interests in Greece and had been besieging Constantinople again in 1423.

Barsbay next turned his attention to Arabia where politics and religion were being mixed together by Shah Rukh, Tamerlane's successor. Mecca and Medina had been under Mamluk protection since 1269 but now Shah Rukh was attempting to usurp the protectorate by offering to send a new *kiswa*, the protective cloth covering of the *Ka'ba*, to replace that of the Mamluks. Then he offered Barsbay the governorship of Egypt under his suzerainty, as he had granted governorships to the Ottomans and other rulers in Anatolia and the Jazira, despite the fact that his own lands were actually east of Baghdad and Tabriz and direct interference in the politics of the Levant would in fact have been very difficult for him – his empire was not as it had been under his father. Barsbay was so enraged by the insult of Shah Rukh's 'offer' that he had his emissary horse-whipped and nearly drowned in a pond after tearing the governor's robe that Shah Rukh had sent into tiny pieces. Barsbay also realised, once he'd calmed down, that the propaganda value of being the keeper of the Holy Places was also at stake, he could not let it slide into Shah Rukh's hands. He sent a military expedition down to Mecca to ensure the local leaders knew who was really in charge. The expedition also opened Jedda, the port of Mecca, to a larger volume of trade, thereby bypassing Yemen for Indian and Chinese ships and increasing the Sultanate's customs revenues.

In 1432 Barsbay installed John II, the son of Janus, on the throne of Cyprus after the old King's death. He was at the height of his power, but a face from the past now returned to make trouble for him almost until his dying day. Janibek resurfaced in Anatolia in 1435 and in many ways in he focused Barsbay's attentions on the wider problems of the Sultanate's northern border. In the post-Tamerlane period the Turcoman tribal confederations of the Sunni Kara-Koyunlu, or Black Sheep Tribe had settled in Azerbaijan and Iraq while the Shia Ak-Koyunlu, the White Sheep Tribe had moved into the Jazira. To the west of the Ak-Koyunlu lay the two Turkish states of Dulkadir and

Karaman, both of which were under pressure again from the revitalised Ottomans. Janibek first sought the assistance of the Ak-Koyunlu but this enterprise was cut short as his supporters were diverted by a war with the Kara-Koyunlu. He went on to besiege Malatya, the Mamluk border city, but failed again and was imprisoned by a petty Prince of Abulustayn. Barsbay's emissary demanded the prisoner's death but he was ignored; it is certain that Shah Rukh was pulling the political strings in Anatolia at this time and that he wanted to keep the troublemaker at liberty. Barsbay therefore sent off an expedition to Anatolia in July 1436 and Abulustayn was reduced to full vassalage but the renegade Janibek again escaped capture. It took betrayal by princes of the Ak-Koyunlu to finally deliver the fugitive's head to Cairo in October 1437, where the Sultan viewed it safe in the knowledge that he had outlived his tormenter. Perhaps it softened death's sting; Barsbay died on 7 June 1438 and his son al-Aziz Yusuf, to whom he made the senior emirs swear the *baya* to on his deathbed, succeeded him.

It was the usual short reign of a son. A senior Mamluk in his late fifties, Chakmak, usurped the throne in September. The single achievement of his reign was to stay in power and to die of old age in February 1453. His reign, his three naval expeditions against Rhodes, all of which failed and his death, the phenomenally brief reign of his son, al-Mansur, and the usurpation of the throne by the septuagenarian al-Ashraf Inal were all overshadowed by events in the north. The Ottomans had destroyed a mighty Crusading army at Varna in 1444 and the Transylvanian Crusade of John Hunyadi at the second Battle of Kosovo in 1448. In 1453 Constantinople fell to Mehmed II under a shower of heavy artillery; one particular cannon was capable of firing a stone of over one thousand kilograms and had needed sixty oxen and two hundred men to pull it to the siege. Attempts had been made by the Muslims ever since the seventh century to take Constantinople and now the Ottomans had done it. On the streets of Cairo people must have asked what the Mamluks could do to match them.

11

Riding with the Ghosts of the Past

The Dynasty Falls

Anything in which a man passes his time is in vain except for shooting with his bow, training his horse, or dallying with his wife. These three things are right. He who abandons archery after having learnt it is ungrateful to the one who taught him.

Attributed to the Prophet Muhammad

A L-Ashraf Inal's reign was not one of note excepting that the support of the Mamluks enabled the bastard son of John II of Cyprus to usurp the throne against the claim of his half-sister. By giving their support the Mamluks ensured the continuance of tribute from the island even after it fell under Venetian control through James's marriage to a Venetian noblewomen and then later death. This was fortunate in the extreme as soon enough the Sultanate would need every penny it could get. The fall of Constantinople to Mehmed's big guns had sparked an artillery arms race in the Middle East and the Mamluks were poorly positioned to win it.

Inal died in February 1461 and his son al-Mu'ayyad Ahmad succeeded him for a grand total of four months when Khushqadam, one of Shaykh's old Mamluks, seized the throne and brought the Sultanate back into the hands of the household of the first Circassian Sultan, Barkuk. But of course this was just one of the now many households of Mamluks still in existence in the state. We have seen how many of the Sultans had reached ages well beyond the medieval average for soldiers – Kalavun was nearly seventy when he died after many years of hard campaigning and Chakmak and al-Ashraf Inal both reigned in their seventies. The plague still exacted a heavy toll on the Mamluks but generally only on the new arrivals, so another problem with the state was that there were now too many veterans, still politically active if not so militarily, and all expecting a cut of the state's revenue. These veterans were quite easily persuaded to undertake coups and indulge in corruption to support grandiose lifestyles and to support what were by now large extended families. Children of Mamluks were in theory forbidden to inherit the offices of their fathers but a *waqf* or endowment for religious and charitable purposes could be made by a Mamluk, and his executors – who were, of course, his children – managed the endowment and thereby ensured their own livelihoods. This is not to suggest that the essential idea of *waqf* was corrupt. Some of the most wonderful religious monuments in Cairo were erected as a result of Mamluk endowments and any number of *maristans* or hospitals owed their origin and maintenance to the *waqf* of Sultans and great emirs. The problem was that an emir had to amass wealth in his lifetime in order to divest these riches upon his death and that required moneymaking to be placed over and above his military role. The *maydans* were empty and crumbling and training was neglected. The reflections of Ibn Khaldun written down in the late fourteenth century show how the Mamluks were perceived even after the decline that took place during and after the reign of al-Nasir:

> From this Turkish nation and from among its great and numerous tribes, rulers to defend them and utterly loyal helpers, who were brought from the House of War to the House of Islam under the rule of slavery, which hides in itself a divine blessing. By means of slavery they learn glory and blessing and are exposed to divine providence; cured by slavery they enter the Muslim religion with the firm resolve of true believers yet with nomadic virtues unsullied by debased nature, unadulterated with the filth of pleasure, undefiled with the ways of civilised living and with their ardour unbroken by the profusion of luxury.*

* In Lewis, pp. 97–9.

By the middle of the fifteenth century the Mamluk military institution was in danger of becoming little more than a paralysed pageantry and, as if this was by now the only way to mark themselves out as the great cavalry warriors they were supposed to be, an edict denying the riding of horses to ordinary citizens was proclaimed in 1451. The corruption and disloyalty among the higher emirs inevitably affected the lower ranks and insubordination reached new heights unseen even in the pay riots and AWOL incidents of al-Nasir's reign. Killing and robbing of citizens was not uncommon; al-Ashraf Inal was stoned by his own Mamluks as he made a public sacrifice. Only two Sultans of this last period, Kayitbay and al-Ghawri, were able to do anything to pull the armed forces up from this nadir, and whilst some of their solutions harked back to tradition, others were innovative, iconoclastic and very much from outside the world of Mamlukdom.

So there were more and more Mamluks in their dotage at the top creaming off the state's surplus, but now there was no surplus. The plague had continued to ravage Egypt's peasants, grain was scarce for want of anyone to plant it and maintain the irrigation required, and the revenue from *iqtas* fell proportionately. The problems were compounded by monopolising of produce, corruption of coinage by the treasury and price fixing by the great emirs. Meanwhile, as the Ottomans had shown at Constantinople, warfare was becoming technologically more and more advanced and consequently more and more expensive. With this in mind and also the expense of the proper training of a Mamluk, it is not entirely surprising that the Mamluk army fell from being an elite force to being, at times, a second-rate army in the late fifteenth century. The fact that it was still able to inflict defeats on powerful foes was because this fall was being made from the heights of near-perfection achieved under the Bahris and that a relatively small elite army was less affected by reduced economic conditions than large conscript armies would have been.

Khushqadam managed, despite all the above problems, to have a relatively peaceful reign, although it is probable that he developed pneumonia from the continual wearing of armour, even in bed, to ward off assassination attempts, and died of it in October 1467. Khushqadam had been a Greek, he was followed by Yalbay, a compromise candidate from among the Circassians, whose wrangling continued even after his coronation. Yalbay made two mistakes: he failed to pay his Praetorians the accession bonus that had by now become expected and he had 120 Bedouin rebels hung drawn and quartered, immediately firing the Bedouin into further revolts. The Sultan was blamed for these revolts and was pushed aside for another 'outsider' – the Albanian Temurboga. Yalbay was imprisoned in Alexandria and died of plague there. The new Sultan lasted less than two months and thereby broke the record for the shortest tenure of power for a Mamluk Sultan by one day. He appeared happy to be handing on what seemed to be a poisoned chalice to the emir Kayitbay.

Kayitbay had been twenty years old when he entered the Sultanate as a Mamluk, he became a lancing instructor in the *tibaq* and later a palace guard under the Sultan Barsbay. He had been a *khassaki* of Sultan Chakmak and under Khushqadam had been created emir of one hundred; he had held the ceremonial parasol over Temurboga's head during his coronation and in all this time he had never shown any political ambitions or been involved in any of the endless intrigues that were the bread and butter of higher Mamluk government. His reputation was of a man who held to the ideal of *khushdashiyya* and kept a friendship, he was also married to a daughter of the Sultan Inal and had the support of the Inaliya Mamluks. He was to guide the Mamluk Sultanate for nearly thirty years, a mature Sultan again, he was fifty-four when he ascended the throne and over eighty when he died. He is said to have refused the throne several times before finally accepting, but Ibn Taghribirdi, a contemporary, wrote that Kayitbay casting the Sultan's turban away again and again and being pressed by his colleagues to take the throne was a performance between him and his *khushdash* Yashbeg, who, it seems, played Marc Anthony to his Caesar.

In the beginning Kayitbay's reign looked no more likely to last than had his predecessor's, but by a intuitive combination of showing loyalty to those who had brought him to power, extending calculated friendship to those whose loyalty might be gained and exiling those who were beyond the political pale he managed to secure himself reasonably quickly and accrue revenue from the appropriation of dissidents' funds. He was temperate but could, as in the words of Ibn Taghribirdi, 'emit thunder and lightning' when required. He was also the first Sultan to ride unescorted around Cairo since Khushqadam.

Kayitbay first turned his attentions to the Bedouin of Egypt. Mamluk control had become so tenuous in the Nile Delta that tribesmen had actually looted shops in Cairo's suburbs before a detachment of Mamluks was organised to repel them and then carry out retaliatory actions. Punitive actions on a grand scale were used against the Bedouin of Upper Egypt but Mamluk atrocities acted more as vengeance than as any real deterrent to revolt. Arab women and children were sold as slaves despite *sharia* law prohibitions on the selling of Muslims and ringleaders were roasted, flayed and buried alive or simply impaled. Kayitbay's instrument for these crimes was Yashbeg, his friend, but a man of a totally dissimilar character to the refined, pious and charitable Sultan whose spiritual purity was as important to the chroniclers of the time as was his military success.* Such was the level of Mamluk malevolence that the revolts died away in the short term but the problem was never really resolved. Indeed, when Yashbeg repeated the exercise in Syria it brought the Bedouin out in revolt and in support of the retired Sultan Temurboga. Temurboga was easily captured and re-retired, presumably in a more secure rest-home, but there were worse dangers beyond Syria already erupting.

The old lands of Armenia had long been under vassalage of the Mamluks but in 1468 a Turcoman, Shah Suwar, renounced the ties to Egypt and began to gather around him Turcomen

---

* It must be remembered that most Islamic historians of the Middle Ages were religious scholars. Their general attitude to warfare was that God, being all powerful, gave victory rather than the actions of men. This explains why they are so weak on military matters and so appreciative of pious rulers such as Kayitbay.

who had either had enough of Mamluk rule or who had been displaced by the push east of the Ottomans, the other centralised state to their west. An expedition left Cairo on 7 March under the *atabeg* Qulaqsiz to put the upstart down. As the Sultans of this period had been fairly uniformly middle-aged or old, the *atabeg* was by this time basically a field marshall exercising the full powers of the Sultan in the field.

Suwar had moved down into the hinterlands of Syria and the forces met at the city of 'Ayntab. Suwar was displaced and retreated, but the fighting was fierce and it seems that Suwar was enjoying support from the Ottomans who were attacking the Karaman to Suwar's west and were happy to have a belligerent force to their foe's east. Then on 14 June Kayitbay received news of a disaster, Suwar had retaken Ayntab and when the Egyptian expeditionary force had gone out from Aleppo to meet him it had been ambushed on the way, Suwar had captured the army's scouts and left it blind before attacking it with a cavalry force. The Mamluks had had superiority in numbers and had nearly turned the battle three times but in the end the *atabeg* had surrendered himself and many other senior officers for ransom. Those emirs who had refused to bow before Suwar were executed. One senior emir, Uzbek min-Tutukh, escaped the field with a small force and reached Aleppo.

Kayitbay was dumbfounded, a large force led by seasoned officers had been destroyed by a minor ruler with a small army of bandits and nomads; it was at this point that he showed his true character. Kayitbay was never to be a great military strategist or a genius of the battlefield but he was able to imbue his subordinates with confidence and had the capacity for facing daunting circumstances and for maintaining the morale of the army and state found in all great war leaders. He called on every man to come to the protection of Syria, Yashbeg promised to pay bonuses for all the officers out of his own purse and the ransom demands of Suwar were refused. A rapid response force of five hundred Mamluks was to be sent to Syria immediately to restore confidence and prevent raids by Suwar and was then to be followed by a larger force. Retired Mamluks had to be called up, horses and mules were forcibly appropriated from the populace and emergency taxes were levied. Kayitbay had to call the army to review several times before he could get enough troops for the two detachments.

The 'flying force' did not set out until 24 October and by then Suwar had taken the fortress of Daranda on the Euphrates and the populace of northern Syria were looking pleased to accept him over their Mamluk lords. One of the keys to the Mamluk recovery in Syria following Ghazan's invasion of 1300 and Tamerlane's in 1402 had been the loyalty, however begrudging, of the Syrian peasants, now that looked to be slipping away too as a result of years of rapacious taxation and corruption.

Uzbek min-Tutukh was made joint commander of the second force and took the title of *atabeg*. The chronicles record Uzbek as being without ambition and a solid friend to Kayitbay throughout his reign, although it is notable that during Kayitbay's difficulties in raising the second part of his expedition against Suwar both Uzbek and the other army commander Kurkumas refused to serve without up-front bonuses of the kind that Baybars would only have paid to emirs after success. The second force set out in February 1469 amid good news of famine and desertions among Suwar's army and reached Aleppo within the month. Uzbek and Kurkumas pushed into Suwar's territory and began to burn and loot his towns and fields. Suwar therefore had to submit to an engagement and in a brief cavalry battle his forces were routed and his brother was killed. The brother's head was sent to Cairo and the Mamluks chased Suwar all the way to the Ottoman border. They thought they had him trapped in a narrow gorge and there was an argument among the senior officers whether to pursue him into the ravine or not.

When Kurkumas forced the issue half the army deserted and set off back to Aleppo. Such disobedience would have been unimaginable in earlier years but perhaps Kurkumas couldn't lead as the emirs of old had. Certainly, his decision to enter the ravine without reconnoitring it first wouldn't have inspired confidence and it led to a second disaster for the Mamluks against Suwar. Uzbek, in a letter to Yashbeg, tried to excuse himself for his part in the catastrophe that led to the death of Kurkumas. A good part of the force had been crushed under boulders rolled down from the tops of the ravine by Suwar's men and their subsequent attack on the Mamluks caused a panicked retreat of the survivors from the gulch. Uzbek explained, 'I had admonished the army not to proceed via the narrow gulch, but they did not agree with me. When we reached al-Durband, the Turcomen accompanying Suwar accosted us. An uncounted number of them were killed. But the affair ended badly when they slashed the tendons of camels and mules, thus preventing any Mamluk from egress.'*

The Mamluk army broke into a mob upon its return to Aleppo, there had been no pay for four months and the troops were hungry and mutinous. Kayitbay sent money but his emissary was stoned by the troops, and things were looking bad for the Sultan by the end of the year. The Mamluk army was being exposed bit by bit, it seemed, as a paper tiger. But then fortune smiled on the Sultan. Suwar's army had been badly damaged by the campaign against him and had also been beaten off by the garrison of Malatya; there were rumours that he had been badly injured by an arrow shot at him by one of his own men and he was also being attacked by neighbouring tribes. Suwar released his hostages from the first campaign and sued for peace. It seemed that Kayitbay's determined approach had won the day, so Suwar's overtures were rejected. Yashbeg started to prepare an expedition, which left on 26 March 1470. He made a slow march up to Aleppo with his two thousand troopers. He used a flying column of cavalry to ride ahead and bring Suwar's forces into the open where his main force could meet them in pitched battle. The campaign had its problems; Suwar was a wily foe and at one point doubled back on himself to raid Malatya a second time, this time, however, he captured the garrison commander and gave him a slow death by impaling him on a tree, but by August Yashbeg had the upper hand and there was a decisive confrontation at the River Jayhan in November 1471.

---

* In C. Petry, *Twilight of Majesty: The Reigns of the Mamluk Sultans al-Ashraf Qaytbay and Kansawh al-Ghawri in Egypt,* Seattle: University of Washingon Press, 1993, p. 65.

Suwar's troops stood on one bank of the river and he threw insults at the Mamluks ranged against him on the other side. It was all designed to make them rush at his forces but Yashbeg held his officers on a tight rein. He knew that Suwar was unready for the engagement but had no choice but to meet the Mamluks who had been burning and looting his towns. His army was hungry and on the point of breaking up and only a swift victory would hold it together. Yashbeg sent scouts out to make contact with the Turcoman bands that made up Suwar's army and soon enough they were deserting him for the Mamluks. Suwar escaped, however, and remained at large for months; eventually Yashbeg outraged many of his fellow emirs when he offered safe passage to Suwar but then had him swiftly incarcerated as a traitor. Suwar and all the male members of his family who could be found were taken to Cairo and paraded, naked and seated backwards on camels, through the streets before being hung, drawn and quartered. Their body parts were hung from the city's gates.

The campaign had been expensive and damaging to the kudos of the regime. Gibbon, in his *Decline and Fall of the Roman Empire*, wrote at length of the importance of the, 'terror of the Roman arms', and the dangers aroused by the disappearance of this façade of military superiority. Suwar had exposed gross failings in the Mamluk military machine and knowledge of such weakness could only encourage more trouble from both the Turcoman confederations and the Ottomans. Kayitbay had consequently to tread very carefully when tackling even the minor rulers of eastern Anatolia. Fortunately, he possessed great tact and discretion. This diplomacy was tested in 1473 by the contest to his north between Mehmed II, who since his conquest of Constantinople had been as relentless as Tamerlane in his campaigning, and Uzun Hasan, the leader of the Ak-Koyunlu.

Uzun Hasan's confederation had been growing in size, he now possessed a vast army and his dominion was pushing onto the Mamluks' northern borderlands in Syria and into Anatolia. Mehmed II, meanwhile, had been pushing east through Anatolia and whilst his army had struggled – to his fury – against the old enemy of the Ottomans, the Karaman, in 1468 he was now ready to meet Hasan's ambitions head on. Kayitbay had stood aside during the war of 1468, despite envoys from Karaman to his court asking for assistance. He was a new Sultan and hadn't yet fully quelled all the resistance to his reign either within the Mamluk government or inside Egypt. Now in 1473 he had to think again about the Ottomans. They were dangerous foes and a defeat at the hands of the Ak-Koyunlu would certainly restrain Mehmed II from interfering in the marches between Anatolia and northern Syria, but in November 1472 Hasan had crossed the Euphrates with a large army and taken Malatya from Kayitbay. Kayitbay's faithful lieutenant Yashbeg was given the task of dislodging Hasan, which he carried out with aplomb, finally driving him back over the Euphrates in April 1473.

The same month saw an Ottoman diplomatic mission to Yashbeg in Syria offering assistance in the war against the Ak-Koyunlu. Ibn Iyas records that the mission came, 'bearing copious gifts and letters, so that friendship should be established between the Ottoman and Mamluk Sultans, on account of Uzun Hasan'. Also at this time an Ottoman embassy to Kayitbay's court in Cairo showed the Sultan captured letters from Hasan to the Pope and the Doge of Venice proposing that they should assault the Ottoman and Mamluk Sultans by sea while Hasan attacked them by land. The Ottomans also reported to the Sultan that Uzun Hasan had been heard to proclaim himself as the new Tamerlane. This was quite enough to make Kayitbay give his word that the Mamluks would remain neutral in the conflict, so when the Ottoman army moved along the Euphrates to meet Uzun Hasan in battle they were met near Malatya by eleven of Kayitbay's ambassadors on camels and given further reassurance of Mamluk non-aggression. With their southern flank therefore secure, the Ottomans turned northeast to meet Hasan's army. When the head of Hasan's son, Prince Zeynel, arrived at Kayitbay's court as a gift from Mehmed II, he might have rejoiced at the fact that an extremely dangerous enemy of his kingdom had been dispatched without his having to deploy a single soldier against it. But that wasn't the full story of what was happening to the north of the Mamluk lands.

An officer of Hasan's army had cried out, 'Son of a whore, what an Ocean!' when he had first spied the Ottoman army and yet Ottoman chroniclers recorded that Mehmed II had been so worried about the size of Hasan's forces that he had called for extra prayers, fasts and religious observances to be carried out all over the empire before the battle, so the Ottoman force deployed must have been tremendously large.* In this period, the number of Royal Mamluks in the Sultanate had fallen from a high of twelve thousand under al-Nasir in the 1320s to under half that figure at the beginning of Kayitbay's reign. Kayitbay bought around eight thousand new men during his reign but the plague may as much as halved this replacement. Furthermore, despite his defeat on 11 August, Uzun Hasan was reported as being happy simply to have escaped the battlefield because, 'having never seen a battle with handguns and cannon he was helpless before the Ottomans'.† If Kayitbay didn't see the great Ottoman victory of 1473 as an omen of real danger to his realm, Mehmed II would have confirmed it for him by his later actions. Caffa, the Black Sea port of the Genoese, fell in 1475 to the Ottomans and Mengli Girey, the Khan of the Golden Horde, was reduced to Ottoman vassal status, with Mehmed going to war with the Circassian tribes on Girey's behalf in 1478. The ending of Genoese presence in the Circassian region and the reduction of the Golden Horde to service under Mehmed put the supply of Mamluks for Egypt from its preferred source at the very least in jeopardy and at the worst in the hands of a potential enemy at a time when the Sultan needed to reinvigorate the army.

By 1480 it was obvious that Mehmed's attentions were turning to the Mamluks. In June 1480 he attempted to take Rhodes from

---

* Uzun Hasan was perhaps the most dangerous foe that Mehmed ever had to face during his reign because, like Tamerlane, his confederation was the antithesis of the Ottoman centralised state and could attract disenfranchised Turcoman elements from the Ottomans. Mehmed's campaign could have ended as disastrously as Bayezid's 1402 campaign. However, it did not, because the Ottomans were by this juncture technologically far superior to their adversaries and the Sultan had ensured that his forces were loyal to him alone.
† Imber, p. 217.

the Knights of Saint John, whom he had accused of piracy against Muslim merchant shipping. What is very obvious, though, is that Rhodes lies opposite Alexandria and that its seizure was part of a larger strategy to first secure the sea passage from Constantinople to Egypt before making war on Egypt in 1481. The campaign failed against Rhodes's impressive citadel and the dogged resistance of the Knights, but Kayitbay had obviously read the signs. A letter of September 1480 from the leaders of Naples to the Duke of Ferrara states that 'the Sultan [Kayitbay] has sent to reassure the Grand Master of Rhodes, promising him every help and assistance against the Turk'.* At the end of April 1481 Mehmed II gathered all his Asian levies to Konya, later Ottoman chroniclers write that he 'was preparing to attack in person the Mamluk Sultan, who was at loggerheads with the lords of Aleppo and Damascus'. But it was in fact impossible to know where the Sultan wished to go. Not even his generals knew; Mehmed II was dying and even whilst doing so he wished to campaign. He died at Izmit in Anatolia on 3 May 1481.

No one in his lands mourned. His conquests and his wresting of over twenty different states from his enemies had required harsh levels of taxation and thirty years of almost continuous campaigning for his army. What he had left the Ottomans, though, was a very dangerous legacy for all their neighbours. The Mamluks of the thirteenth century had seen themselves as the champions of Islam, almost divinely ordained to defeat the Mongols and Crusaders, and Baybars and Kalavun had given them the leadership and military capability to do it. In the same way Mehmed II had left the Ottomans a great and growing imperial consciousness, especially through his conquest of Constantinople. And through his centralisation of the Ottoman State and regularisation of its army, his reordering of its financing, his expanding of the Janissary corps and investment in a powerful fleet, artillery both for the field and for sieges and in handguns, he had given them the means to realise the ambition of empire.

Kayitbay had spent the 1470s purging the Inaliya of any opposition to his reign and used the novel technique of

---

* Imber, p. 247.

putting disgraced emirs up for sale as if they were slaves in the market all over again, in order to complete their fall from power and raise revenue. He also toured the Sultanate to check its defences personally. Alexandria's defences were added to, a tacit admission of the superiority of the Ottomans at sea. Things were reasonably calm for a decade and Kayitbay started a reform of the military. In an attempt to make up for his dwindling manpower and for the cost of training Mamluks he formed an infantry unit, the *awlad al-nas*, from Nubians, Egyptian levies and sons of Mamluks. Knowing that it was impossible to make these men into effective archers he instead armed them with the primitive arquebuses available to him. Barsbay had obtained guns from European merchants as early as 1451 and, whilst the capabilities of the weapons were well below what could be achieved with a compound bow, fifteenth-century *Furusiyya* manuscripts still describe and illustrate the use of these new weapons. The Sultan was delighted when he received a shipload of more modern firearms from Ferdinand of Naples in 1482 and on the whole these were good years, but a great blow to the regime came in 1480 with the death of Yashbeg in what can only be called an adventure.

Yashbeg had been approached by the son of Uzun Hasan in June 1480 and told about the distracted condition of the Ak-Koyunlu since its defeat at the hands of the Ottomans back in 1473. Yashbeg was enticed into taking a force with him into the Jazira in an attempt to secure the leadership of the confederation for himself. He had the tacit agreement of Kayitbay for the venture as the Sultan was becoming more and more concerned over Yashbeg's ambition. Also, since Mehmed's victory of 1473, it had become obvious that the Mamluk defence policy in the marches of using buffer states recognising Mamluk suzerainty between themselves and the Ottomans had become compromised. Kayitbay gave him a force of five hundred Mamluks and had a political rival of Yashbeg's, Azdamar, killed for him before Yashbeg set out – a soothsayer had told Yashbeg that an Azdamar would murder him. The expedition ended abruptly and badly as soon as it crossed the Euphrates into Ak-Koyunlu territory. Yashbeg attempted to storm the walls of the frontier fortress, al-Ruha; the assault failed and the fortress's garrison then sallied forth and broke his forces and he was captured. The garrison commander sent a black slave into his cell to cut off the Mamluk's head. Just before he was decapitated Yashbeg asked his executioner's name. 'Azdamar', came the reply. Kayitbay was stunned by news of Yashbeg's death, he had been his closest ally and when Yashbeg had been at death's door from a fever in 1469 Kayitbay had attended to his care personally. He also had to send his remaining intimate, Uzbek, to Syria for fear of an Ak-Koyunlu invasion as a result of the tribes' seeing the head of the Sultan's most feared lieutenant paraded through their lands. They did in fact make an abortive attempt on Malatya but otherwise the border remained quiet.

Confrontation with the Ottomans in eastern Anatolia had been delayed by the death of Mehmed II and there were diplomatic initiatives from his son, the new Sultan Bayezid II, aimed at keeping the peace between the two Sultanates. Bayezid's problem was that his accession was disputed by a younger brother, Jem, who had gathered support from the Turcoman tribes still used as auxiliary forces in Anatolia by the Ottomans and then called for a share of the empire. Jem's forces were quickly defeated but he was not captured and remained a thorn in his brother's side for years to come. He fled from Bayezid to the Mamluk Sultanate in August 1481. Kayitbay received him, but without formality, in the courtyard of the Cairo citadel rather than the throne room. He also remained seated when Jem was presented and it was obvious that the Sultan was going to great lengths to ensure that his support for Bayezid would be heard of in Istanbul. Put simply, Kayitbay did not treat Jem as a Sultan because he wanted to avoid war with Bayezid at all costs. Jem was, however, given the freedom of the city and remained in Egypt for several months. When he came to Kayitbay with plans for the invasion of the Ottoman Empire in March 1482, however, there was no support forthcoming, indeed the senior emirs felt that he was building castles in the air such was the degree of unreality in his planning. He was allowed to leave the Sultanate but received no material support and was defeated by his brother a second time in August 1482, this time fleeing to the West, where he ended up being housed in the Vatican and being used by the Papacy and the Venetians as a check on his brother's European ambitions right up until his death in 1495.

It is certain that Kayitbay made a strategic error in not backing Jem: doing nothing was worse than doing something. Baybars had used dissident Mongols and displaced Kurds as well as the first Egyptian Caliph in ventures into Mongol lands just to upset 'normal business' for his foes. He understood that the Mongol aim was the reduction of Syria and that anything he could do to distract them from that endeavour was worthwhile, but Kayitbay misread totally the Ottoman strategic view. His policy attempted neutrality in the Jem affair but neutrality wasn't possible simply because the coming war between the Ottomans and the Mamluks wasn't about princes, it was about who would be dominant in eastern Anatolia and subsequently in the Middle East. The Ottomans saw themselves now as the heirs of all the Roman lands as they were now the successors to the Byzantine Empire and this of course, before the Arab invasions, had included Egypt and Syria. So Kayitbay should have been bolder and bloodier in the Jem affair but the Mamluk strategy and philosophy had always been, generally speaking, conservative in its approach to the defence of the realm. The exceptions to this had been Baybars's and Barsbay's campaigns of 1277 and the 1420s, neither of which aimed at permanent conquest. Their thirteenth-century Syrian coastal defence policy had encouraged this mindset, and by the fifteenth century the Mamluks were committed to preserving both an ideological and territorial heritage that only embraced Syria and Egypt with as little change as possible. Change meant risk and regimes that are in their senescence find change abhorrent. Late fifteenth-century Mamluk grand strategy was therefore effectively limited to holding to the borders and to only interfering in Anatolia enough to maintain what has been called a 'triple line defence'* against the invasion of Syria from the north. A

---

* S. Har-El, *Struggle for Domination in the Middle East. The Ottoman–Mamluk War 1485–91*, Leiden: EJ Brill, 1995, pp. 35–54.

key element of this was the geography of the area. The Taurus Mountains and the Euphrates were natural barriers limiting the freedom of approach of any invader, so control of the passes out of the mountains and of the fordable areas of the river was vital. Hence there was direct control and Mamluk garrisoning of Tarsus, Serfendikar, Ayas and Malatya. The next line was the vassalage of Turcoman principalities in Cilicia and in what had been Armenia, which controlled key areas of passage through the mountainous region. The third and outer part of this defence had been the friendly or at least anti-Ottoman state of Karaman, but this had been effectively destroyed by Mehmed II in 1470, leaving only a few pockets of Karaman resistance, the petty Turcoman lords of southeastern Anatolia and the Mamluk garrisons between the Ottomans and Syria proper.

As early as 1484 Bayezid started working to take the Mamluk defence plan apart with threats of invasion coupled with promises of protection – in a word, extortion – against the Turcoman lords of southeastern Anatolia. Bayezid had a free hand as Hungary was at war with the Habsburgs and a treaty had been formed with Venice. Kayitbay sent an embassy to Istanbul at the end of the year with gifts and suggestions of truce and cooperation between the two Sultanates, but Bayezid kept the mission waiting for his response and then in June 1485 Kayitbay received word via the *barid* that the Ottomans were moving on Sis and Tarsus. Uzbek was sent north with a scraped-together and reluctant army. More and more the Egyptian Mamluks were loath to leave Cairo and communications with the Syrian garrisons were impeded by Bedouin revolts. This said, the force comprised three thousand ageing Royal Mamluks and a large number of the *khassakiyya*. The presence of such an imposing force was enough to bring some of the wavering petty Anatolian lords back into the Mamluk camp and then in March 1486 amazing news of a great victory near Adana was brought to Cairo. The Ottomans lost forty thousand men on the field and the commander was captured along with numerous battle standards. Uzbek sent the heads of two hundred Ottoman officers back to Cairo to announce his triumph. An inscription in Cairo dedicated to Kayitbay tells the story:

He sent the Victorious Armies to the country of Rum to repel their armies and when the two armies met, the Victorious Armies attacked them like lions, encircling them without leaving them room to escape and putting them to flight like fearful donkeys. They captured the commander of the armies, Ibn Hersek and others and left the flesh of the dead prey to the hyenas, wolves, vultures and eagles. They brought the captives in chains and fetters, their banners are now laid inverted in the Royal Courtyard. Such a day has never been recorded in the history of former kings.*

A battle that was recorded by contemporary Western writers as the greatest defeat the House of Osman had ever suffered had been won, but the war went on, which was the problem of confrontation with the Ottomans. In the past the Mamluks' superior military abilities had defeated the Mongols even when outnumbered three to one because the Mongol state was badly managed and never developed either a viable war economy or a credible strategy to tackle the Mamluks in the long term. With the Ottomans it was different. The new foe was a centralised state with an effective trade and manufacturing base to finance belligerence and proper academies to train both Janissaries and an officer class. It was also populous in terms of the men who could be pressed into military service whilst the Mamluk army, by the very nature of its peculiar foundation, could not grow exponentially without massive investment in new *julban* or slave recruits. This expansion was required at a time when, as we have seen, the Sultanate's economy was in almost permanent crisis and the slave routes from the Black Sea region had been severely impeded by the Ottoman expansion under Mehmed II. Even with Kayitbay's new non-Mamluk arquebusier regiments and the employment of Bedouin cavalry the army couldn't match the manpower of the enemy; this battle of numbers was unwinnable and with the neglect of the *Furusiyya* exercises there could be no reliance on individual capability making up for lack of numbers. In fact, on the whole, it is surprising how long the Mamluk army did manage to resist the Ottomans.

---

* In Har-El, p. 133.

By January the Ottomans had replaced their losses with a fresh field army consisting of Christian troops from Europe who were exempted from the *jizya* for service in Anatolia and by April 1487 they had reoccupied Adana and the fortress of Ayas. The border garrisons of the Mamluks fell back to Aleppo. Their exposed positions had become untenable because the petty princes surrounding them had all turned, once again, to the Ottoman side. The *julban* who had been sent to Aleppo to make up for a paucity of forces rebelled over pay and many deserted, but the governor of Aleppo's veteran forces were enough of a threat to call a halt to the Ottoman advance and produce a temporary stalemate. This lasted until early 1488 when the Ottoman fleet appeared off the coast near the Mamluk fortress of Bab al-Malik. Bayezid was attempting to open a new front south of the Mamluk frontline fortresses of the Taurus Mountains and to block any opportunity for the Mamluks to transport troops by sea from Syria into Cilicia. Then a force comprised of three thousand heavy cavalry and six thousand Janissaries, with light cavalry, irregulars and Christian levies bringing its total up to about sixty thousand men pushed down through the petty principalities again, coming the same way that they had come the year before. Sis fell under a heavy artillery barrage, its garrison was captured and Cilicia was conquered by April 1488. Here the Ottomans stopped and began to fortify their positions. They knew the Mamluks would have to come through the narrow Syrian Gates in order to push them from Cilicia; they would be pummelled while doing so by fire from the Ottoman fleet.

This was the situation facing Uzbek in July 1488 as he brought an army north from Aleppo to challenge the Ottomans. An advance party made up of the troops of Hama was sent into the Syrian Gates first, along with Bedouin cavalry, but it was decimated by artillery fire from the Ottoman fleet and from fixed positions in the mountains above as it struggled through the narrow pass. Uzbek retired, but then on 9 August he decided to push his army through the pass. The situation was far from ideal as there was a river to cross, morale was low as the troopers looked ahead to see a pass being turned into a killing zone by the Ottoman artillery and retreat was not an option once he was committed to the move. He moved ahead, though, and he got lucky. A gale blew up in the bay and the Ottoman fleet was forced to head for deep water, several ships were wrecked and bedraggled survivors made it ashore only to be slain by jubilant Mamluk troopers. Morale was restored as the storm was attributed to divine anger with the Ottomans for bringing Christian troops into a Muslim war. Some twenty-five Ottoman vessels that had been anchored near the coast and chained together were stormed and captured by the Mamluks.

Uzbek moved on up the coast road into Cilicia and pushed on to Adana where the Ottomans came out to meet him on a plain two miles from the city. After consulting with his emirs Uzbek decided to attack at once as the Ottomans had arrived after the Mamluks on the field and were still disordered. A classic 'five' or *hamis* was taken up by Uzbek's forces – centre, right wing, left wing, vanguard and rear guard, with the Royal Mamluks in the centre and the Bedouin cavalry held in reserve. Damascenes made up the right wing and Aleppans the left. The Ottomans hastily pushed their heavy cavalry to their centre and covered their preparations with a line of Janissary archers and arquebusiers. Light skirmishers and archers sat ahead of the main Ottoman army. Uzbek similarly placed his arquebusiers in front of the Mamluk van. The Ottoman wings were formed on the right by the Anatolian and on the left by the European levies as well as forces of the petty Anatolian princes.

As the armies clashed, the Ottoman left wing advanced quickly and struck the Damascene Mamluks hard; Uzbek's right wing was failing under the assault of the Europeans and to his front the Janissaries were taking a heavy toll of the arquebusiers, but his Royal Mamluks were standing strongly against both the Janissaries and the Ottoman heavy cavalry. Then the governor of Damascus executed a superb piece of troop movement under intense pressure from the European levies. He could see that his men were about to give way and indeed were on the point of submitting so he led them quickly from the right, riding behind the entire Mamluk line to join the left wing where the Mamluks of Aleppo were beginning to make headway against the Anatolians of the Ottoman right wing. His move was daring and executed with such speed that it turned the battle. The Royal Mamluks under Uzbek, seeing what was required of them, manoeuvred to extend their line to their right to cover the Damascene withdrawal and to prevent the army from being outflanked. They were then not only able to hold the Europeans on their right side and the Janissaries to their front but also then to move forward as a whole into the gap that was growing between the Ottoman centre and right wing.

Under this triple assault the Ottoman right wing disintegrated into confusion and panic as the Anatolians began to flee the field. Meanwhile, the Europeans and Janissaries had managed to regroup to take advantage of the Royal Mamluks' left oblique and finally outflank them. They rushed around the rear of the Mamluk army and crashed into Uzbek's Bedouin rearguard, which fled before them. The battle had begun at noon and it was now late afternoon. The Royal Mamluks had continued a rapid advance, thereby outpacing the Janissaries and Europeans' attempt to attack their rear and had reached the Ottoman camp and sacked it. So mobile had the battle been, though, that Uzbek's forces were dispersed all over the field and the army was in danger of losing all cohesion. He decided on withdrawal, as did the Ottoman commander, Ali Pasha. Night was coming on as Uzbek attempted the recall of his scattered forces and a difficult retirement through the pass. The Royal Mamluks were ambushed by marines of the Ottoman fleet that had returned to the shoreline with the passing of the storm, but otherwise the retreat went well and the Mamluks made it to the safety of the foothills of the mountains.

It must have seemed like a defeat to the Mamluk commander but over on the other side of the field the Ottomans were counting their dead and deciding that their forces had been so weakened by the battle that continued occupation of Cilicia was now untenable. Thirty thousand men had fallen, to a loss of four thousand Mamluk troops, and after ringing his camp with artillery carriages Ali Pasha organised his army for evacuation through the Taurus Mountains. Uzbek regrouped and followed their retreat cautiously. Then he brought up his siege cannons and began an investment of Adana that would take three months to conclude but didn't hold back the commencement of victory celebrations in Cairo, which lasted for a week.

In Istanbul Bayezid was furious. Ali Pasha was exiled and captured deserters were executed. Uzbek eventually took Adana when one of its ammunition magazines exploded. He also managed to get a whole detachment of Janissaries to desert to the Mamluk cause. They later paraded in Cairo before intrigued crowds and joined the army. Uzbek pushed deep into Anatolia burning and looting as he went. He only stopped in September 1490 at Kuwara because his troops refused to go any further, his supplies were used up and his line of retreat was tenuous. He returned by short marches to Aleppo and then to Damascus. Kayitbay was said to be have been angry at his field marshal's withdrawal from the frontier, but upbraiding a general who had enjoyed success of such magnitude was virtually impossible for the state's titular head and Kayitbay placed a ceremonial hero's robe upon Uzbek's shoulders when he returned to Egypt.

Uzbek returned to the field in March 1490 with an army that was slowly evolving. Men of the *halqa*, the old second-tier cavalry division, had been enticed with promises of extra pay to become arquebusiers. Kayitbay also began to mount his musketeers on camels to speed their deployment to the battlefield, where they would then dismount as it was impossible to use the guns from the saddle. Here we enter an area of controversy centring on the use of firearms and artillery in the Middle East at the end of the fifteenth century. The question is, why guns didn't just completely supplant the bow in this period as they so obviously did later, and why didn't Mamluk troopers take up its use? Put simply, any advantage that the gun had over the bow in this period is not actually that easy to find and even in 1517 when the Mamluks were finally destroyed by the Ottomans their defeat had more to do with the massed field artillery of the Ottomans rather than the muskets ranged against them. The compound bow was as accurate as the common musket at this time and four arrows could be dispatched to every bullet fired in terms of reloading time. There was also no smoke to obscure the aim of the archer, and arrows disable a man immediately, even if only a flesh wound is sustained whereas bullets may not. Arrows are also easily made and do not require a developed industrial base for mass manufacture unlike bullets. In terms of range, even the muskets deployed at Waterloo only had a range of 130 metres, whilst Mamluk light war arrows could be shot up to 250 metres. Furthermore, the gun in this period simply couldn't be used from the saddle and by taking up firearms the Mamluks would have given up one of their greatest military assets – mobility.

So why did the gun eventually triumph on the battlefield? Of course firearms improved, but there was more to it than that. The gun was the great leveller; skilled archery was the domain of highly trained soldiers in the peak of physical condition, it took months to develop the skills required to be a battlefield archer and years to reach the level of skill acquired by a Royal Mamluk – it is entirely unsurprising that over a third of all the *Furusiyya* literature produced under the Mamluks directly relates to training with the bow – whilst a rifleman could be taught 'cheaply' in a compressed timeframe, with no need for athleticism on the part of the soldier; 'normal' standards of fitness could apply. For the Mamluks, then, the musketeers were auxiliary forces, not because of misguided attachment to the past on their part but because the skilled mounted archer was still the main player on the battlefield. Indeed it is notable that despite the common notion of the Janissary as a musketeer par excellence even in 1510 they were still in the process of changing over from compound bows to firearms.

To avoid being intercepted in the narrow passes around the Syrian Gates Uzbek entered Anatolia via Abulustayn and began to lay waste every principality that had recognised Ottoman suzerainty. There were brutal rapes and massacres of civilians in what amounted to a campaign of terror designed to bring Bayezid around to the idea of peace. Appalling as such an idea was, it worked. Bayezid despatched an embassy with the keys of Ottoman-occupied fortresses in Mamluk territory to Kayitbay in May 1491. A prisoner exchange was concluded and Mamluk suzerainty in both the marches of Anatolia and over the Holy Places of Arabia was recognised. A return embassy to Istanbul took place soon after and an accord was signed recognising the pre-eminence of the Mamluk Sultan over the Middle East. A peace that really only meant a cold war was secured; it would outlast both Bayezid and Kayitbay. Bayezid then moved immediately against the remaining rump of the Ak-Koyunlu in 1492 without fear of interference from the Mamluks. In truth Kayitbay's victory was a pyrrhic one, it had left the state exhausted, if victorious, and he needed peace perhaps even more than Bayezid did.

The year 1492 was a plague year. Two hundred thousand people died in Cairo alone, visions of the Prophet were reported, foretelling annihilation if the wrongs done by the Mamluk caste were not corrected and it was reported that *jinn*, devils, had been released by Allah to punish the depraved. There was a sense of despair in the country. Full-scale food riots broke out, led by *julban* Mamluks and Kayitbay nearly died after being thrown from a horse he was trying to break. His loyal emirs had rallied around to keep the government stable and Kayitbay's bravery in continuing to rule whilst recovering from compound fractures of his leg had encouraged the populace but it was evident that he was ageing and there were grave doubts about the future. The plague carried off many senior emirs of ministerial rank and aided the political fortunes of Kansawh, a joint commander on the 1490 expedition against the Ottomans; his rise was the reason for a lot of the pessimism pervading Egypt. He had married Uzbek's daughter and was expected to make a grab for power as soon as the old Sultan breathed his last, despite the fact that Kayitbay had an heir, his young son, al-Nasir Muhammad. Kayitbay promoted the emir Aqbirdi to his privy council in an attempt to check Kansawh's power but the move did little to reduce his influence. A degree of paranoia showed in the eighty-three-year-old Sultan in 1494 – probably as a result of the loss of so many close friends to the plague – and he turned on his son, suspecting him of plotting and sent him to sweep the *julban* barracks.

Whilst Egypt's physical condition improved from 1494 to 1496, Kayitbay started a decline into fevers that ate away at him. There were attempts on Kansawh's life by the *julban* at

Aqbirdi's instigation whilst Kansawh and Uzbek encouraged a faction to kill Aqbirdi, and a small army of their supporters assembled at Uzbek's quarters ready to do so. The succession battle threatened to tear the army and state apart and Kayitbay's response was one that was both unusual and surprisingly effective. He went down to the army's review platform and had a simple proclamation read out, summoning all the Sultan's loyal forces to muster. The call struck a chord of affection for the old Sultan, so close to death, within the men and many of them turned from thoughts of civil war back to a man who, for many of them, had been as a father. Kansawh and Uzbek's force melted away and for a brief period everything that was honourable and gallant about the Mamluk way triumphed over the everyday gore of politics. Kansawh went into a self-imposed political exile to await events but Uzbek went to his old friend in white robes after ritually washing himself. He stepped through Aqbirdi's supporters, despite the obvious threat, and approached the Sultan, asked for permission to retire to Mecca, and when given consent left almost immediately for Arabia.

Chivalry sometimes comes to the fore in the affairs of men, more often it is just the tinsel to obscure the bloodiness of reality and Kansawh was back at his intrigues only a few months later, in July 1496. He managed to convince Kayitbay to grant him a public audience at which he was publicly exonerated. Shortly afterwards, his Mamluk recruits stormed Aqbirdi's palace. Kayitbay tried the same technique that had quelled the first revolt but this time no one came. The Mamluks had obviously decided that he was already in his mausoleum, at least politically, and it was time to choose sides. The Sultan, barely able to stand, stayed at the review platform for hours, looking out onto the empty square. Eventually he struggled onto his horse and retired to the citadel. The last thing he heard before slipping into a coma was that Aqbirdi was in hiding. As the Sultan was dying on 5 August the senior emir Timraz sought his permission to invest al-Nasir Muhammad as Sultan but there was no response from the old man. Timraz went ahead anyway, putting the fourteen-year-old on the throne so he could take up real power behind him before Kansawh could do so, but he wasn't strong enough to keep his place and Kansawh had him captive within hours and had killed most of Aqbirdi's supporters within another day.

The Sultan died on 7 August and the embalmers were shocked by how wretched and thin his body had become. He was interred in his mausoleum with a lack of ceremony that stood at odds with the magnificence of the edifice; the crowds were too busy watching the Caliph investing al-Nasir under Kansawh's watchful eye to attend the burial. There is no doubt that Kayitbay was a great man. After a shaky start he had seen off the Turcoman threat and halted the Ottoman drive into southeastern Anatolia and his imaginative restructuring of the army had given him the manpower to achieve these victories. That he was unable to fully arrest the decline of Mamluk power was not his fault; the problems of corruption, economic decline, plague and the increasing power of its prime enemy, the Ottomans, all pre-dated his reign and were beyond the power of even such a long-reigning Sultan to correct without massive institutional reform. While such reform might have saved Egypt, it would have almost certainly destroyed Mamlukdom, as the slave soldiers become gentry were by this stage in fact an integral part of the state's malaise. All Kayitbay could do was maintain the highest personal standards and hope that by doing so he would cause others to act in the same way, with his personality holding the country together, despite the state's massive internal difficulties. Al-Malik al-Ashraf Abu'l Nasr Kayitbay al-Mahmudi received this verdict from Ibn Iyas:

> He was serene and dignified, correct in decorum, invariably respected, projecting an aura of majesty to official ceremonies. Highly intelligent, sound of judgement, skilled in state affairs particularly when corrupt officials warranted dismissal. Yet he always reflected carefully before implementing a decision.
>
> Renowned for his bravery, adept as a cavalier, he was proficient in all military arts, and yet obsessed with a lust for money.
>
> After violent fits of temper, he calmed rapidly. His fury always dissipated – an attractive trait.
>
> Overall, the good qualities outweighed the bad; he was the best of the Turkish monarchs, especially when compared with

those who followed him. Although tainted by greed, he was the noblest of Circassian rulers, their finest.*

Al-Nasir, in his brief reign, showed some of his father's firmness of character and he pushed ahead with reforms to the army but these led to his assassination near Giza by Kansawh and other magnates who were offended by the Sultan's advancement of his Nubian musketeers. The Sultan had found the riflemen to be effective in Upper Egypt where the Mamluks had to campaign almost continually now just to hold on to some semblance of control, but his perceived preference of them over the old order excited Mamluk xenophobia and Kayitbay's son was murdered on 31 October 1498. Kansawh ascended the throne; by this time, though, he was less popular among the emirs and was a virtual puppet until he was displaced by the emir Tumanbay, who bombarded the Cairo citadel with mangonels in June 1500. Kansawh left Cairo hurriedly in disguise, to be replaced by another of Tumanbay's creatures, Janpulat. Then in January 1501 Tumanbay declared himself Sultan and drove Janpulat from the city, only to have the same thing done to him by a hastily formed junta just three months later. During this period of kingmaking in 1497, the rounding of Cape Horn by the Portuguese and their appearance in the Indian Ocean passed by unnoticed.

The junta elected al-Ashraf Kansawh al-Ghawri for the throne. It is likely that he was seen merely as a stopgap Sultan by emirs who fancied themselves as kings. He was over sixty when he took the throne after running through the same show of reticence that Kayitbay had performed, where the chosen Sultan doth protest too much. Ibn Iyas's description of the new Sultan shows that al-Ghawri was attracted to what we would expect of a man in his later years. 'He loved to observe flowers and fruit trees . . . he enjoyed planting shrubs . . . he delighted in the singing of birds, the scent of blossoms . . .' And yet he was able to secure his grasp on power with some rapidity, despite having been little more than a reliable if somewhat harsh governor of Tarsus and Malatya during much of Kayitbay's reign before

---

* In Petry, pp. 15–16.

becoming a captain of the bodyguard under Kansawh. Even his throne name of al-Ghawri was only a reference to his *tibaq*, the barracks of al-Ghawr and he muttered that throne names were pointless if the Sultan was just the plaything of magnates. The first attempt on his Sultanate was made by Tumanbay, the elderly ex-Sultan, but the plot was discovered and as Tumanbay fled through the city at night he fell from a wall, breaking his leg, and was hacked to death by al-Ghawri's *khassakiyya*. The new Sultan heeded the warning; he set himself to survive through limiting the power of the magnates and he hoped to achieve his goal through reducing their family wealth to the treasury's benefit, undertaking just enough judicial murders to prevent conspiracies forming, and through modernising the army whilst calling it back to its disciplined past. Despite this last laudable aim al-Ghawri inspired the spite of almost every contemporary chronicler. Ibn Iyas's description continues:

> His faults were legion . . . he seized the patrimony of orphans unjustly, he appointed sheikhs over the local provinces, charging them large sums for their offices and they in turn assessed the fief holders double. The Sultan installed the governors of Syria in like fashion demanding large sums every year. He renewed taxes in a fashion unprecedented by his predecessors. His greed knew no limit, for he even stooped to extorting drivers of water-bearing draft animals and gardeners at the Citadel, forcing them to sell the dung of their beasts and to turn the money over to the reserve fund . . .*

Well, where's there's muck there's brass, and al-Ghawri needed brass and silver very badly. Certainly the Sultan was disposed to luxury, we are told that every one of his fingers was covered with emerald and ruby rings, but such is the nature of kingship that trinkets are required to awe and startle the populace and fellow regents. Al-Ghawri also had other plans for the money he squeezed from the state. As discussed earlier there was an artillery arms race going on and the Mamluks,

---

* Petry, pp. 120–1 Ibn Iyas's inheritance from his father was sequestered by al-Ghawri so the source of the writer's ire is not difficult to ascertain.

although they had had a head start – having used siege cannon as early as 1419 – were by 1500 quite some distance behind the Ottomans especially in terms of mobile field artillery. The problem was complex. First, the materials required for casting cannon were not to be found in Egypt. Copper had to brought from European merchants as the only extensive mines in the greater Mediterranean region were in the Tyrol, and wood for carriages and saltpetre for charge were drawn from Anatolia and the Black Sea region, areas which were now very much under Ottoman control. Furthermore, the whole process, even discounting materials, was expensive because of the high rate of failure of cast cannon during testing; it has been suggested that the Islamic interdict on bells that deprived the Muslims of a tradition of casting led to this production problem.* The Ottomans, of course, could grab Christians for their experiments, Mehmed II's guns for the siege of Constantinople were cast by a Byzantine captive, but the Mamluks didn't have a Western front. The distressing results of poor casting have been recorded for us by Ibn Iyas:

> The Sultan went . . . and they tested in his presence the cannon they had cast, when they fired the powder from them they all exploded. Their bronze flew through the air, and not one of them was sound. There were about fifteen cannon. The Sultan was increasingly upset on that day, he had intended to give a feast to the emirs and spend the day rejoicing, it was not to be.†

Al-Ghawri got around this problem to some degree by buying cannons from Europe, of course this was extortionately expensive, as was his building of a new *maydan* in order to reinvigorate the army's training programme. From 1503 the Sultan had another new expense to cover as the Portuguese had set up Cochin as a port in India and threatened to cut the oriental trade of Egypt. The rapid construction of warships was required for the protection of the Arabian Peninsula as the Portuguese

---

* Cf. R. Irwin, 'Gunpowder and Firearms in the Mamluk Sultanate Reconsidered', in M. Winter and A. Levanoni, *The Mamluks in Egyptian and Syrian Politics and Society*, Leiden: EJ Brill, 2004, p. 129.
† In Holt, *The Age of the Crusades*, p. 199.

next tried to enforce the very trade embargo that the European powers had failed ever to impose in the Mediterranean against the Sultanate in the Red Sea. Al-Ghawri fortified Jeddah with an arquebus regiment and sent his new fleet into the Indian Ocean to assist the ruler of Gujarat, who was fighting off the Portuguese in 1505. The fleet defeated the Portuguese fleet in January 1508, its arquebusiers more than matching the riflemen of the Portuguese vessels, but it suffered a reverse in February 1509 off Diu Shawwal and returned to Egypt.

The help of Bayezid II was sought and in this mutual Holy War against the Europeans the Ottoman–Mamluk differences were forgotten as Bayezid, before his death in 1512, sent timber, iron and gunpowder to al-Ghawri. The fleet was enhanced by more vessels built in the Gulf of Suez and it set out again in 1515 with an additional complement of two thousand Ottoman sailors sent by the new Sultan Selim. The expedition fought its way down through the Red Sea to Yemen in June 1516 and took Zabid and Aden. Yemen was secured by the fleet's efforts but was to end up as an Ottoman protectorate by virtue of the simple fact that the Mamluk Empire fell to Selim in 1517; perhaps he knew exactly what he was doing when he sent his mariners out with the Mamluks. Ibn Ayas's accusations of money madness against the Sultan are then hard to countenance when placed against the expenses the treasury had to bear; even the writer's own diatribe against the Sultan's high custom duties actually gives us a very strong indication of what was happening to the Sultanate at this juncture: 'The prefect of Jeddah collected from the Indian merchants a tenth of their income, an act discouraging them from entering the port at all – which thus fell idle. Their goods became scarce in Egypt, and the town was deserted. Similarly, the ports of Alexandria and Damietta were abandoned because Frankish merchants ceased entering them. European merchandise also disappeared.'*

Ibn Ayas gathered evidence of trade decline but drew the wrong conclusion. The reason for the disappearance of trade was Venice's new policy of détente with the Ottomans,

---

* In Petry, pp. 120–1.

reopening Asian trade through the Dardanelles, and European Ocean trade that simply went round the Middle East via Cape Horn. Egypt was denuded of its trade revenue. Added to this were further visitations of plague, self-seeking and corruption among the higher magnates that reached such appalling levels that al-Ghawri threatened to abdicate if they didn't rein in their rapacity to a more moderate level of absurdity. There was also insubordination among the *julban* so atrocious that the Sultan almost decided not to even raise his own corps of Royal Mamluks as Sultans always had done, feeling that their dubious loyalty wouldn't be worth the effort and expenditure, as well as almost constant rebellion among Turcoman and Bedouin tribesmen. In short, all the old evils were still there and were enough to precipitate a cash crisis of such magnitude that it is to be wondered that al-Ghawri was even able to keep the Sultanate running. In an attempt to reinvigorate the troops' loyalty to the state he introduced a new oath sworn on a Koran of the third Caliph Uthman and he continued to attempt reform. In 1503 it was proudly recorded that the officer corps had finally reached its full complement of twenty-four emirs of one hundred and seventy-five emirs of forty – a survey of the armed forces hadn't been undertaken for years beforehand.

In Syria things were looking increasingly ominous. Despite al-Ghawri's efforts at suppressing sedition, by 1504 the governors of Aleppo and Damascus were acting almost as autonomous rulers without reference to Cairo. They had taken advantage of the dotage of Kayitbay, the Bedouin revolts in both Egypt and Syria and the ongoing financial crisis in the Sultanate to make their move. Although al-Ghawri kept up the pretence of control in the province he knew that it was a façade and that Syria could not be relied on to stay loyal in the event of an engagement with the Ottomans or the new Turcoman enemy to his north. This new enemy replaced the Ak-Koyunlu, who had withered on the vine after Uzun Hasan's death in 1478. It was a Shiite confederation of Turcoman tribes created in 1501 under the charismatic Shah Ismail Safawi. The mystical Shah gained leadership over nomadic and independent-minded Iranian Turcoman tribes who considered the Mamluk and Ottoman fixed government systems anathema. His confederation also attracted the allegiance of nomads of Azerbaijan and the eastern Jazira.

The Safavids, as the confederation came to be known, exploded into the Mamluk consciousness in 1502 from almost nowhere, with their rapid advances into the petty Anatolian states that separated the Mamluks from the Ottomans. Then, before al-Ghawri could even muster a response, they had gone again, retreating eastwards, and peace returned to the region for five years. Just as they were almost forgotten, the Safavids hit again in 1507, invading Abulustayn, and getting as far as Malatya. Al-Ghawri responded in force. He mustered fifteen hundred Mamluks under the command of five emirs of one hundred, Bedouin irregular cavalry and rifle infantry. But, just as this force was preparing to leave, emissaries arrived from Shah Ismail begging forgiveness for the incursion into Mamluk territory, which was claimed to be a mistake. The emissaries were somewhat coarse and rustic and looked out of place in the sophisticated Cairo court. This may have influenced al-Ghawri's decision not to take the Safavids too seriously. He forgave the incursion and other later smaller ones that the Safavids made into Anatolia. Even in 1510, when the area around al-Bira was raided by the Shah's men, al-Ghawri only sent an emir of ten as his emissary to the Shah's camp to order his withdrawal.

Then intelligence came to the Sultan that changed his perspective of the Safavids entirely: messengers had been captured during a reprisal raid into the Shah's borderlands and letters addressed to European monarchs had been found suggesting joint action between the Shah and the West against both the Mamluks and the Ottomans. A closer watch was placed over the Safavids and then in June 1511 their emissary delivered a gift to the Sultan. Shah Ismail had killed the Khan of the Crimean Tatars, the successor state to the Golden Horde, in a personal duel and then had his skull fashioned into a drinking goblet. This was the Shah's gift to al-Ghawri. The Sultan was appalled by this treatment of one of the Mamluk's historical allies but kept his cool, he knew that their continued push into Anatolia would soon force the Safavids into a confrontation with the Ottomans and at this point the Ottoman–Mamluk peace pact was solid. Maybe the Ottomans would do the dirty work of dispatching the Shah for the Mamluks. Certainly the new Ottoman Sultan was just the man for such a task. Sultan Selim, soon to be given the sobriquet of Selim the Grim, was much more like his grandfather than his father and never likely to resort to peaceful means when war was an option.

From 1511 to 1514 things were peaceful but the situation within the army was worsening, in many ways peace and inactivity had always been the Achilles' heel of the Mamluk system, whenever the soldier slaves had no external enemy they made their masters their foe and their bonuses and pay their *casus belli*. It was only fear of a succession crisis and the chances of receiving no pay whatsoever in such a situation that kept the Mamluk troopers from deposing al-Ghawri, there were endless riots and many of them were instigated by senior officers. A particular bone of contention was the Fifth Corps of infantry riflemen that al-Ghawri was expanding to cover the Red Sea front against the Portuguese, as the Mamluks thought its growth was depriving them of bonuses and new arms. The Sultan threatened to resign his office several times, once even addressing the troops, 'if there is any among you whom you wish to enthrone, I shall relinquish the Citadel to him and retire to my mosque, where death will be welcome'. Such bluster kept them from throwing him out but there were serious doubts whether the army would ever follow al-Ghawri, or any other man, into the field in proper order. In truth, and putting standard soldierly bellyaching aside, the army was in a ramshackle condition by this point. Even al-Ghawri's *khassakiyya* complained bitterly to the Sultan:

> For five months meat and fodder rations have been delayed. The granaries hand us wheat that is so rotten our horses won't touch it. Our stipends from you do not suffice to rent a house or a stable, to pay a groom, or to buy clothing or uniforms – all of which are costly. Throughout your reign we have never been properly provisioned. We are now famished and go naked!*

---

* In Petry, p. 189.

Meanwhile, the Safavid state continued to grow and by 1514 posed a very real threat to both Ottoman Anatolia and Mamluk Syria. Selim, now secure as Sultan, acted in 1514, invading Abulustayn even though it was a Mamluk protectorate, and chasing Shah Ismail into Azerbaijan. The two sides met in a colossal battle at Chaldiran in 1514 and the Shah was defeated with a great slaughter being inflicted on his men by the Ottoman field artillery. The noise of the guns alone was enough to send the Shah's cavalry into panicked retreat. Despite some difficulties in his diplomacy with Selim prior to the battle, al-Ghawri managed to maintain Mamluk neutrality leading up to a battle that cost Selim thirty thousand in dead and appeared, at first, to have shattered the Safavids completely.

However, the Shah was not finished by a long way and it was at this point that al-Ghawri made a fatal diplomatic foray. Concerned over the Ottoman occupation of Abulustayn and this final erosion of the buffer states protecting Syria, he made contact with Shah Ismail to suggest a mutual defence pact against Selim. Perhaps he just meant to give Selim pause for thought but if so he had misread the new and fearless Sultan's character totally.

Al-Ghawri massed his forces in May 1516 in northern Syria simply to act as a threat to the Ottoman southern flank as Selim was preparing to move east again against the Shah but Selim would not tolerate such intimidation and he sent to al-Ghawri to withdraw from the frontier zone. Perhaps Selim had heard about the army sent to threaten him. Only 944 Royal Mamluks could be found for the expedition and the Egyptian army as a whole only consisted of about five thousand men. It was supplemented by Bedouin camel cavalry, whose animals' ears were stopped up to prevent them being terrified by the artillery. It was a common saying in Egypt that one Mamluk was worth a thousand infantrymen but it was still hard to see how such a tiny force could hope to match Selim's vast army of two hundred thousand men. Al-Ghawri could not even send his new Fifth Corps for fear of leaving the southern flank exposed, but he did pick up local Syrian infantrymen to bolster his paltry force on the march north. Negotiations were begun but Selim sent differing signals, at one point addressing al-Ghawri as a father and asking for pardon for his occupation of Abulustayn and then changing to arrogance and derision for the Mamluk Sultan, so that al-Ghawri felt that Selim was just playing for time in order to deal with Shah Ismail before turning south to annex Syria. He was encouraged in this belief by the governor of Aleppo, Khair Bey.

Given the dissent that was openly displayed in the dishevelled Mamluk army, the reported defections of emirs taking sail from Alexandria to join Selim's court and the fact that the Sultan had had practically to treat the governor of Damascus as an equal in order to get his support, al-Ghawri should have done everything in his power to avoid a confrontation at least until the Safavids had engaged Selim. It would even have been better to withdraw into Syria to stretch the Ottoman lines of communication but the lessons of the past, of Homs in 1281 and Marj al-Suffar in 1302 were not heeded, perhaps they could not be. In 1260 Mamluks in Aleppo had called upon Homs and Hama to join them in rebellion but the answer had been, 'we are with the ruler of Egypt, whoever he may be'. Now it was very different; any withdrawal from northern Syria would see not its fortified places acting as a thorn in Selim's side but more likely their defection to him.

Negotiations broke down finally when a courier sent by al-Ghawri to Shah Ismail was intercepted by the Ottomans and Selim turned to face the Mamluks. Battle was joined at Marj Dabiq, north of Aleppo, on 24 August 1516. Al-Ghawri deployed the forces of Damascus on his right and the forces of Aleppo on his left. His Egyptian veterans made up the centre. The *julban*, unlike the recruits of the past, were not trusted enough to be in the van and stood behind the Royal Mamluks. Selim's vast army formed up with its field artillery unit positioned just to its rear, in the centre. The gunners linked their gun carriages together to form barricades against cavalry charge.

Al-Ghawri's Royal Mamluks under his *atabeg* Sudun made the first charge on the Ottoman line and such was the speed and ferocity of their onslaught that the Ottomans were initially stunned as the veterans penetrated through to the artillery, rounding the carriages set as barricades, pouring arrows into the gunners and cutting down riflemen. Then Damascus joined the charge and seven of the Ottomans' standards were captured as Janissaries fell under the onslaught of lance, sword and *khanjar*. At noon the battle looked winnable and al-Ghawri came forward with the *julban* but then both Sudun and the governor of Damascus, Sibay, were killed – probably by cannon fire – and the *julban's* charge petered out, leaving the Royal Mamluks and the Mamluks of Damascus fighting alone and leaderless. Selim used this welcome respite from the Mamluk onslaught to organise the advance of his right wing to be matched by the pre-arranged desertion of Khair Bey, the governor of Aleppo. Al-Ghawri watched in horror as his left wing simply disintegrated. He cried out, 'fight on and my share is yours!' and then was struck dumb, no more words could come as he suffered a massive stroke. An emir caught the royal standard and kept it aloft as the Sultan fell from his horse, but the army collapsed as news of the Sultan's death and Aleppo's desertion spread over the battlefield. Many of the *julban* escaped the battlefield but the carnage among senior emirs and the Royal Mamluks was terrible. The governors of Safad and Homs had fallen and the brave Royal Mamluks had been annihilated; the field was covered with their gold embossed swords and daggers, many were picked up by Ottoman officers and kept for generations by the same family as revered objects.

Al-Ghawri's body was never found, it was most probably buried secretly by his *khassakiyya*. The Caliph was found by the Ottomans, wandering dazed from the battlefield. Aleppo fell bloodlessly, shutting its doors to fleeing Mamluks but opening them to the Ottomans. At Damascus *julban* were hunted down by gangs of citizens and killed and the city welcomed Selim in October 1516. The old loyalties that had allowed the Mamluks to hold onto and recover the cities of Syria after 1300 and 1402 were long gone.

The coronation regalia had been lost with al-Ghawri and there was no Caliph to enthrone him but Tumanbay, al-Ghawri's nephew and his most trusted emir, was called back from Upper Egypt to take the throne on 11 October 1516 and we can be sure that his reported reticence was genuine. Selim was unsure about attempting Egypt's conquest. He had lost a large part of his forces in the battle to the furious charges of the Egyptian veterans, and the march across the Sinai would stretch his communication lines at a time when he still hadn't fully secured his eastern flank against the Safavids. He was encouraged to take on the campaign by Khair Bey, who was now his adviser in all things Mamluk and would become his vassal ruler. Selim nicknamed him *al-kha'in*, the traitor.

Tumanbay let the Ottomans come almost to Cairo before making a stand. He met them at al-Raydaniyya on 23 January 1517. Tumanbay had been a keen advocate of field artillery and he now gathered every gun he could find in Egypt for the country's defence. Perhaps he placed too great a reliance on them. Certainly his guns took a heavy toll on the Ottomans but his entrenched position was then outflanked by their cavalry and rolled up. Uzbek had done the same to the Ottomans in 1486 and Tumanbay, as a cavalryman, should have known better. Every cannon needed to be washed and cooled down with vinegar and water between each shot and every wash brought the mounted enemy closer and closer. Tumanbay was routed and the Ottomans entered Cairo, but he scraped together another force of Arabs and Mamluks out in the desert. He tried to negotiate using the threat of Arab revolt, but Selim was adamant that only complete surrender would suffice. The few Mamluks remaining with him surrounded Tumanbay and angrily demanded that he take the field once more, and for the last time Mamluk troopers followed the standard of their Sultan and set a volley of arrows flying before charging with their lances couched. The battle took place among the Pyramids of Giza and ghosts of the men who had been the nemesis of the Ilkhans and of the Crusaders might well have ridden at Al-Malik al-Ashraf Tumanbay's shoulder as a dynasty was swept away by the fire of the Janissaries, the new slave soldiers.

EPILOGUE

THE DEVIL'S TRICKS

THE FATE OF THE MAMLUKS

When the Ottoman Sultan learnt that the people did not believe that Tumanbay had been taken, he was angered, and sent him across to Cairo. He passed through Cairo, greeting the people along the way until he reached the Zuwayla Gate, unaware of what would befall him . . . When he realised that he was about to be hanged, he said to the people around him, 'say the *Fatiha* three times for me'. He spread out his hands and said the *Fatiha* three times and the people said it with him. Then he said to the executioner, 'do your work'. When they put the noose around his neck and raised the rope, it broke and he fell on the threshold of the gate. It is said that the rope broke twice and he fell to the ground. When he died and his spirit went forth, the people cried with a great cry, and there was much grief and sorrow for him.

Ibn Iyas, d. 1524*

THE MAMLUKS' SULTANATE ENDED with the death of Tumanbay and Selim vowed their annihilation. Mamluks captured at Giza were beheaded and the Ottomans searched Cairo, hanging any civilian who hid a Mamluk and summarily decapitating any Mamluk they caught before displaying his head on a pole. But then the Sultan made an abrupt volte-face, Khair Bey was made viceroy of Egypt and an amnesty was called. Mamluks came out of hiding to be enrolled in their own regiment but they received the lowest pay of any

---

*   In Holt, *The Age of the Crusades*. The *Fatiha* is the first chapter of the Koran. It is used as a prayer for the dying.

soldiers in the Ottoman army, all costumes and pageantry associated with the past were banned and Khair Bey personally cut off their beards, telling them to shave like the Ottomans. Their humiliation seemed complete and they were used simply as tax-farmers and as a local defence force, but then in May 1518 they were employed, ironically, to put down a Janissary revolt in Cairo and the Sultan began to show a greater reliance on them. Selim had moved from his policy of elimination to incorporation, simply because the vast expanse of land he had conquered stretched his troop requirements. He had effectively inherited the Mamluks' conflict with the Portuguese and the continued threat to Syria from the Franks in the eastern Mediterranean and from the Safavids.

They were eliminated to a man in Syria by Selim's son, Suleyman, in February 1521 after they revolted against his rule but eight hundred Egyptian Mamluks took part in the same Sultan's conquest of Rhodes in 1522 and Ottoman writers were by this time already beginning to mythologise the Mamluks' endeavours. Sons of Ottoman grandees read, as part of their education, stories of the Persian Prince Baybars, who as the last of the Khwarazm Shahs avenged his father on the Khan Hulegu, and of the handsome and arrogant Kalavun, who mocked Baybars's unfortunate looks. The stories told of how the Circassians were descendants of the Arabs and how the last Sultan, Tumanbay, had lectured Sultan Selim on the cowardliness of guns versus the nobility of the sword and bow. The great battles of the past were reduced to chivalric bouts of single combat and whilst Kayitbay was praised and his defeats of the Ottomans conveniently forgotten, al-Ghawri's reign and his betrayal of the old heroic ways were condemned. The manufacture and spread of these tales throughout the Ottoman aristocracy allowed the Ottomans to usurp the heritage of an older and nobler military heritage, just as the Romans had been able to do with that of Greece. In later years there were Mamluk festivals in Istanbul; collecting swords of the old slave soldier dynasty became extremely fashionable and *Furusiyya* manuscripts were treasured and marked with the *tughra* of many of the Ottoman Sultans. So the Mamluks continued on as minor functionaries in the Ottoman Egyptian administration and as characters in Ottoman historical fantasies, but as the Ottoman Empire crumbled the Mamluk emirs began once again to accrue power. New novices were bought from Georgia via a rejuvenated slave trade and great households formed again. A situation arose not dissimilar to that of the Islamic Empire of the ninth century, with Egypt paying only lip service to Istanbul and operating almost independently of the Sultanate.

Napoleon's arrival in the Middle East in 1798 made the Mamluks into curios for European travellers, writers and painters and also sealed their fate. His modern army destroyed the army of Egypt at the Battle of the Pyramids in a matter of hours. The French were forced to leave after only three years by a joint British–Ottoman expedition that then also went to war with the Mamluks. Bonaparte took a Mamluk named Rostom Razmadze with him as a personal bodyguard. He served the French Emperor until 1814, as did a Mamluk force that Napoleon formed from captured Mamluks and Janissaries before his departure. In 1803 the Mamluk Company joined the Imperial Guard and after fighting impressively at Austerlitz their company was granted a standard; Goya depicted their charge against the Madrilene in 1808 in his work of 1814. Napoleon took two companies of Mamluks into the Belgian campaign of 1815. These men, fighting in Napoleon's last campaign, were also the last Mamluk force to fight as a battle unit.

The British and Ottoman assaults on the Mamluks in 1803 and a failed revolt by the emirs against the new Ottoman viceroy Muhammad Ali in 1805 led the Georgian Mamluk leaders to write to the Russian government requesting a return to their homelands. There was no response from the Tsar, who certainly didn't want armed Georgians returning to an area he was in the process of subduing and it had now also become evident to the rulers of the Middle East that the old ways could no longer hold. Just seeing how Napoleon's army conducted war had made it startlingly obvious to them just how far behind the West they had fallen.

The Mamluks and Janissaries were seen as part of the problem and as an obstruction to any army modernisation that might take place and they shared the same fate. Sultan Mahmud II massacred his Janissary corps in 1826; Islamic teaching allows the use of the Devil's tricks to fight the Devil and both Mahmud and Muhammad Ali, who was by 1810 practically an independent ruler in Egypt, had decided that European-style armies were the answer to the challenge of the new Crusaders.

The Mamluks were pushed from Egypt in 1811. Their leaders had been invited to feast with Ali, but as soon as they were all inside the Cairo citadel the gates were locked and they were gunned down by riflemen shooting from the turrets above. There was a further massacre in Cairo's streets of Mamluks and their families; a few men managed to flee to Sudan where they set up a mini-state that continued to import slave soldiers, but they were eventually destroyed by an Ottoman expedition in 1820. The final extinction of the soldier slaves who had emerged at the end of antiquity marked the beginning of the modern Middle East but history hasn't totally swallowed them up. Mamluk mosque lamps, beautiful and ethereal, carry a Koranic inscription, 'The lamp enclosed in glass: the glass as it were a brilliant star', a suitable testament to men who attained perfection in the military arts.

BIBLIOGRAPHY

Al-Sarraf, S., 'Mamluk Furusiyah Literature', *Mamluk Studies Review*, vol 8, no 1, 2004.

Amitai-Preiss, R., 'Mamluk Espionage Among the Mongols and Franks', *Asian and African Studies*, vol 22, 1988.

Amitai-Preiss, R., *Mongols and Mamluks: The Mamluk-Ilkhanid War, 1260–1281*, London: Cambridge University Press, 1995.

Ayalon, D., 'The Mamluk Novice: On his Youthfulness and on his Original Religion', *Revue des Etudes Islamiques*, vol 54, 1986.

Ayalon, D., 'The Military Reforms of Caliph Al-Mutasim, Their Background and Consequences', in D. Ayalon, *Islam and the Abode of War*, London: Variorum Reprints, 1994.

Ayalon, D., 'Studies on the Structure of the Mamluk Army–III', *Bulletin of the School of Oriental and African Studies*, 1954.

Boyle, J., 'Dynastic and Political History of the Ilkhans', in J. Boyle (ed.), *The Cambridge History of Iran, Volume Five*, Cambridge: Cambridge University Press, 1968, ch. 4.

Dauvillier, J., 'Guilliame de Roubrouck et les Communautes Chaldeenes d'Asie, in J. Dauvillier, *Histoire et Institutions des Eglises Orientales au Moyen Age*, London: Variorum Reprints, 1983.

France, J., *Victory in the East: A Military History of the First Crusade*, London: Cambridge University Press, 1994.

France, J., 'Technology and Success of the First Crusade', in V. Parry and M. Yapp (eds), *War, Technology and Society in the Middle East*, London: Oxford University Press, 1975.

Har-El, S., *Struggle for Domination in the Middle East: The Ottoman–Mamluk War 1485–91*, Leiden: EJ Brill, 1995.

Hillenbrand, C., *The Crusades: Islamic Perspectives*, Edinburgh: Edinburgh University Press, 1999.

Holt, P., *The Age of the Crusades: The Near East from the Eleventh Century to 1517*, London: Longman, 1986.

Holt, P., *The Memoirs of a Syrian Prince*, Wiesbaden: Steiner, 1983.

Holt, P., *Early Mamluk Diplomacy 1260-1290: Treaties of Baybars and Kalavun with Christian Rulers*, Leiden: EJ Brill, 1995.

Imber, C., *The Ottoman Empire 1300–1481*, Istanbul: Isis Press, 1990.

Irwin, R., *The Middle East in the Middle Ages: The Early Mamluk Sultanate*, London: Croom Helm, 1986.

Irwin, R., 'Gunpowder and Firearms in the Mamluk Sultanate Reconsidered', in M. Winter and A. Levanoni (eds), *The Mamluks in Egyptian and Syrian Politics and Society*, Leiden: EJ Brill, 2004.

Joinville, Jean de, *The Memoirs of the Lord of Joinville*, translated by E. Wedgewood, New York: Dutton, 1906.

Levanoni, A., *A Turning Point in History: The Third Reign of al-Nasir Muhammad Ibn Kalavun*, Leiden: EJ Brill, 1995.

Lewis, B., *Islam from the Prophet Muhammad to the Capture of Constantinople*, New York: Harper & Row, 1974.

Little, D., 'The Fall of Akka in 690/1291: The Muslim Version', in M. Sharon (ed.), *Studies in Islamic History in Honour of Professor D. Ayalon*, Leiden: EJ Brill, 1986.

Maalouf, A., *The Crusades through Arab Eyes*, translated by J. Rothschild, London: Al- Saqi Books, 1984.

Marozzi, J., *Tamerlane. Sword of Islam, Conqueror of the World*, London: HarperCollins, 2004.

Morgan, D., 'The Mongols in Syria 1260–1300', in P. Edbury (ed.), *Crusade and Settlement*, Cardiff: University of Cardiff Press, 1985.

Morgan, D., *The Mongols*, Oxford: Blackwell, 1990.

Nicolle, D., 'Arms of the Umayyad Era: Military Technology in a Time of Change', in Y. Lev (ed.), *War and Society in the Eastern Mediterranean, 7th to 15th Century*, Leiden: EJ Brill, 1997.

Petry, C., *Twilight of Majesty: The Reigns of the Mamluk Sultans al-Ashraf Qaytbay and Kansawh al-Ghawri in Egypt*, Seattle: University of Washington Press, 1993.

Petrushevsky, I., 'The Socio-economic Condition of Iran under the Ilkhans' in J. Boyle (ed.), *The Cambridge History of Iran. Volume Five*, London: Cambridge University Press, 1968.

Rabie, H., 'The Training of the Mamluk Faris', in V. Parry and M. Yapp (eds), *War, Technology and Society in the Middle East*, London: Oxford University Press, 1975.

Scanlon, G., *A Muslim Manual of War*, Cairo: American University at Cairo, 1961.

Smith, J., 'Mongol Society and Military in the Middle East: Antecedents and Adaptations', in V. Parry and M. Yapp (eds), *War, Technology and Society in the Middle East*, London: Oxford University Press, 1975.

Thorau, P., 'The Battle of Ayn Jalut: a Re-examination', in P. Edbury (ed.), *Crusade and Settlement*, Cardiff: University of Cardiff Press, 1985.

Williams, A., 'Ottoman Military Technology: The Metallurgy of Turkish Armour', in Y. Lev (ed.), *War and Society in the Eastern Mediterranean, 7th to 15th Century*, Leiden: EJ Brill, 1997.

SUGGESTED FURTHER READING

The works used in the construction of this book are the obvious starting point for any reader interested in further reading about the Mamluks, the Mongols, the Ottomans and the other numerous characters that have graced us with their presence in the period covered in these pages. For those readers who wish to pursue their studies a little further, the following works are suggested. Most are readily obtainable but because of the relative immaturity of English-language studies into both the Mamluks and Mongols some could be considered 'specialist'.

Abulafia, D., *Marseilles, Acre and the Mediterranean 1200–1291 in Italy, Sicily and the Mediterranean 1100–1400*, London, 1987.

Alban, J. and Allmand, C., 'Spies and Spying in the Fourteenth Century', in C.T. Allman (ed.), *War, Literature and Politics in the Later Middle Ages*, Liverpool, 1976.

Amitai-Preiss, R. and Morgan. D. (eds), *The Mongol Empire and its Legacy*, Leiden, 2000.

Atil, E., *Renaissance of Islam: Art of the Mamluks*, Washington, DC, 1981.

Boase, T. (ed), *The Cilician Kingdom of Armenia*, Edinburgh, 1978.

Bosworth, C., 'The Political and Dynastic History of the Iranian World 1000–1217', in J. Boyle (ed.), *The Cambridge History of Iran. Volume Five: The Saljuq and Mongol Periods*, Cambridge, 1968.

Boyle, J. (translator), *Ata Malik Juvaini. The History of the World Conqueror*, 2 vols, Manchester, 1958.

Boyle, J. (translator), *Rashid al-Din. The Successors of Genghis Khan*, New York and London, 1971.

Boyle, J., *The Mongol World Empire 1206-1370*, London, 1977.

Budge, E. (ed. and translator), *The Chronography of Gregory Abu'l Faraj, Commonly Known as Bar Hebraeus*, 2 vols, London, 1932.

Cahen, C., 'The Mongols and the Near East', in K. Setton (ed.), *A History of the Crusades, Volume 2*, Madison, NJ, 1969.

Cahen, C., 'The Turkish Invasion: The Selchukids' in K. Setton (ed.), *A History of the Crusades, Volume 1*, Madison, NJ, 1969.

Cahen, C., *Pre-Ottoman Turkey*, translated by Jones-Williams, London, 1968.

Chambers, J., *The Devil's Horsemen: The Mongol Invasion of Europe*, London, 1979.

Cleaves, F. (translator), *The Secret History of the Mongols*, Cambridge, MA, 1982.

Crone, P., *Slaves on Horses: The Evolution of the Islamic Polity*, Cambridge, 1980.

De Rachewiltz, I., *Papal Envoys to the Great Khans*, London, 1971.

Edbury, P. and Rowe, J., *William of Tyre, Historian of the Latin East*, Cambridge, 1988.

Ehrenkreutz, A. 'Strategic Implications of the Slave Trade between Genoa and Mamluk Egypt in the Second Half of the Thirteenth Century', in A. Udovitch (ed.), *The Islamic Middle East 700–1900: Studies in Economic and Social History*, Princeton, 1981.

El-Azhari, T., *The Seljuqs of Syria during the Crusades: 1070–1154*, translated by Winkelhane, Berlin, 1997.

Fink, H. (ed.), *Fulcher of Chartres: A History of the Expedition to Jerusalem 1095–1127*, Tennessee, 1969.

Firro, K., *A History of the Druzes*, Leiden, 1992.

Gabrieli, F., *Arab Historians of the Crusades*, translated by E. Costello, London, 1969.

Glubb, J., *Soldiers of Fortune: The Story of the Mamlukes*, New York, 1973.

Hookham, H., *Tamburlaine the Conqueror*, London, 1962.

Housley, N., *The Later Crusades: From Lyons to Alcazar. 1274–1580*, Oxford, 1992.

Humphreys, R., *From Saladin to the Mongols: The Ayyubids of Damascus 1192–1260*, Albany, NY, 1977.

Inalcik, H., *The Ottoman Empire: The Classical Age 1300–1600*, translated by N. Itzkowitz and C. Imber, London, 1973.

Inalcik, H., *The Ottoman Empire: Conquest, Organisation and Economy*, London. 1985.

Jackson, P., 'The Crisis in the Holy Land in 1260', *English Historical Review*, vol 95, 1980.

Kennedy, H., *The Prophet and the Age of the Caliphates: The Islamic Near East from the Sixth to the Eleventh Century*, London, 1986.

Koprulu, M., 'Life along the Border and the Founding of the Ottoman Empire', in G. Leiser (ed. and translator), *The Origins of the Ottoman Empire*, New York, 1992.

Lindner, R., *Nomads and Ottomans in Medieval Anatolia*, Indiana, 1983.

Little, D., *An Introduction to Mamluk Historiography*, Wiesbaden, 1970.

Morgan, D., 'The Great Yasa of Chingiz Khan and Mongol Law in the Ilkhanate, *Bulletin of the School of Oriental and African Studies*, vol 49, no 1, 1986.

Morgan, D., *Medieval Persia*, London, 1988.

Peters, P., *Jihad in Medieval and Modern Islam*, Leiden, 1997.

Pipes, D., *Slave Soldiers and Islam: The Genesis of a Military System*, New Haven, CT, 1981.

Richard, J., 'Une Ambassade Mongole a Paris en 1262', in J. Richard (ed.), *Croises, Missionaires et Voyageurs*, London, 1983.

Saunders, J., *The History of the Mongol Conquests*, London, 1971.

Sivan, E., *L'Islam et la Crosaide: Ideologie et Propagande dans le Reactions Musulmanes aux Croisades. Librairie D'Amerique et D'Orient*, Paris, 1968.

Spuler, B., *History of the Mongols*, London, 1972.

Thorau, P., *The Lion of Egypt: Sultan Baybars and the Near East in the Thirteenth Century*, translated by P. Holt, London and New York, 1992.

Vemadsky, G., 'The Mongols and Russia', in G. Vemadsky (ed.), *A History of Russia, Volume 3*, New Haven, CT, 1966.

Wittek, P., *The Rise of the Ottoman Empire. Royal Asiatic Society Monographs, Volume XXIII*, London, 1967.

Yapp, M., 'The Golden Horde and Its Successors', in P. Holt, A.K.S. Lambton and B. Lewis (eds), *The Cambridge History of Islam*, Cambridge, 1970.

INDEX